Testim(

In *Why You Were Born*, Pastor David Johnston gently takes you on a journey into the knowledge of God's Word to reveal the answers every man, woman, and child so desperately need to know—that they are special, unique, and loved—and an important part of God's plan. But this is not just one of those "feel good" books. Pastor David takes you by the hand and shows you how to overcome your past and step into a future full of hope, promise, and divine purpose.

—Dr. Jerry Williamson
President, Go To Nations

Why you were born helped me reposition my mind in relation to hurts I faced. It brought a level of deliverance that was needed to free me from unforgiveness, bitterness and resentment. God used this teaching to help me navigate past painful experiences and prepare me for a new role in life.

—Kent A Jacob
Senior Pastor, Covenant Life Ministries
Trinidad and Tobago

If I hadn't been a Christian before seeing and hearing *Why You Were Born* I certainly would have become one. I found out who I really am. It is life changing.

—Mark C
Christian Bookstore Owner

Realizing the truth in *Why You Were Born* not only helped me wrestle with my own life challenges but equipped me to help my patients through theirs.

—Dr. Paul Shirley, MD

Thank you for speaking life into me through *Why You Were Born*. Truth is alive to me by Gods spirit through your faithfulness.

—Kent Staples
Educator and Coach

WHY YOU WERE BORN

A Blueprint for Discovering Your Life Potential

DAVID L. JOHNSTON

Why You Were Born

Published by HigherLife Development Services, Inc.
PO Box 623307
Oviedo, Florida 32762
(407) 563-4806
www.ahigherlife.com

ISBN: 978-1-951492-21-2 (Paperback)
ISBN: 978-1-951492-20-5 (Ebook)

Printed in the United States of America
10 9 8 7 6 5 4 3 2 1

Dedication

I dedicate this book to the single most important person – YOU!

Dear Reader, this book is to you, for you and about you. What others think of you is of little concern compared to what you think of you. Other people may have an opinion about you, the good, the bad, the ugly. But don't become a prisoner to their thoughts and opinion. Don't live your life held captive to other people's expectations for you and thoughts about you.

In the quiet, you can have serious thoughts about yourself. In reading this book I hope you choose to shake off all outside data, unmanipulated and uncoerced where even the memories of what others have said or done to you are summarily dismissed. Use your time reading this book to have a heart-to-heart with yourself – just you, mentally and emotionally naked, pondering and contemplating the meaning of you, your life and your future.

It is in this stillness that you will meet your Maker. You will hear Him speak to you – in a still small voice – a voice that is not brash, rash or harsh – just there as a voice to encourage, support, direct, sometimes correct but always LOVE you in consummate, immeasurable ways.

What does it take to "Know Thyself" as the ancient maxim inspires us to do? The answer can only be found in knowing the One who created you in the first place, your "personal Designer." I'm not writing to tell you the answers to who you are, but to get you in contact, personal contact, intimate contact with Him.

God be with you on your journey.

David L. Johnston

There are two important days in your life: the day you were born, *and the day you found out why!*

—Mark Twain

Table of Contents

Introduction

It's About You

This book is about you, just you, the real you, the only you, the magnificent you. And you, my friend, have intrinsic and inherent value. You are not valuable simply because of the sum of your parts. Your existence is much more profound than your mere biological arrival.

René Descartes, the French philosopher and mathematician, known as the father of modern philosophy, is famous for his statement made in 1637: *Cogito ergo sum,* which translates: "I think, therefore I am."

And yet, simply knowing that you exist is hardly sufficient or inspiring. What you need to know about yourself is that you are not a copy. You're not a clone. You are an original, a "first edition," if you please. There is *no one like you*. No one can ever take your place. You are indispensable.

> To be "true to thyself" is virtually irrelevant if we do not know the "self" to which we should be true.

Regardless of the circumstances of your birth, you are not an accident, a biological mistake, or the mere product of passion in the night. How you think about your "self" is vital and will be reflected in how you treat yourself, how you treat others, and how you live your life. You need to know the truth about yourself, no matter how wonderful it is. To be "true to thyself" is virtually irrelevant if we do not know the "self" to which we should be true.

How will you discover your real self? The answer lies beyond the rationale of parents or peers. In fact, if you want to remain frustrated for your whole life, just try being what everyone else thinks you should be. Terrifying, right?

However, there is a place of genuine self-realization. It awaits you. Where can it be found? Is it found in the corridors of academia? The annals of history or philosophy? On a psychiatrist's couch? At the séance of a spirit medium? Shall we pluck it from our family tree? Or shall we just give up and spend our lives in the meaningless passage of time?

The answer is "no!" A thousand times, "no!" This book is about you. I get to walk beside you for a while. Together we will search; and if we search, we will find. Let me be your comrade. Let's lock arms and minds, maybe even hearts. Let's go forward together. Where do we start?

Who in the whole wide world can explain the mystery of you? From whom can we get such wisdom?

An ancient venerable philosopher both asked and answered this question. Here's the question. His answer will follow.

> *"But where shall wisdom be found? and where is the place of understanding?*
>
> *Man knoweth not the price thereof; neither is it found in the land of the living.*
>
> *The depth saith, It is not in me: and the sea saith, It is not with me.*
>
> *It cannot be gotten for gold, neither shall silver be weighed for the price thereof.*
>
> *It cannot be valued with the gold of Ophir, with the precious onyx, or the sapphire.*
>
> *The gold and the crystal cannot equal it: and the exchange of it shall not be for jewels of fine gold.*
>
> *No mention shall be made of coral, or of pearls: for the price of wisdom is above rubies.*

> *The topaz of Ethiopia shall not equal it, neither shall it be valued with pure gold.*
>
> *Whence then cometh wisdom? and where is the place of understanding?*
>
> *Seeing it is hid from the eyes of all living, and kept close from the fowls of the air.*
>
> *Destruction and death say, We have heard the fame thereof with our ears."* (Job 28:12-22)

Let's note the following in summary:

- No amount of money can get wisdom.
- No living person knows the answers.
- Wisdom cannot be found in the depths.
- No amount of gold or silver or precious jewels can procure it.
- The price of wisdom is worth more than rubies (which are presently four times the value of diamonds).
- Not even 24K gold can purchase this wisdom (the ability to understand you).
- The wisdom is hidden from every living person.
- Death and destruction have only heard how famous wisdom is.

Now here comes the answer, the answer of how to find the wisdom to answer the great mysteries of life and particularly the mystery of you.

> *"God understandeth the way thereof, and he knoweth the place thereof."* (Job 28:23)

There it is: the first open door to finding the One who has the wisdom, who can explain the mystery of you, and the answer to life's most important question: *Why was I born?* God is the only One smart enough to answer the questions of your life. Why should that surprise any of us?

We are about to walk on holy ground. We are entering sacred

territory. *El Shaddai,* the Lord God Almighty, the God of heaven, beckons us with open arms. He's very anxious to be in contact with you once again. He's been with you before, even though you might not have known it. He welcomes you now. Don't be fearful. You will be in safe hands: His! And I'll just walk beside you for a little while. Later, I'll leave you with Him, just the two of you, and it will be divine.

Here we go. We are tapping into vital information that comes from Him. Don't let the strangeness of new territory scare you. We are going back to you, to your real roots. We're going back to the "you" that existed before you were born. Don't be nervous. You were there, and so was He.

Chapter One

You, Before You Were Born

It started in darkness. It was an amazing moment. It happened in the quiet. It happened in secret. No human eyes beheld the scene. A mystery was unfolding, happening in real time and space. No one could see. For weeks, no one would know. Even then, they wouldn't know much. But you were there…all of you. You had to wait…and wait…and wait some more. A housing was being built; a body for you to live in was emerging, molecule by molecule, cell by cell, here a little, there a little. Sure, it was miniscule at first, but you didn't mind. You didn't have any control over the process, but Somebody did. You were not alone.

Like a seed planted in soil, you were planted in your mother's womb. I'm guessing you already know where babies come from, so I'll skip the details, but when a man and woman get together sexually, there is a good chance a baby will soon be on the way. I don't want to gross you out, but when your father and mother were…you know…doing it, they were not likely thinking about you. I'm sorry to disappoint you. They knew nothing about you—nothing. You were not on their mind. They didn't even really see you until about 270 days later.

Someone else did see you, however. It was your real Father. He was there. He is the One who designed your biology. He made the rules about how new humans are made. Sperm plus egg equals baby. That's what makes a baby's body, but that is *not* what makes the person. Many have the mistaken notion that God might have made the first man and woman, but that men and women have been the ones making babies ever since. Wrong! Check this out.

> *"Know ye that the Lord he is God:* ***it is he that hath made us****, and not we ourselves."*
> (Psalm 100:3a, emphasis mine)

It is God who puts the real person inside the body of the baby. You got your body from the merging of your earthly father and mother. But the "you" that was put into that baby's body was made by God. *You came from God*. That is precisely why Jesus taught that the proper way to pray is to say, "**Our Father which art in heaven...**" (Matthew 6:9; Luke 11:2). God is literally your Father. He made you.

It's true that you live in a body and that you have intellect and emotion, but the *real* you is a "spirit." That's why God is referred to as "the Father of spirits" (Hebrews 12:9). Only God is able to create a person. Earthly fathers and mothers only create the flesh and blood in which we (who are actually spirits) live. In death, the real you will leave your body, but the real you will live on (more details on that later).

Let's go back now to that sacred place, that sacred moment, when you entered that baby's body sent from God. It was dark. What was the darkness? It was the darkness of your mother's womb. No one could see you except God. Darkness does not hide us from God.

> *"Yea, the darkness hideth not from thee; but the night shineth as the day: the darkness and the light are both alike to thee."* (Psalm 139:12)

Come gently and reverently with me to the next verse, the next truth about your creation:

> *"For thou hast possessed my reins: thou hast covered me in my mother's womb."* (Psalm 139:13)

God was there in your mother's womb, not only observing, but controlling, your entrance into that baby's body. The phrase, "for thou hast possessed my reins," means that God was personally steering, controlling, and forming the real you. Now look at the next verse, in which David is explaining the same thing of himself that was true of you:

> *"I will praise thee; for I am fearfully and wonderfully made: marvellous are thy works; and that my soul knoweth right well.*
>
> *My substance was not hid from Thee when I was made in secret, and curiously wrought in the lowest parts of the earth."* (Psalm 139:14-15)

These, beloved friend, are the very words you can and should be saying about yourself: "I am fearfully and wonderfully made." This is the truth about you before you were even born. Can you look at yourself and say, "Marvelous are Thy works"? Yes, you can. Yes, you must. Yes, it is true. Praise should leap from your heart and soul and be shouted forth by your voice. You are a work of God to be marveled.

Do not miss the issue here. David said, "This my soul knoweth right well!" Do you know this "right well"? Have you got it down in your soul? In your mind? In your understanding? In your emotions? Have you got it? You must get this! You must! You simply must! Do you know this is *right*? And do you know it *well*?

One of the words for "wisdom" in the Bible means "to pound in." That's how you learned the multiplication tables. You pounded them in. Now, years later, you don't need to stop to figure them out. You simply know that seven times nine equals sixty-three. You know it because you pounded it in. That is what you must do with this truth. Pound it in. Get it. Settle it. Forever!

You and I are still walking forward. We've got more to share, but before we leave the moment of your real arrival, your real creation 270 days before you were born, let's see more of what was taking place in the seclusion, the secrecy of your mother's womb. Read Psalm 139:15 again.

When you were being made, you were under watchful eyes, the eyes of God. Accumulating around you was "substance." A botanist or scientist could probably tell you better the details of that substance. But whatever it was, thick or thin gelatinous material was being gathered around you to give you a body, and it was being watched by God. The "stuff" your body was being made out of didn't even have shape yet perfected, but God was watching. The next verse reads thus:

> *"Thine eyes did see my substance, yet being unperfect."* (Psalm 139:16a)

Before you had self-awareness, God was aware, *very aware*, and very involved. So, what did God do besides watch? He created you and placed you in your mother's womb, and now He's been watching the formation of your body. But what then?

> Before you had self-awareness, God was aware, very aware, and very involved.

He made, or caused to be made, records of you and of the event. God keeps books. The Book of Life is mentioned eight times in the Bible. That book, my friend, has a starting page with your name on it. In chapter 1, in real time, as the members of your body were being shaped, each of them was written. They were written during that entire 270- day process. Some of your body parts got written down before they were even perfected or completed. Such was your Father's zeal for you. Here's the Scripture that shares this with us:

> *"And in thy book all my members were written, which in continuance were fashioned, when as yet there was none of them."* (Psalm 139:16)

That page in that chapter, in that book (the Book of Life) contains a list about you. You may well see that Book someday. I know I intend to see the pages that tell about my life. And I want you to see yours. Each of us is adding to that record every day we live by everything we think and say and do, and by every motive in our hearts. All of it is going into the record book.

The truth about you is astonishing, amazing, remarkable, extraordinary, even stunning—that you were created by God and placed in your mother's womb, made a part of the Book of Life—and as you were being physically assembled, an eternal record was being made of each step in the process, and it was written with such excitement over you that the recording angels could hardly wait for the perfection of your body parts before writing them down. Go ahead. Be excited!

But there is more!

Even though you were not yet self-aware, from the instant you were created God was thinking about you.

> *"How precious also are thy thoughts unto me,*
> *O God! How great is the sum of them."*
>
> (Psalm 139:17)

Notice the word, "also" here. "Also" means "in addition to" or "furthermore." As well as creating a comprehensive record about you, God was pondering, musing, contemplating, and thinking of you. God was using His mind to focus on your development and attributes.

God was using His mind to focus on your development and attributes.

To be thought about by others bolsters our sense of self-esteem. It's nice, really nice, to know that someone is thinking of you. We get cards or notes, texts or e-mails, tweets or posts on social media. The pleasantness of these communications comes from the realization that we are being considered or thought about. It makes us feel significant. This significance is enhanced based on the significance of the Sender. Thus, a note from a grateful child, a message from the city mayor, even a personal expression from the president adds to the significance of the message. Now try to imagine this: God Himself was and is thinking about you! Wow!

God, Mister Big, Numero Uno; the Creator of the universe and the stars of the heavens; Designer of the earth, the land, the seas, the birds of the air, the flowers of the fields, the fishes of the sea, and the beasts of the fields, every tree, plant, insect—*He* thought about *you*. God is properly referred to as the *Most High* forty-eight times in Scripture. The psalmist David simply said,

> *"O Lord my God, thou art very great; thou art clothed with honour and majesty."* (Psalm 104:1)

Imagine with me for a moment that we have a PET scan (a positron emission tomography) of God's brain. If you could inspect the thoughts of God, past and present, what would you find? The answer is…you. You were there! You were there!

How many times were you in the thoughts of God? Well, we just read that, didn't we? Let's look at it again:

> *"How precious also are thy thoughts unto me, O God! How great is the sum of them!"*
> (Psalm 139:17)

How many times did and does God think about you? The writer inquires, "How great is the sum of them?" Ready yourself for the answer. You are about to view ultimate magnificence. There are not enough superlatives in any thesaurus to convey or portray, picture or present, describe or detail, relate or represent, this unsurpassed, unequalled, unparalleled, unrivaled reality. The only way to communicate them is by the cognitive process of analogy, and God answers the question. How great is the sum of God's thoughts toward you?

> *"If I should count them, they are more in number than the sand."* (Psalm 139:18)

If you were sitting in front of me, I could show you a high-definition picture of a handful of sand. I would ask you to try to imagine how many grains of sand are in that one handful. I'd give you some time to stare, and stare some more. I did this myself as a child. My father and mother would pack a few sandwiches, fill a gallon jar with Kool-Aid, and we'd drive to the beach about fifteen miles away. Lake Erie had lots of beaches, but our favorite was near the pier at Turkey Point. Mom would lay out the family blanket and Dad would set out the goodies that he had carried in a homemade insulated box. It was playtime.

However, instead of running toward the water, I would often just pick up a handful of sand and stare. I'd try to imagine how many grains of sand were in my little hand. I'd separate my fingers and watch the sand stream through my homemade hourglass back to the beach. The bright sun would send light sparkles in many a direction. I'd look at the pier about 200 feet away and try to imagine how many grains of sand there were between myself and the pier. I'd never heard of a trillion or a googol, a number followed by one hundred zeros, or a googolplex, a number followed by a googol of zeros, or a googolplexian, a number followed by a googolplex of zeros. I had no numbering system like that, so I would just say to myself, "There are more grains of sand here than there are numbers in the world."

If you were sitting in front of me, you would see a handful of sand—and then I'd show you real-life photos of the Sahara and more. Even if we could count the grains of sand around the Great Lakes, the oceans of the world, the thirty-three deserts of the world, which cover one-third of the earth's land surface, God's thoughts about *you* are *more in number* than that!

> *"O Lord, thou art our father; we are the clay, and thou our potter; and we all are the work of thy hand."* (Isaiah 64:8)

How could this be? That is a worthy question. The answer is simple, but it lies beyond measure, beyond calculation, beyond description, beyond imagination, and yes, certainly beyond comprehension. The answer is summed up in one word: God.

God has over twelve thousand titles and descriptions. Each of them is peerless and without parallel. Such is the greatness of His person. In a PET scan of God's mind, an inspection of His thoughts, what would find you there? You! How often would you be there? How many thoughts of you would you find in the mind of God? More in number than the grains of sand. You are there.

Why were you born? Because God wanted you! He wanted you:

Here,
Now,
At this time in history,
Living in a body whose gender was decided for you,
Embedded in a mother He assigned to you,
With strengths and weaknesses He preferred you to have.
He wrote the specs on you.
He doesn't make mistakes.
Divine wisdom devised you.
He c-r-e-a-t-e-d you!

He has a purpose for you, for your life, and for your eternity! Be careful how you respond to this vital information. The danger is that you would think it utterly impossible; that it's merely a fairy tale, a make-believe idea, a myth, a fiction, a falsehood, a fallacy, a fraud, a tale, a prevarication, a pretense, or an outright lie.

You might think that it's too wonderful to believe. You're not alone. David, the psalmist, to whom this was revealed, had the same response and the same problem. Here is what he said:

> *"Such knowledge is too wonderful for me; it is high, I cannot attain unto it."* (Psalm 139:6)

The Message renders it this way:

> *"This is too much, too wonderful—I can't take it all in!"* (Psalm 139:6 MSG)

When we began this walk together, I promised you that I would tell you the truth about yourself, no matter how wonderful it was. This would give you more detail than the simple sentence, "God loves you." He is crazy about you. You are the object of His affections. You and I should be ecstatic by now: utterly enraptured, euphoric, and thrilled. Use whatever description fits.

These truths, properly responded to, should put you on cloud nine, so to speak, or in the seventh heaven.

The right response is to shout an unequivocal "Amen!" If you do, it's as if God sends an angel down out of heaven with a golden hammer and a silver nail and fastens that truth to your life. You will never be the same again.

Before we move on, let's review the documentation of the facts:

> *"I will praise thee; for I am fearfully and wonderfully made: marvellous are thy works; and that my soul knoweth right well...*
>
> *When I was made in secret, and curiously wrought in the lowest parts of the earth...*
>
> *How precious also are thy thoughts unto me, O God! How great is the sum of them!*
>
> *If I should count them, they are more in number than the sand."* (Psalm 139:14,15,17-18)

Chapter Two

To Like You or Not to Like You: That Is the Question

Her name was Bonnie. She just showed up one night after a Thursday night chapel service at the Teen Challenge Center in Toronto. My father was the director and I was a young minister at the time. Dad would lead the chapel services, and I would go out into the streets and preach, hoping people would be touched and come in.

Dad was just finishing up when Bonnie snuck timidly in the back door. I was sitting in a chair on the other side of the room, which wasn't very far away as it wasn't a very big room. The chapel sat about twenty-four people altogether. A lot of kids like Bonnie would wander in and out, but for some reason I noticed her.

I can still remember the scene vividly. The red carpet on the floor. The blackboard pushed to the side of the room that my dad and I would draw diagrams on or where we'd write things we wanted people to remember, trying to help them learn about the love of God. Most of all though, I remember the rostrum near the front where a big Bible lay open for any to investigate. I remember how lovingly and reverently my dad used to turn the pages when he taught from it.

The instant I saw Bonnie I knew she was a runaway. She just had that look. She wasn't quite sure where she was. She almost tiptoed in as if she didn't belong there or anywhere, for that matter. It had been a while since she'd had a chance to clean herself up and probably longer since she'd eaten. She was the type who wouldn't have wandered in if she hadn't been desperately casting about for help.

It was then that I also noticed her cradling her wrists, continually pulling her sleeves down to hide them. Through her fingers, I could see long horizontal scars that were just beginning to heal—the kind someone makes when trying to kill themselves. At the same time, there was still some light in her eyes. Bonnie wasn't gone yet.

I crossed the room and greeted her, which was when I learned her name. I asked her where she was from and some other questions she didn't seem to want to answer. I could tell that the longer we talked, the more she wanted to turn and run out of the building, so I cut to the chase and asked her if there was anything I could do to help.

"Oh, I'm fine," she lied. "I don't need anything." Then, sort of as an afterthought, she said, "I'm not really worth your help anyway."

"Hogwash," I said. (To be truthful, I used the BS words in an effort to shock her.) She'd been turning to go, but stopped and looked back at me in surprise.

"What?" she asked.

"Hogwash. No, double hogwash," I countered. She looked at me blankly, but her eyes pleaded. "May I show you something?" I asked. She shrugged.

I walked over to the big Bible on the rostrum and motioned for her to follow. She did. Then I opened the book to some of its most worn pages—a section I had heard my father quote many times—Psalm 139. I began to read from the first verse.

"O Lord, thou hast searched me, and known me." I paused. "Each place where it says 'me,' I want you to imagine *your name* in there. I want you to imagine that it says, 'O Lord, You have searched me—Bonnie—and You have known me, Bonnie.'"

Bonnie's forehead scrunched. "Okay," she said tentatively.

I continued, "Thou knowest Bonnie's sitting down and her rising up. Thou understandeth her far-off thoughts. God, You've searched out Bonnie's path, and You know where she lies down to sleep, You are acquainted with all of Bonnie's ways."

As I read, I continued to look back and forth from the Bible to her face. I walked her through each phrase, telling her in the simplest terms I could, how much God loved her—even when she was in her mother's womb—how God had carefully woven her together, how she was His work of art, how she was the object of His affections. I watched as each phrase sank in, one by one.

Then something dark and terrible washed over her face. Suddenly, she jumped at me, fingernails flailing. I fell back, putting my hands up to protect myself.

"Can your God make me a virgin again?" she screamed in anguish. She was hysterical. As gently and as quickly as I could, I reached out my hand and touched her forehead.

"Jesus," I whispered.

She crumpled to the floor in a puddle of tears. She sobbed and sobbed.

I knelt on the floor beside her and waited until she took a breath and had the chance to hear my words. "Yes," I said. She looked up at me again, puzzled anew. "Yes," I repeated. "Jesus *can* make you pure again. He can't change the past, but He can wipe away the guilt and the shame," I went on. "In fact, He gave His life for that very thing. He gave His life for that very 'Bonnie' we were just reading about. The 'Bonnie' God loved and planned good things for from the day she was conceived." I went on to tell her of the cross, the blood of Jesus, and more about God's love for her personally.

The moments grew into minutes and the minutes into an hour. In the end, sitting on that red carpet in that tiny chapel, Bonnie received three things: forgiveness, cleansing, and reinstatement to her right relationship to her loving Father God.

She didn't leave that place the same as the girl who had come in.

My hope is that you won't leave this book the same person now reading these words either. God had a reason Bonnie was born, and He has a reason you were born. He has a plan and a purpose. He has gifted you and appointed a purpose for your life.

There's a reason you were born. This book is to help you find that out.

It Starts with Liking You

Like Bonnie—for various reasons, from things we've done to trauma we've experienced, to the nose that stares back at us when we look into a mirror—many of us don't really like ourselves. We tend to either look down on ourselves or we hunger for recognition so much that we go out into the world to force others to notice us. We may think looking down on ourselves is some form of humility, or we may think we have no worth until we've accomplished some great thing. Both are tricks to keep us down. If we don't like ourselves the way God made us, then we won't even try to reach the heights God purposed for us; we won't pursue the dreams He knit into us in our mothers' wombs. Instead, we try to get fame and glory for ourselves, following a world system meant to enslave us. Neither path holds the freedom and fulfillment God planned for us the very day He began knitting us into being.

What if you don't like yourself because of a traumatic background? What if you don't like yourself because you were mistreated or even abused as a child? What if you don't like yourself because you were rejected? Or what if you don't like yourself because you were deserted by one or both of your parents? What if you don't like yourself for any of a thousand other reasons?

I have some really wonderful news for you:

> *"For I* ***(God)*** *will* ***restore*** *health unto thee, and*
> *I will heal thee of thy wounds, saith the Lord;*
> *because they called thee an Outcast, saying, This is*
> *Zion, whom no man seeketh after."*
>
> (Jeremiah 30:17, emphasis and additions mine)

I love the word *restore*. Have you ever had a computer that went haywire? You reboot it, and it gets *restored*. Once it's restored, it functions properly again, doesn't it? (Usually, anyway.)

No matter what has happened to you, no matter how you've been broken or damaged, disgraced or shamed—God wants to restore you, to return you to your original design. Look at what He said above: "I will *restore* health to you: mental health, emotional health, and spiritual health. I will heal your wounds." There's nothing broken He can't fix. That's why we call Him Savior. That's why we call Him Redeemer. *Blessed* Redeemer. He says: "I will restore your health. I will heal your wounds because everybody's treating you like an outcast, like there's something wrong with you, but *I* know better."

There's nothing broken He can't fix.

Look at what else He says:

> *"And I will restore to you the years that the locust hath eaten, the cankerworm, and the caterpiller, and the palmerworm, my great army which I sent among you. And ye shall eat in plenty, and be satisfied, and praise the name of the Lord your God, that hath dealt wondrously with you: and my people shall never be ashamed."* (Joel 2:25-26)

Everything that's tried to chew you up and spit you out, that wants to ruin your days, your weeks, your months, and your years, *He will restore*. God will bring you back to a restored point—as if none of that had ever happened. You'll eat plenty, and you'll be satisfied. You'll end up praising the name of the Lord, your God, because He will have dealt wondrously with you, and you will never be ashamed.

Here we are, created by God Himself, the One who is above all positions and degrees, the One with whom there is no rival, competition, or comparison, the ultimate Being. He made us, He was with us from our conception when no one else even suspected we existed, and He planned out a destiny and purpose for our lives that would have ripple effects for generations to come. And what is our typical human response? We look at what God created and intended to accomplish— marvelous things—and we look down on it. We despise ourselves. We scoff at and belittle the very work of His hands. We look down on ourselves in a way we wouldn't even let a person treat a dog. That said, will we bow before the God who created the universe in adoration, or will we spurn the work of His hands? (That work is you, by the way.)

Ephesians 2:10 tells us that we are "his workmanship, created in Christ Jesus unto good works." The *International Standard Version* translates this verse in this way:

> *"For we are* ***God's*** *masterpiece, created in* ***the Messiah Jesus to perform good actions*** *that God prepared long ago to be our way of life."*
>
> (Ephesians 2:10 ISV, emphasis mine)

This begs the question: If God says each of us is His work—His unique and special masterpiece—who are we to disagree?

The Bible even warns about the arrogance of rejecting the work of His hand. The Bible repeatedly says, "Woe to them." The word woe or woes appears 107 times in 98 verses in the King James Version of the Bible.[1] Woe is an exclamatory crying out, a lament of caution, often prolonged, based on the intrinsic urgency. It refers to situations that have caused great distress, and warns us to take care and remain alert and attentive, vigilant, prudent, discreet. We must take heed. Here is a critical thing to heed: there are three serious woes of which the prophets warned us. It was their way of saying: "Big trouble is looming for any who do not take heed to these truths."

One example is this:

> *"Woe unto him that striveth with his Maker!"*
>
> (Isaiah 45:9a)

You do not want to contend with God. Talk about a losing

1 "'Woe' or 'Woes,'" Blue Letter Bible (Blue Letter Bible), accessed February 7, 2020, https://www.blueletterbible.org/search/search.cfm?Criteria=woe+OR+woes&t=KJV)

proposition! You will lose if you strive with the Maker of the universe (and your Maker). There's no room to disagree with His statements about making you and His big plans for your life—plans that will impact eternity. (See Jeremiah 29:11 again.) He produced, fabricated, fashioned, constructed, and built you. He brought you into existence. It just follows that if you like Him, and if you respect Him, you will like what He made. That means you had better like *the you* He originated. If not, *"Woe!"* You're headed for big trouble if you don't change course.

But that's not all He said in this passage. He goes on to say:

> *"Woe unto him that striveth with his Maker! Let the potsherd strive with the potsherds of the earth. Shall the clay say to him that fashioneth it, What makest thou? Or thy work, He hath no hands?"*
> (Isaiah 45:9)

Let me paraphrase: "Will the pot say to the Potmaker, 'Hey, you did a lousy job?' Will the clay tell the Potter His business? Will you carry on a dispute with your Maker? Will you tell God that His hands are clumsy and that He messed up when He made you?"

The idea is pretty laughable, isn't it? Who could say such things to God? Who could criticize a design about which we understand so very little? Why would we criticize the art of an Artist we really love? "Oh, those other things You made are beautiful, but this one—this *me*—this is unlovable." Of course, you can't say that! It makes no sense!

Let's look at another verse, this time in a more modern paraphrase to bring out its meaning:

> *"Who in the world do you think you are to second-guess God? Do you for one moment suppose any of us knows enough to call God into question? Clay doesn't talk back to the fingers that mold it, saying, 'Why did you shape me like this?' Isn't it obvious that a potter has a perfect right to shape one lump*

> *of clay into a vase for holding flowers and another into a pot for cooking beans?"*
>
> (Romans 9:20-21 MSG)

That is why you should really, really like yourself. You were formed in the hands of the Artist that makes no mistakes, the hands of the Sculptor that makes no blunders. For God, even the potsherds—the broken pieces of pottery—have a beautiful purpose. We may not understand it, but what would be the fun of it if we did? There would be no mystery to solve! However, we do need to trust the Artist. At the core, the question is: Will you decide to accept your "self"—the you that God made—or will you decide to reject your "self"—the you that God made? Which do you think is more likely to propel you to your intended destiny? To accept the creation of the Divine Planner or reject it? How can you reject the you of your destiny, and still be all you were destined to be?

Upon your answer to this fundamental question, your future will be determined. My advice, in the strongest of terms, would be for you to say, "I will praise Thee; for I am fearfully and wonderfully made: marvelous are Thy works; and that my soul knoweth right well" (Psalm 139:14). Say it every time you look in the mirror and every time you see a picture of yourself. You can't imagine how much good that will do you!

It helps. It's good to remember it's not really about *you*. It's about Him and what He made. You will either be grateful for the way God made you or not. You will either celebrate yourself or criticize yourself. Suicide does not begin with a bottle of pills, a razor blade, or a rope. Self-destructive behaviors begin by criticizing what God has made. If the devil can get you to despise God's creation, then he can destroy you. If, however, you think of yourself and treat yourself the way you would regard and treat anything else God made, self-destructive behaviors won't even cross your mind.

The person who does not like him or her self will spend the rest of their lives trying to be like someone else, always comparing themselves with others, and feeling they fall short. Or they will fall into the ditch on the other side of the road, always trying to prove they are better than everyone else by putting others down. It is thus that superiority or inferiority complexes are created. Neither are healthy.

We weren't meant to look to the right or the left to figure out who we are. We were meant to look *up*. Look to your Father in heaven who loves you. Get your worth from Him. Then you can look to the right and the left to help others, to look up to receive that same love and approval. That's the origin of true humility. You don't have anything to prove because God loves you, but, in response, you want to be everything you can be because you want to reciprocate that love. True humility doesn't say, "I'm nothing." It says, "I'm loved. Even if I'm a little imperfect and broken, I'm on the path to something better, something my God has had planned for me before I was even a twinkle in my parents' eyes!"

It's Not Your Parents' Fault Either

If that's not enough, then here are two further *woes*:

> *"Woe unto him that saith unto his father, What begettest thou? Or to the woman, What hast thou brought forth?"* (Isaiah 45:10)

Some of us blame our parents for what we've become in our lifetimes. That's not a helpful choice. Here God says *woe* to those who blame their father, and a further *woe* to those who blame their mother. Self-rejection plus blame is still self-rejection, no matter whose "fault" it is.

But what if our parents *did* do bad things to us? Why is it woeful to blame them for what you've become when who you are now is at least partially the result of how they brought you up? The attitude we are supposed to have toward our father and our mother is well-known, but unfortunately not often lived out. From the beginning, we are instructed, thus:

> *"Honour thy father and thy mother."*
> (Exodus 20:12a)

Honoring your father is the antithesis of indicting him for "begetting" you. Honoring your mother is the polar opposite to incriminating her for what she "has brought forth." Your father and your mother were indeed the conduits, the instruments that God used to bring you into the world. God is saying here that anybody who had a significant role of bringing this "one of a kind" *you* into the world should be esteemed. The rejection of your father and mother, regardless of their faults and failures, brings to us these *woes*.

Disregarding the woe warnings will bring damage and destruction into our present and future lives.

> *"Whoso curseth his father or his mother, his lamp shall be put out in obscure darkness."*
> (Proverbs 20:20)

This simply means that our light, our ability to influence others the proper way, will be obscured and clouded. We will not have a positive effect on those around us if we can't respect others. And if you can't respect those to whom you are closest, then you won't ever really respect anyone, especially yourself. In contrast, if you honor your father and mother, you will not have woes, but blessings. As the apostle Paul wrote:

> *"Honour thy father and mother; which is the first commandment with promise;*
>
> *that it may be well with thee, and thou mayest live long on the earth."* (Ephesians 6:2-3)

What is the essence of the promise Paul is referring to here?

- It will be well with you; you will have success in every area of your life; the condition of your spirit and your conscience and your example will propel you forward.
- You will live long on the earth; you will have fewer health issues; your spirit and this right condition of your mind that comes from the proper honoring of your

parents will prompt, induce, stimulate, and encourage you forward because the spiritual clutter that comes from dishonoring parents will not contribute to your physical and emotional demise.

The health of your relationship with your parents will affect the health of your body and your success—if you honor them, you will live long *and well!*

The Heart of the Question before Us

The heart of the question here is not merely, "Why should you accept yourself?" The question is: "*Will* you accept yourself—*joyfully, enthusiastically, even fanatically*?" Because it's not just about getting by, it's about being all you were intended to be.

My best advice to you is to be exuberant, cheerful, and energetic about you. Why? Because you were designed by God Himself. You are the work of His hands. You are loved, desired, and sought after. You are His masterpiece, created to do good on the earth.

> Since feelings come from thoughts, you can only change your feelings by changing your thoughts.

> *"I have loved thee with an everlasting love: therefore with lovingkindness have I drawn thee."*
> (Jeremiah 31:3)

I know very few people who don't need to upgrade how they think of themselves. If we're to do it right, we're to think of ourselves like God thinks of us:

> *"Not...more highly than he ought to think; but to think soberly, according as God hath dealt to every man the measure of faith."* (Romans 12:3)

Since feelings come from thoughts, you can only change your feelings by changing your thoughts. That's the benefit of reading this book and spending time with me here. You get a chance to change the thoughts you have about yourself.

How can you be sure that what I am telling you is the right way to begin thinking about yourself and pondering why you were born? Because these thoughts come from God Himself. They are *the facts*. They come from the Holy Bible. They are *the truth*. Who can calculate the human pain of a life based on false illusions? Believe these things and the pain will begin to go away. Depression will be vanquished. The truth of the matter is that you have better things to do than fight with yourself. God has a wonderful plan for your life.

There is a penetrating insight in 1 Timothy. In this book, Paul tells Timothy,

> *"Let no man despise thy youth."* (1 Timothy 4:12)

Paul also instructs the young Timothy, thus,

> *"Flee also youthful lusts."* (2 Timothy 2:22)

Paul is instructing this junior progeny on how to handle and help people. He tells him not to get into strife, to be gentle, to be able to explain what he preaches when asked, to be patient with people, to be meek, and then instruct "those that oppose themselves" (2 Timothy 2:24–25). That's an interesting way to say it, don't you think? "Those that oppose themselves." It is possible, as we've been discussing, that people can hold counterproductive views about themselves. Self-destructive behaviors abound in our culture, and I believe this is the source of many of them. The non-acceptance of one's self, the non-celebrating of one's self, fits into the category of holding views that oppose one's self. If not confronted and debunked, such opposition will irritate and corrupt any good in a person's self-image and life.

There is good news, however. God is on your side, even when you are not. He is always *for* you, never against you.

> *"When I cry unto thee, then shall mine enemies turn back: this I know; for God is for me."*
>
> (Psalm 56:9)

Why not join Him?

Of course, there is also someone who is against you, as we've already mentioned.

> *"Your adversary the devil, as a roaring lion, walketh about, seeking whom he may devour."*
>
> (1 Peter 5:8b)

So, if God is for us and the devil is against us, who is going to win? I like what the old-time preacher said: "I believe in *election*. God votes for you, the devil votes against you, but *you* get to cast the deciding vote." In the end, the deciding vote is yours. Will you be *for* you? Or will you be in the number of "those that oppose themselves"?

To like you or not to like you? That is the question. What is your answer?

I'd suggest agreeing with God. If you still can't let yourself do that, go back to the beginning of this chapter and Psalm 139, and read it like I read it to Bonnie. Put your name into the verses every time it says "me" or "my." Do that until you can agree with God about how special you are to Him.

At the same time, it's worth looking at the lives of some people who had a lot more going against them than you do, and see what they did with what God gave them. I think you'll be as amazed and moved by their stories as I have been. They are truly inspiring. Additionally, be sure not to miss Supplement 2 which lists thirty consequences of not liking yourself, as well as what to do about that. :-)

Chapter Three

You Are Not a Mistake

"I am come that they might have life,
and that they might have it more abundantly."
(John 10:10b)

Nick Vujicic was born with no arms and no legs. At sixteen, Ryan Troutman was in a car accident that left him brain-damaged and in a coma for six weeks. He remained in the hospital for a year and a half as he struggled to retrain his body to walk and speak. Gianna Jessen survived a saline abortion attempt on her life. (In a saline abortion, a corrosive fluid is injected into the mother's womb with the intent to burn the baby inside and out and cause its death within twenty-four hours.) An eight-second *YouTube* video labeling Lizzie Valesquez as the ugliest woman in the world went viral when she was seventeen. It was viewed by over 4.8 million people, many of whom left comments telling her to kill herself. Ji Seong-ho was a starving boy in North Korea whose limbs were run over by train after he collapsed on the tracks from exhaustion, as if things weren't bad enough when he was starving to death! Rebecca was sexually molested and abused from age five to seventeen by a trusted friend of the family.

How would any of these people become someone of note?

In a moment, I will tell you more of their stories, but first a fundamental truth must be understood. Their lives are living proof of this truth:

> *"And we know that all things work together for good to them that love God, to them who are the called according to his purpose."* (Romans 8:28)

I know this will stagger your mind, your intelligence, your reason, and your heart. Those who underestimate the "God Factor" will never get it, but you can comprehend it.

Can God turn no arms and no legs into something good? Even something *very* good? Can God make something wonderful out of a saline-burned baby? You bet He can! Can God turn ugliness into beauty? Can God take a tortured boy, who was run over by a train, and turn him into a statesman who can save thousands? Can God take a beaten-down, molested child and turn her into a successful advocate and rescuer of hundreds of other sexually assaulted and damaged children and women? The answer is a resounding, "Yes!" This is why we call Him the Redeemer!

Let's look a little closer at this astonishing truth. It's flabbergasting. It's dumbfounding! It's breathtaking! But just before we move on, let's look at several other wordings of this often untold and mind-boggling Scripture:

> *"We can be so sure that every detail in our lives of love for God is worked into something good."*
> (Romans 8:28 MSG)

> *"Moreover we know that to those who love God, who are called according to his plan, everything that happens fits into a pattern for good."*
> (Romans 8:28 PHILLIPS)

God is a tragedy-to-triumph fanatic. He makes everything good!

God is accurately referred to as "the Father of mercies and the God of all comfort" (2 Corinthians 1:3 ISV). After that, it is said of Him that He:

> *"Comforteth us in all our tribulation, that we may be able to comfort them which are in any trouble, by the comfort wherewith we ourselves are comforted of God."* (2 Corinthians 1:4)

The same verse in other versions is translated this way:

> *"He comes alongside us when we go through hard times, and before you know it, he brings us alongside someone else who is going through hard times so that we can be there for that person just as God was there for us."* (2 Corinthians 1:4 MSG)

> *"He comforts us in all our troubles so that we can comfort others. When they are troubled, we will be able to give them the same comfort God has given us."* (2 Corinthians 1:4 NLT)

Here's the truth:

- God has a comfort, an answer, a solution, a fix, a recovery act for every test, trial, tribulation, tragedy, or trouble of every and any sort. That's the meaning of "God of all comfort" and that's the magnitude of "comforts us in all tribulation."
- God's purpose in supplying the solutions to us is so that we can pass on the solutions He personally gave us to others who are in the same situation we once experienced. Our influence is enhanced. We have greater potential after a difficulty than we would have had without it. It's being able to say with conviction, "I would rather be with God in the dark than in the light without Him."

You become God's purveyor of hope to others. Your purpose and meaning in life—the reason you were born—cannot be thwarted, frustrated, derailed, or foiled. You cannot be impeded, hindered, obstructed, stymied, or defeated by anyone or any seeming tragedy *if you will respond to God.* He is the God who can "make everything work together for your good" if you love Him and walk according to His plans.

Nick Vujicic

Take Nick Vujicic as an example. He was born without arms or legs. He was born with tetra-amelia syndrome. Can you imagine living life without limbs? Yet Nick has become a symbol of triumph against all odds. His videos have been watched over a hundred million times.

> **You become God's purveyor of hope to others.**

It wasn't easy for him. For years, he was harassed and tormented at school. At the age of ten, Nick attempted suicide. However, Nick, the boy born without arms or legs, had an encounter with God, who is (remember) "the God of all comfort." That changed everything. During an interview on *Oprah*, he summarized his life:

"I know that God didn't give me this pain, but what the enemy tried to turn into bad, God made it into good. I want everyone to know that we are wonderfully and fearfully made by God. And until you can actually understand that we are all wonderfully and fearfully made by God, you will always be trapped and chained and stopped, but when you have the incredible power of faith in action, nothing can hold you back and you are beautiful just the way that you are—no worries."

With regard to being connected, he said, "I can't get married. I can't even hold my wife's hand. What connection am I going to have?" But then he declared, "You know what? All things come together for the good for them that love Him." (However, on February 12, 2012, Nick married Kanae Miyahara.) He went on to say, "Being without arms and legs is all about choice. I had parents who were my heroes. They said, 'You can always be angry for what you don't have, or you can be thankful for what you do have. Do your best and God will do the rest.'" He went on to say, "Because I gave my life to Jesus Christ and [underwent] the renewing of my mind, I knew I could be unstoppable."[2]

Nick graduated from university at age twenty-one with a bachelor of commerce degree, with a double major in accounting and financial planning. He founded Life Without Limits, an international nonprofit organization and ministry. He also founded Attitude Is Altitude, a motivational-speaking company. He starred in the film *The Butterfly Circus* and was awarded Best Actor in a Short Film by the Method Fest Independent Film Festival.[3]

Nick has written eight books, including *Life Without Limits*; *Love Without Limits*; *Be the Hands and Feet: Living Out God's Love for All His Children*; and others. Nick and his wife, Kanae, now have two sons and twin girls. You simply must see and hear his story. You can easily search his name on *YouTube*. He is living proof of how God can take what seems like the worst situation and turn it into the best.

Ryan Troutman

Ryan Troutman is a business sales rep at my local Apple store. A car accident left him in a trauma hospital and in a coma for six weeks. His time in rehabilitation lasted over eighteen months. He has written the details of his experience in his book, *Second Chance Story*. He transparently tells of the battles he lost and the battles he won.

When your brain doesn't work, neither does your body. Ryan had to start from scratch. Ryan once described it to me thus: "I was trapped inside my own body. My eyes were open, but I could not respond. I simply stared off into space and was unable to communicate. I was unable to walk, talk, use the restroom, or feed myself. I was a sixteen-year-old, 120-pound baby." Meanwhile, Ryan's parents suffered with him. The issue for Ryan became, in his words, "how to complete life's puzzle or even how to put the first two pieces together."

---

2 Tabernacle United Methodist Church, "Nick Vujicic on Oprah." YouTube video, 3:30. January 25, 2016. https://www.youtube.com/watch?v=hmvtuB0gtGg

3 ILiveInANoMansLand, "The Butterfly Circus [Short Film HD]." YouTube video, 22:35. October 12, 2011. https://www.youtube.com/watch?v=p98KAEif3bI

Ryan did put it together; and although he has worked for Apple for more than seven years at this time, his eyes sparkled when he told me how he now lives to help others survive and thrive in spite of brain damage. He has a nonprofit dedicated to helping people around the world. I think he personifies the adage of how to turn lemons into lemonade. Who knows the scope of his help to others? The solutions he found and has handed on will give a meaningful life to many.

Gianna Jessen

Gianna Jessen survived the silent holocaust of the abortion industry. A doctor attempted to perform an instillation abortion on her: A chemical solution including salt was injected into her mother's womb, which was intended to asphyxiate and blind the fetus, burning it inside and out, then cause contractions in the mother, which would then expel the deceased infant in twenty-four hours. The lifeless body could then be thrown away. However, Gianna was still alive when she emerged, and because of the Born Alive Infant Protection Act, which had recently been passed into law, the doctors were required to do all they could to save her life. She was two and a half pounds at birth, and a lack of oxygen to her brain had left her with cerebral palsy. Despite her poor prognosis, she lived, and the abortionist who had intended to toss away the lifeless fetus had to sign her birth certificate instead.

She spent three months in the hospital before being placed in foster care. Despite being dismissed from the hospital, doctors believed she would never be able to raise her head on her own. Instead, she began walking at three with the aid of a walker and braces, and today she walks on her own with only a slight limp. She has even run marathons. (Oh, and she's also an accomplished singer!)

Her first months were spent in a "mean" foster home in which she was hated, but she eventually was placed in a loving home, and later discovered how greatly she was loved by God.

As a result of that encounter, she now calls herself "God's girl." She admits that she is weaker than most of the rest of us, but she has a message. She speaks regularly, offering hope to masses of hurting, forgotten, and discarded people. She tells her audiences how God can make the most miserable thing beautiful. She challenges men to stand up and be men because she believes God made them for greatness. She calls on them to defend women and children, even those yet to be born. "You women," she says, "are not made for abuse, but you are made to be fought for."

She told Mike Huckabee the following on his television program: "So you can imagine how I feel when I hear the argument: 'If the baby is disabled, we need to terminate the pregnancy.' Well, who are you, healthy person, to look at me and decide for me what my quality of life is? You have *no idea* how beautiful my life is because I have something to overcome— because I actually *need* Jesus."[4]

What a will to make the most of what God has given to a person, don't you agree? Oh, that the rest of us would do as much with what God has given to us! "As for me," she says of her life, "I hope to make God smile."[5] I wept the first time I heard her speak. She has appeared on numerous televisions shows, in numerous nations, and has testified several times in the halls of government. (You can hear her story for yourself on *YouTube.*)

Lizzie Velasquez

And then there's Lizzie Velasquez. When she was sixteen, an eight-second video of her went viral, labeling her the ugliest woman in the world. It was viewed by over 4.8 million people. The comments below this viral video asked such things as: "Why didn't your parents abort you?" and "Can't you just find a gun and kill yourself?" They called her a monster and something that should be "destroyed with fire." Can you image what it would be like, as a sixteen-year-old girl, to stumble across a site like that

---

4 Huckabee, "Gianna Jessen's POWERFUL Abortion Survival Testimony." YouTube video, 8:00. January 20, 2018, https://www.youtube.com/watch?v=pwpJTY1pEns.

5 Jennifer Johnson, "One of the Best Pro-life Speeches EVER! Gianna Jessen abortion survivor Full video," YouTube video, 15:41. August 21, 2013, https://www.youtube.com/watch?v=hOWMmx6eBjU.

with your picture on it and read comment after comment, not only degrading you, but telling you that you don't even deserve to be alive? She determined to read every comment, looking for at least one person who would stand up for her. She didn't find a single one!

Lizzie looks the way she does because she was born with a disease called neonatal progeroid syndrome. It inhibits weight gain and leaves a person with weak bones and a weak heart. She was 2.1 pounds when she was born, she has zero body fat, and she has never weighed more than 64 pounds in her entire life. The disease also caused blindness in one of her eyes. She is one of only three people in the world known to have this disease.

Never able to get beyond emaciated, Lizzie was bullied in grade school and constantly ridiculed, mocked, and berated for an appearance over which she had absolutely no control. She was called things like "skinny bones," "grandma," and "pork chop legs." In high school, things only escalated. How could such a person ever be happy? How could her life have meaning or purpose? How could this "trashed girl" ever have a livelihood? Did God create her just to be ridiculed?

Lizzie's answer would be a resounding "No!"

"God is the reason why I'm here," she tells audiences today. "God is with me, and if He's not leaving this path, neither am I. I'm not going to let that video, or those people, become the definition of who I was meant to be."

During her junior year in high school, Lizzie was asked to address the freshman class of four hundred students about her condition. Instead of the anticipated chaos and rowdiness expected from young students, the room listened in rapt attention. Most were silent, but many wept. At the conclusion of her speech, students lined up to hug her and thank her for how her story had touched them. It was in the midst of this that Lizzie realized her purpose in life: She was called to be a messenger of hope and lead a constructive movement against bullying. God did have a purpose for her after all!

Today, she is the author of three books and the producer of numerous videos. Her TEDx Talk in Austin, Texas on self-image has also gone viral, with more than 7.1 million views the last time I looked. In it, she says of the bullies who tormented her all those years, "Tell me those negative things…I'm gonna turn them around and use them as a ladder to climb up to my goals."[6] In Mexico, more than 10,000 gathered to hear her story. In Washington, D.C., she influenced Congress in the creation of the Safe Schools Improvement Act.

Her message is simple: "We were all put on earth for a purpose. Be brave! Find your purpose! Succeed! ...I feel that Jesus put me in this little body to show people that no matter what size you are, or where you come from, or what you go through, there is a God who is there, who will never leave you. And that will surpass any obstacle."[7]

Ji Seong-ho

Ji Seong-ho was born in North Korea. In his teens, Ji Seong-ho used to scavenge coal that had tumbled out of trains and try to trade it for food for his family. In one instance, while jumping from one train car to another, he lost consciousness due to hunger and fell through the gap between the cars. When he awoke, he discovered only "a piece of very thin flesh was holding my leg to the rest of my body. Blood was gushing out." He realized immediately that he needed to stop the bleeding. When he tried to work on his leg, he realized that three of his fingers on his left hand had been sheared off. His younger brother was able to help him stem the bleeding, get him into a cart, and to a hospital. Had it not been for the pleading and crying of his mother, the doctors would have left him to die. To save costs, they used no anesthesia when they amputated his leg and hand.[8]

---

6 TEDx Talks, "How Do You Define Yourself? | Lizzie Velasquez | TEDxAustinWomen
Brave Starts Here," YouTube video, 13:10. January 16, 2014, 13:10. https://www.youtube.com/watch?v=QzPbY9ufnQY.

7 Ibid.

8 Paul Bond, "North Korean Defector-Turned-Radio Broadcaster Reveals Cruel Treatment: Hand, Leg Removed Without Anesthesia," The Hollywood Reporter, April 20, 2015, https://www.hollywoodreporter.com/news/north- korean-defector-turned-radio-789919.

Once he survived and had healed enough to walk with a crutch, he was back to foraging for food, which included smuggling rice from China, a criminal offense in North Korea. Eventually, he was caught and arrested. In prison, he was beaten worse than others who had committed similar crimes. He was told by an agent, "You went over to China hobbling on crutches. You've dishonored the leader by doing that in a foreign land. Sons of bitches like you are throwing mud on the face of our leader, who is doing all he can to provide."

Just how could a young man like this have any real purpose in life? What would his answer be if you asked him, "Why were you born?"

And yet, Ji never gave up his hunger for freedom. In 2006, he and his brother escaped to South Korea, walking with the help of wooden crutches made by his father. He fell in among a group of Christians who helped him obtain prosthetics and find a way to provide for himself and his brother. A few years later, he established a group, Now Action and Unity for Human Rights, to speak out about human rights. He began rescuing North Korean defectors trapped in China. He traveled a 1000+ miles across China and Southeast Asia, spreading his message of hope and deliverance. He has since addressed the British Parliament.

Meanwhile, his father, previously a member of the "regime," was caught trying to escape, and he was tortured and murdered. Though Ji Seong-ho now has an artificial limb and can walk on his own, he brandished those same father-made wooden crutches when he was hailed in the Presidential State of the Union Address.

Ji became a Christian. He now lives in Seoul. His purpose? The reason he was born? To rescue defectors from the tyranny of the rogue nation of North Korea and broadcast the truth of deliverance (the gospel) throughout the region.

And Rebecca

Rebecca was tormented, violated, assaulted, manipulated, exploited, and degraded for twelve long years. When she was only five, the perpetrator, disguised as a "friend of the family," started to influence the life of this innocent child. A full-grown adult, he began to engineer, orchestrate, choreograph, and program her little mind in such a way that she would be held captive by him at his will and whim for twelve years: for four thousand, three hundred, and eighty-three days.

Unscrupulously, he held her as in a vise; he held her by enticements and fear. It's hard for me to tell Rebecca's story. I wept inwardly (and at times outwardly) as I interviewed her for an hour and a half on (of all days) Valentine's Day. The details of the torture and sexual exploitation should never be conveyed or graphically described. I know that's contrary to our degraded culture, which seems amused and entertained by degradation. Thank you, Helliwood! In the Bible, these acts are called "the works of darkness," and we are well informed that "it is a shame even to speak of those things which are done of them in secret" (Ephesians 5:12).

In civil dialogue and academic terms, Rebecca's situation is referred to as complex trauma, the result of a prolonged, repeated experience of interpersonal trauma in a context in which the individual has little or no chance of escape. She describes it as living in a war zone from which there was no escape; a lack of safety on multiple levels; loneliness that simulated being exiled from everyone else; manipulated into silence by threats that you wouldn't believe. The candy was poison and the poison turned to pain, pain beyond the physical that reached to mental and emotional depths unspeakable. She was a trashed human, relegated to a garbage can and feeling like she belonged there.

Rebecca! Now what? She connected with God. Jesus became her friend. She learned who she really was. She got the truth about herself, and it was wonderful. Unspeakably terrible things might have happened to her, but she animatedly declared, "What happened to me does not define me. I am a daughter of the Most High God." Every time a lie would come into her mind, she would repeat this phrase. She "pounded in" the truth, and she no longer lives with a damaged version of herself. Her advice to would-be survivors is: "Put all the pieces of your broken heart into the hands of God. He knows how to mend them and put them back together in a beautiful way."

I asked Rebecca if there were any long-term consequences from her abuse. She said, "No, I'm happy; I'm blessed. I love my life. I love what I do." I asked, "What is that?" Without hesitation, she responded, "I help others." "How so?" I asked. She replied, "I help abused and damaged girls to not just merely survive but recover, so that they thrive in life. I tell them to never give up and be sure to connect with God."

I had two more important questions for her. "First, did going through what you went through help you to be more effective in helping others? She responded, "Definitely." And dear reader, that is the essential point of this chapter, that no matter what hurt, damage, abuse, or tragedy you've experienced, our wonderful God wants to fix whatever is broken, heal whatever is hurt, and empower you to be more effective in life than you otherwise would have been.

My final question for Rebecca was, "Rebecca, what is your purpose in life now?" Her answer was simply profound and profoundly simple. She said, "It is to love." I ended the interview by asking Rebecca how she would pray for an abused girl if one should walk into my office right now. This is how she prayed. (Maybe this prayer is for you.)

> Dear God, Thank You for Your love. Thank You for what You created Your daughter to be. God, we know You are here, that You are with us; You are with her. God, we may not feel Your presence but we know You are here. We ask for Your help. We ask for Your guidance. We ask for Your wisdom.
>
> I ask that Your daughter would know that even in dark moments, she is not alone. I ask You to give her others who would help, defend, and protect her, even angels who would protect her. Help her to know what You truly created her to be. You love her and You still do miracles today. Amen!

What Will Your Story Be?

What will the story of your life be? Why were *you* born? I'm sure it was for some greatness that may be too wonderful for you to believe. And yet, each of the people I've written about in this chapter probably had far more circumstances opposing them than you do. Finding that belief in themselves—seeing themselves through the eyes of God instead of being limited by human perception—they continue to achieve wonderful things every day of their existence. Truly, the world is a better place for having them in it; and as handicapped and deformed as the world might see them, they have instead expressed the beauty of lives trusting in God.

I sincerely want you to know that nothing, absolutely nothing, can destroy your God-implanted purpose, if you will only reach out and take hold of it. No tragedy, no setback, no circumstance, no bully, no demon, no nothing can prevent God's purpose. As Lizzie Velasquez proclaimed, "*You* are the biggest influence in your life, not anyone else."[9] God is on your side, and "if God be for us, who can be against us?" (Romans 8:31).

So, what about you? Have you only been told what's wrong with you your entire life? Do you feel like you're "less than" for some reason? Do you only count all the reasons you're not important and believe you don't deserve some kind of happiness in life? And at the same time, looking at the lives of Nick, Ryan, Gianna, Lizzie, Jo, and Rebecca, do you really think that any interference can prevent you from achieving the reason you were born, if you will plug in to your purpose in life as they did theirs? No! I'm telling you, no! Nothing can defeat you if you pursue your dreams with God.

You have as much, if not much more, going for you. Despite their "defects" and debilitating circumstances, each of these individuals found a way to not only *like* themselves, but also to turn the obstacles they faced into stepping-stones toward success, and making a difference for others. Life plagued them with lemons,

9 TEDx Talks, "How Do You Define Yourself? | Lizzie Velasquez | TEDxAustinWomen
Brave Starts Here," YouTube video, 13:10. January 16, 2014, 13:10. https://www.youtube.com/watch?v=QzPbY9ufnQY.

and they have each become experts in making the most wonderful lemonade.

Why would God want any less for you?

If you will but respond to the simple truth that *you plus God can triumph in life*, then who knows what you can accomplish? The Bible tells us the angels in heaven actually sit on the edge of their seats, watching in anticipation of seeing God's plans for the earth revealed through our lives (Ephesians 3: 9-10). What are you going to do with the gifts, the life, and the purpose you've been given?

God intends to partner with you to help you fulfill your purpose, the reason you were born.

None of us is alone. God intends to partner with you to help you fulfill your purpose, the reason you were born. There is no adversity too great, no devil so strong, no circumstance so overwhelming that can keep you from achieving the reason you were born, if— and "if" is the hinge upon which the gates of heaven swing—*if* you will believe and live these four truths:

1. God has a purpose for you.
2. God will make a way when there seems to be no way.
3. God will teach and train, comfort and equip you, if you will turn to Him and follow Him with all of your heart.
4. You are then called to teach, train, comfort, and equip others, using what God has given you.

There is only one *you*. Who is that *you* supposed to be? It's time to take off the limits and start dreaming again. What has God purposed for your life?

Chapter Four

Uniquely You

"Are not two sparrows sold for a farthing? And one of them shall not fall on the ground without your Father. But the very hairs of your head are all numbered. Fear ye not therefore, ye are of more value than many sparrows."
(Matthew 10:29-31)

No one has it all. That is, no one but God. It could be debated that *even He misses you*, that He is lonely for you and for humanity. He wants you to be part of His wholeness, to participate in His big plans and be engaged in His magnificent future intentions for the universe.

No one *is* it all. We need one another. We are to be properly conjoined. We are social.

We need to meet and merge and overlap and participate with others in the big scheme of things. We need others. Recognizing the dignity in others should never diminish the dignity of ourselves. Our culture seems to think and act otherwise. Instead of loving and appreciating one another, we compete or we conform. We try to outdo, we become rivals, and so we contend and vie for superiority of one over the other. Or we try to fit in. We try to look and act like others, and we try to be like a particular group because we feel it will get us liked. We try to be a carbon copy of someone else. An anonymous quote advised, "Be yourself, everyone else is already taken."

It happens in families, in schools, in sports, in business, and even in churches, and it can turn ugly, very ugly. Competition, for instance, is the cause of wars and fights between individuals as well as nations. We create winners and losers. In the fracas, we lose track of our real selves.

We obsess with competing and comparing. Fears are born in us, fears of inadequacy and inferiority. The caustic vitriol of perceived threats leaks into every attitude, thought, and emotion. Contention becomes the agenda, and true introspection becomes impossible and distorted to blinding levels of myopia. We vacillate between seeing ourselves as inferior or superior, between thinking too much of ourselves or too little. This faltering irresolution can last a lifetime. The danger is that we may never discover our genuine selves. As French mathematician Blaise Pascal put it, "We are only falsehood, duplicity, contradiction; we both conceal and disguise ourselves from ourselves."[10]

On the other hand, we can conform to some ideal in the hope of being accepted and lose the ability to think, decide, and act for ourselves. We're so hungry for love because of some brokenness of our past that we're willing to do anything to fit in and feel wanted. That's how people fall into cults or buy into an ideology that sounds good outwardly but is only there to control people. It happened in Hitler's Germany. It fuels racism, classism, and a lot of other unhealthy, divisive-isms. It takes away personal responsibility for being ourselves and says, "If you just believe these things and conform to them, you'll be taken care of and be happy." But true happiness only comes from being who you were created to be. Fulfillment only comes from grabbing hold of your unique destiny and pursuing it through pursuing God with all your heart.

God doesn't use a photocopy machine to make people. He starts from scratch each time and makes each person unique.

The Trap of Comparing Yourself with Others

A lot of people make the mistake of trying to figure out their self-worth and form their identities by comparing themselves to other

10 Blaise Pascal, "Blaise Pascal Quotes," BrainyQuote (Xplore), accessed February 7, 2020, https://www.brainyquote.com/quotes/blaise_pascal_159844)

people. They go to great lengths to fit in, stand out, or stand above. Too many wish they were something or someone else, rather than embracing the beauty and wonder of who they were created to be.

How do *you* compare with others? The answer is *"You don't!"* You are incomparable. Wanting to be *better than*, *greater than*, or *higher than* others is a trap, as is wanting to be just like someone else. It will destroy your peace, and it will lead to a diminished respect for yourself *and* others.

Scripture emphatically warns against it:

> ***"For we dare not make ourselves of the number, or compare ourselves with some that commend themselves: but they measuring themselves by themselves, and comparing themselves among themselves, are not wise.***
>
> *But we will not boast of things without our measure, but according to the measure of the rule which God hath distributed to us, a measure to reach even unto you.*
>
> *For we stretch not ourselves beyond our measure...*
>
> *Not boasting of things without our measure."*
>
> (2 Corinthians 10:12-15a, emphasis mine)

What's so bad about comparing ourselves with others? The answer is that we lose track of *who we are*. We try to emulate the others whom we admire instead of seeking to become our true, unique selves. We wish to be like others, act like others, think like others, look like others.

We have forgotten the value of the ancient Greek aphorism, "Know thyself," used by Socrates, Aeschylus, and Plato. Among other things, it was a warning to pay no attention to the opinions of others. Rendered into Latin as *nosce te ipsum* or *temet nosce,* it was a maxim also employed by the critic Alexander Pope, Benjamin Franklin, Emerson, Coleridge, and many others.

Comparing ourselves with others (and their comparing themselves with us) leads to boasting, bragging, gloating, and puffery. The above passage in other translations describes the activity as "comparing, grading, and competing" that leads to making "outrageous claims." What you *may* boast about is "according to the measure of the rule which God has distributed to us"—about the jurisdiction in our lives that God has given uniquely to each of us.

Your uniqueness is not a point of competition.

Again, your uniqueness is not a point of competition. The fact that God has given you something He hasn't given others in no way diminishes them, nor does His giving them something He didn't give you diminish you. Does God have favorites? Does He prefer one person above another? *Absolutely not!* Peter, speaking of what the Holy Spirit inspired him to preach, declared,

> *"Of a truth I perceive that God is no respecter of persons."* (Acts 10:34b)

God does *not* respect one person above another, one gender above another, one race above another, one age group above another, or one child above another. And yet God's view of each person is *not* a low view. In Psalm 8 the question is asked,

> *"What is man, that thou art mindful of him? and the son of man, that thou visitest him?"* (Psalm 8:4)

Let's personalize this verse, as we have before. Put your name into the blank space:

> *"What is _______ that Thou (O God, Almighty) art mindful of him/her?"* (Psalm 8:4)

Who are *you* that God Almighty should think about you? (You need to know the answer to that question.) *You really are a somebody!* Imagine great big wonderful God thinking about little ol' you!

Okay, now use your eraser, take your name out, and put someone else's name in there.

The answer of what God thinks about the person you just penciled in is the same answer as it is for you.

Now, one more time, erase that name and put in the name of someone you don't like or someone about whom you have spoken poorly to someone else—someone you have loathed or ridiculed. Go ahead. Put their name in there. Do you think God has changed the answer?

With God, there is no human trash. No highers or lowers—no goods, betters, or bests. He is *not* a respecter of persons. He treasures each human individual. May I learn never to disrespect a man, woman, boy, or girl for whom Christ died!

You can repeat this exercise with regard to the second question asked in the Scripture: "What is the son of man, that thou visitest him?" Who are you, you son or daughter of a man, that God would visit you? Come to you? Talk to you? You must really be a somebody—*and you are.* But so are the other two people you wrote in the blank above. So is anyone else you know that you can pencil in there? God has the same respect for any and every other person whose name you might put in there.

So, what's the answer? What does God think of you and the others you named? The next verse gives us the answer.

> *"For thou hast made him a little lower than the angels, and hast crowned him with glory and honour."* (Psalm 8:5)

Let me reprint this for you to fill in again too:

> *"For thou hast made* __________________________
> *a little lower than the angels, and hast crowned him with glory and honour."* (Psalm 8:5)

Any person whose name you write in there, in God's estimation, is:

- A little lower than angels. (Actually, the word referring to God here is *Elohim*, which means God Himself.)

- Crowned with glory. (That's why sin is so terrible; it makes us come short of the glory.)
- Crowned with honor. (Synonyms of honor are "esteem, distinction, privilege, prestige.")[11]

That's what God thinks about you. That's why He was willing to come to us, and He still does, to anyone who will respond to Him. He means it when He says:

> *"Look! I stand at the door and knock. If you hear my voice and open the door, I will come in, and we will share a meal together as friends."*
>
> (Revelation 3:20 NLT)

You are what God thinks about. *You* are who God deems worthy of friendship. And so is any other person whose name you write into one of those blanks.

You are incomparable, but so are other people. That goes for each and every person you meet.

The Founding Fathers of these United States of America got it dead right:

"We hold these truths to be self-evident, *that all men are created equal.*"[12]

None of us is "better than the other," just different—very different, very distinctive, diverse, unique, one of a kind, idiosyncratic, remarkable, singular, extraordinary, exceptional, peculiar, and noteworthy. This is not about human biodiversity or heritable traits among various population groups. What makes us different from one another lies far beyond gender, nationalism, transracialism, or social groupings of any sort. It is the differences of spiritual endowment. And therein lies your true identity and that of others: that you have been endowed by the Creator!

---

11 "Honor," Dictionary.com (Dictionary.com), accessed February 7, 2020, https://www.dictionary.com/browse/honor)

12 Thomas Jefferson et al., "The Declaration of Independence: Full Text," ushistory.org (Independence Hall Association), accessed January 15, 2020, https://www.ushistory.org/declaration/document/)

Chapter Five

You, Endowed by the Creator

Whether you realize it or not, you have been endowed. *Endowed* means that you have been provided with an asset, a quality, an ability, a talent, a faculty, a set of goods. You didn't have to earn that. It was donated to you. It has been furnished to you, although it is not furniture.

This bequeathed asset is already yours and in your possession. Imagine someone putting a million dollars in your bank account, but then no one notifies you that it is there. You're used to having a low balance, so you don't even inquire about it because you get discouraged each time you do. So, you write no checks and withdraw no money because you don't know what you have. You, a rich person, could die in poverty. But imagine how you would feel at the discovery of that million dollars!

So it is with most of us. Deposited into us and given to each of us at birth was a great treasure. But in all likelihood, most of us have not discovered it. That discovery is what the rest of this book is about. First, let's talk more about endowments, again using the United States Declaration of Independence. It begins with this statement:

"We hold these truths to be self-evident, that all men are created equal, that **they are endowed by their Creator** with certain unalienable Rights, that among these are Life, Liberty and the pursuit of Happiness."[13]

The "self-evident" truth is, first, that you are equal with others. Nobody is better than you (or lesser than you, for that matter). There is no place here for an inferiority complex. You are not lesser than the greatest of persons. Where did the Founding Fathers get this understanding? It may shock us to realize that it came from the Bible, from God Himself. As we read earlier in the Scriptures, "God is no respecter of persons" (Acts 10:34). That simply means that He neither places nor esteems one person above another. No race is above another. No nationality is above another. No gender is above the other. Not even IQ, as we shall learn.

The second "self-evident" truth is that each of us, including you, is "endowed by our Creator." That's where your endowment comes from…God, your Creator. Remember:

> *"Know ye that the Lord he is God:* ***it is he that hath made us, and not we ourselves****; we are his people, and the sheep of his pasture.*
>
> *Enter into his gates with thanksgiving, and into his courts with praise: be thankful unto him, and bless his name."* (Psalm 100:3-4)

Make sure you get this. Nail it down in your thinking. He made you; no one else did! What do you think a proper and adequate response is to knowing this? How do you respond to the fact that God made you and that He has endowed you with a rich treasure? The verse above provides that answer: Be thankful, praise Him, and bless His name. Why don't you get started right now with this proper response? Thank Him! Praise Him! Bless His name! I assure you, it is going to get even better.

Before we leave the Declaration of Independence, let us also observe the words that follow that phrase: "with certain unalienable rights" and "that among these" rights "are Life, Liberty and the pursuit of Happiness." Only these three are named, but there are

---

13 Thomas Jefferson et al., "The Declaration of Independence: Full Text," ushistory.org (Independence Hall Association), accessed January 15, 2020, https://www.ushistory.org/declaration/document/)

many, many more, as implied by the phrase "among these are." Let me name a few.

- You have a right to self-discovery.
- You have a right to know and understand your value, your intrinsic worth, and your endowments.
- You have a right to capitalize on these embedded riches and make the best use of them.
- You have a right to know your purpose and fulfill it.
- You have a right to celebrate what you are and what you have been given.
- You have the right to recognize that you, as an individual, have been "crowned with glory and honour" (Psalm 8:4).
- You have a right to know that God has His heart set on you personally, and that He intends to lift you up and magnify you more than you have ever imagined.

You have a measure that can reach others, and you do not need to stretch yourself beyond your measure to be what you are supposed to become.

You are indispensable. Nobody can ever take your place because God has distributed to you "a measure." (See 2 Corinthians 10:13 again.) You have a measure that can reach others, and you do not need to stretch yourself beyond your measure to be what you are supposed to become.

God designed you—purposely, intentionally, lovingly—so perfectly that He intends for you to live eternally. Unfortunately, you may not have yet grasped the significance of the measure you have. But when you do, you will like yourself because you will know who you are, not what people think of you or don't think of you, but that you really *are* somebody.

At this point, we move to the great redemptive principles of Scripture, principles that are called laws. These are the laws of Calvary, our rules of action:

- Confess your sins, for He forgives them. (1 John 1:9)
- Redemption is through the blood of Jesus that forgives, cleanses, heals, restores, and puts you back in the condition you were in before all of the damage was done. (Ephesians 1:7-10)
- You can live as if it never happened because sin will no longer have any power over you, and you will have no shame. (Romans 6:6)

The drunkard, the woman of the streets, the whoremasters in the high-rise buildings downtown can all come to God because of Calvary. None of us is barred from His salvation.

> *"Ho, every one that thirsteth, come ye to the waters, and he that hath no money; come ye, buy, and eat; yea, come, buy wine and milk without money and without price."* (Isaiah 55:1)

God has never stopped loving you, no matter what's happened to you. He wants to wrap His arms around you and heal you. You will not be ashamed of what or who you are. *You* will like *you*.

Chapter Six

Getting Back On Your Track

Kristin went to church because her parents went to church, but she ended up financially broke, homeless, and addicted to cocaine. She spent years in jail. She got off track at a young age. Influenced by toxic "friends," Kristin allowed herself to be used and abused repeatedly. Could she ever recover? And if so, how?

While in prison for conspiracy and possession with the intent to distribute, she decided that she wanted to be the person she was meant to be before she started making poor choices. In my interview with her, she said that jail was the best thing that ever happened to her because it was there that she got back on track. Here's how she did it.

In the first prison in Brownsville, Texas, there was little or nothing to do. The place was dirty, the toilets had zero privacy, and the food was gross. The days were long with only an hour or so each week to be outside. But it was there—in the loneliness, the emptiness, the vacuum of life, that she did serious thinking, reflection, and contemplation. Her faithful mom had given her a basic Bible that had a concordance in the back. A concordance is like an index to help you find where any given word is used and can be found throughout the pages of the Bible. She began looking up key words, getting insights. Day after day, she searched the

Scriptures by topic. And then an amazing and wonderful thing happened. She says, "As I lay alone in my bunk, I began to experience the presence of Jesus. He became my friend. He was there—every day and every night. I communed with Him. He forgave me." But the hardest was yet to come.

Would she forgive herself? Could she?

Kristin began writing dozens and dozens of letters to everyone she had offended or wronged in some way, everyone whom she had "let down." She confessed her wrongs and asked forgiveness. I know this to be true because I was the recipient of one of those handwritten letters so many years ago. I, like many others, wrote her back, commending her on her faith and assuring her of forgiveness and that all was well between us. This was a courageous action on her part. She demonstrated a sincerity, a genuineness, an integrity that could not be denied, degraded, diminished, or denigrated. Yet, the greatest issue was yet to be resolved—self-forgiveness! Would she? Could she?

> **If God has forgiven us, what right have we not to forgive ourselves?**

Here are Kristin's own words: "I had to forgive myself for damaging that little girl that was inside me." She did just that. She forgave herself. If God has forgiven us, what right have we not to forgive ourselves? Why would we oppose God and thus, ourselves? There's a Scripture describing a group of persons who become self-afflicting and self-abusive.

> *"In meekness instructing* ***those that oppose themselves****; if God peradventure will give them repentance to the acknowledging of the truth; and that they may recover themselves out of the snare of the devil, who are taken captive by him at his will."*
>
> (2 Timothy 2:25-26, emphasis mine)

"Those that oppose themselves." If Kristin were talking to you personally right now, she would, like this Scripture says, instruct you so that you, along with God's help, would get to the truth and recover yourself from this devilish trap. Satan is against you, and he wants you to be against you, too.

Kristin expresses gratitude toward her parents, who have always stood by her. They, too, are faithful followers of our Lord. How do I know this story so well? I recently interviewed Kristin, but she and her parents were a part of my life many years ago. In fact, Kristin recently texted me, saying, "I have carried your teachings with me through my life." What an encouragement to me!

Kristin's story does not end with forgiveness from God and self-forgiveness. Whom God forgives, He also cleanses. He takes away the past, declares it null and void, neutralized, invalidated, negated, revoked, rescinded, reversed, cancelled, terminated, squashed, obliterated, and put out of existence. Never doubt that God, who created something out of nothing, can also create nothing out of something. And when we come to Him properly, that's exactly what He does with our past sins.

> Never doubt that God, who created something out of nothing, can also create nothing out of something.

This is still not the end of Kristin's story. Her story really has three parts: forgiven, cleansed, and reestablished. Kristin is back on track morally and in life. Listen to her words: "Who I now am determines what I now allow in my life." She learned to say no to the temptations to which she once agreed, and she walked away from old, evil "friends" who were really no friends at all.

A few days after I interviewed her, I sent her about thirty pictures of herself and her artwork from her early teenage days. The most profound and heartfelt of them was the final one with her picture captioned with the phrase, "Created to Create!" And that's what Kristin is doing now. She is happily married and owns her own business. But most of all, Kristin is a trophy of God's saving grace, a profound testimony to getting back on track.

What about you?

You can go ahead and feel bad…but not too bad. It happens to us all. We head in one direction and then in another, trying to find ourselves, trying to find what "fits." Sometimes it's late in life before we discover that we can't run a good race on the wrong track. The sooner we figure out what life is about, the better. Discovering the meaning of life is imperative, but equally essential is to discover the meaning of *our life.* The further off track we get, the more difficult it is to come back.

Remember the phrase, "Okay, Houston, we have a problem"? In 1970, the *Apollo 13* mission was 200,000 miles from earth when an astronaut first radioed Mission Control with this declaration or some facsimile of it. It has since become the title of a movie and an iconic manifesto of need for a severe alert. All of us need a day, a time, a moment when we say, "Houston, we have a problem."

So, what's the severe problem? We are off track even though we've tried to convince ourselves otherwise. The feeling of "off track" can become a gnawing, never-ending, and incessant foreboding background to our lives. Who can sum up the repercussions of this? The effects are often marked by living with a backdrop of depression, anxiety, fear, uncertainty, and emotional instability. Life becomes a question mark instead of an exclamation mark. So, what do we do, Houston?

We must do something! If nothing changes, nothing changes. Denial is a coping mechanism that may give a person time to adjust to emotional stress, but living in denial is refusing to accept a truth that is actually occurring in one's life. So, one may say, "not me!" or "It's not my fault" or "It's not important" or "I'll never fail" or "It's not my problem" or "This is the way God made me." The denials can go on and on *ad infinitum*, both in diversity and repetition. Denial means we try to hold on to our own perceptions of reality *regardless of their conflict with the truth*. People tend to engage in distractive or escapist strategies in order to cope. Mental illness looms.

In an upcoming book I'm planning called *Authentic Mental Health*, I underline the need for biblical descriptions and prescriptions. The question here is: What is the biblical description of being off track? So here we go. Here's the description. (Brace yourself, but you will only need to do so temporarily; the solution to the problems is coming.)

> *"All we like sheep have gone astray; we have turned every one to his own way."* (Isaiah 53:6)

Astray means off the correct path or direction; gone awry; adrift; on the wrong route; gone afield, amiss, off course; removed, missing, maybe even AWOL.

There are actually two tracks.

We should be traveling these two tracks simultaneously. One we will call the Moral Track and the other we will call our Life Track.

Getting Back on the Moral Track

This "off track" situation, morally and in life direction, is defined by one biblical word: *iniquity*.

Note the rest of this verse:

> *"All we like sheep have gone astray; we have turned every one to his own way; and the Lord hath laid on him the* ***iniquity*** *of us all."*
> (Isaiah 53:6, emphasis mine)

Iniquity simply means being "not equal to," not equal to what we should be morally.

> *"For all have sinned, and come short of the glory of God."* (Romans 3:23)

> *"They all look to their own way, every one for his gain."* (Isaiah 56:11b)

Iniquity is the biblical word for the modern word *narcissism*. It is the opposite of love. It is self-serving, self-exalting, and selfish. It's when the ego has usurped the rightful place of God in our lives. We live on a stolen throne. We've become god-players with everybody playing god. Doing what is right in our own eyes prejudices us, and disables us from doing the truth. The ego biases our judgment, our decision-making ability. Generally, making a decision based on ego will be a wrong decision. Here's what the Bible says about ego-based thinking:

> *"The way of a fool is right in his own eyes: but he that hearkeneth unto counsel is wise."*
>
> (Proverbs 12:15)

> *"All the ways of a man are clean in his own eyes."*
>
> (Proverbs 16:2b)

> *"For he flattereth himself in his own eyes, until his iniquity be found to be hateful.*
>
> *The words of his mouth are iniquity and deceit: he hath left off to be wise, and to do good.*
>
> *...he setteth himself in a way that is not good; he abhorreth not evil."*
>
> (Psalm 36:2-4)

Getting on Your Life Track

How does one get off course, off of one's path of life, away from one's own proper track? By making choices. We make these choices under the influence of parents or peers, society or culture. Perhaps we have made them under pressure or prematurely, before having an adequate basis for making a wise decision. Whatever the case, we made these choices. And although others may have influenced us, the "buck stops with us." Each of us is a sovereign person who must decide for ourselves. We are responsible for our own choices.

This "gone astray," off-track condition has two implications. The first is a moral track. Getting off track morally will surely get us off our life track as well. God is the greatest asset and resource any person can have. Only He is qualified to define the moral track. What do I mean by "moral track"? It's the determination of right and wrong, good and evil, just and unjust. Why would anyone choose not to know the truth, the whole truth, and *nothing but the truth*? Building a life on that which is untrue, erroneous, faulty, flawed, and fraudulent requires either a great degree of foolishness or evil intentions.

> *"O Lord, I know that the way of man is not in himself: it is not in man that walketh to direct his steps."* (Jeremiah 10:23)

In the book of Wisdom, the second track, your "life track," is referred to as your "path of life." Here is a striking, sensational, and spectacular truth: God isn't simply interested in you being on the moral track, but He wishes to help you get back on your personal life track, and it's wildly wonderful!

> *"Thou wilt shew me the path of life: in thy presence is fulness of joy; at thy right hand there are pleasures for evermore."* (Psalm 16:11)

> *"Now you've got my feet on the life path, all radiant from the shining of your face. Ever since you took my hand, I'm on the right way."* (Psalm 16:11 MSG)

We get to be shown our path (or track). God walks with us on our path, and it's a happy path, one full of pleasurable surprises. It's a happy road. It's an individual path. Others may try to dissuade us, but we can pray,

> *"Teach me thy way, O Lord, and lead me in a plain path, because of mine enemies."* (Psalm 27:11)

No one can take us away from God and His ways except we ourselves.

> *"And I give unto them eternal life; and they shall never perish, neither shall any man pluck them out of my hand.*
>
> *My Father, which gave them me, is greater than all; and no man is able to pluck them out of my Father's hand."* (John 10:28-29)

According to Jesus, *nobody can pluck you out of His Father's hand—nobody! Nobody!*

You're untouchable. Nobody can change your status of being a son or daughter of the Most High God. Further, we should allow no one to entice us, manipulate us, or get us off our life track or path. God wants us to discover and walk this path in cooperation and coordination with Him.

To start that process, we need only reconnect with Him in a proper way. We must keep Him in the God-position of our life. The God-position is the place in our life of ultimate authority. It must be reserved for God alone, not another person, not even our ego (that would make us narcissists). We voluntarily submit to His absolute authority, and we do this without fear. He is the only One strong enough, loving enough, and smart enough to be trusted. We make Him Lord! That means He is Master, Sovereign, Ruler, King. It means we make Him the Boss (although you won't find Him bossy). He will give you clear *wisdom* (the biblical word for *smarts*) for each and every part of your life. Note the following:

> **You plus God is all it takes.**

> *"Trust in the Lord with all thine heart; and lean not unto thine own understanding.*
>
> *In all thy ways acknowledge him, and he shall direct thy paths."* (Proverbs 3:5-6)

You plus God is all it takes. Is there room for your own

creativity? For sure! But creativity doesn't include the right to get off your moral track. That's not being creative. That's being evil. On your life track, your path of life, there will be all kinds of room for your creativity. In fact, God watches with bated breath to see just what you will do with your real self.

Discovering the reason you were born and fulfilling it is really a divine romance! It's your story and His story. Will you be successful? It is absolutely assured.

> *"If God be for us, who can be against us?"*
> (Romans 8:31b)

It may not always *look* that way., but it will work out that way. Perhaps the best thing I can do is give you an example, and the best one I can think of is the story of Joseph, found in Genesis. Let's look at that in the next chapter.

Chapter Seven

The God Factor

Before I tell you the story of Joseph, let's take a look at this promise of God to all of us:

> *"Then shall ye call upon me, and ye shall go and pray unto me, and I will hearken unto you.*
>
> *And ye shall seek me, and find me, when ye shall search for me with all your heart.*
>
> *And I will be found of you, saith the Lord: and I will turn away your captivity."*
>
> (Jeremiah 29:12-14a)

As a young teenager, Joseph was somewhat spoiled by his father. He had a tendency to flaunt his designer clothes, and tell everyone he would be a great success one day. He got this idea from a dream that he claimed came from God. In it, he saw all of his older brothers—and even his parents—bowing down to him.

Since his father Jacob knew the power of dreams, he decided to watch and see what God would do with this child whom he had always prized as special. While the idea that he would one day bow down to his own son did seem a bit boastful and arrogant, he also knew that nothing was impossible with God. Joseph, after all, was a miracle child whom Jacob had thought would never be born because his mother had been barren (unable to have children). Joseph had been an answer to prayer, so his father already had great expectations for him.

The same could not be said of his ten older brothers, however. Joseph's special status with their father had always bugged them, and now their kid brother was telling them they'd one day bow down to him? You can imagine how they must have felt. Jealousy got the best of them. They mocked him, saying, "We shall see what shall become of this dreamer!"

Eventually this teasing turned violent in a field far from their home. Joseph was sent with a message from their father while the other brothers had been toiling all day, tending the herds under the hot Middle Eastern sun. As Joseph (I think I'll just call him Joe) approached, they had already been discussing their little brother's boastfulness, and when they saw him coming, one of them suggested tossing him in a pit, a dried-up well. The idea met no resistance. As soon as Joe was close enough, they ripped the envied coat (a multicolored coat his father had given him) from his back and threw him in the empty well.

While most of the brothers wanted to kill him, the oldest spoke up in his defense, and so they decided to have lunch and think about it. When a caravan of traders came by and the oldest brother was off attending to something else, one of the other brothers suggested they make some money rather than murdering Joseph, so they sold him to be taken to Egypt as a slave. Then, to cover their tracks, they smeared the blood of a baby goat on his coat and showed it to their father. They swore that Joe had been killed by wild animals. They split the money and figured that was the last they would ever see of "the dreamer."

Joe was put on an auction block in Egypt and resold to the highest bidder. A big-time rancher named Potiphar bought Joe, took him to one of his multi-staffed ranches, and put him to work. Despite having been betrayed by his brothers, mocked, thrown into a pit, separated from his father and mother, and sold as a slave in a foreign land, the dream lived on in Joe. He still believed he had a destiny from God. Instead of moping around in doom and gloom at all the awful things that had befallen him, he made the best of serving Potiphar. The result was promotion after promotion until he became the leader over all the other slaves.

The boss was so impressed that he placed Joe in charge

of everything and everyone on all the ranches and over all his businesses. The only person on the ranches Joe didn't have authority over was, naturally, Potiphar's wife. That was no problem for Joe because he wasn't going to give up his dream, his life purpose, for a mere night of illicit passion with the boss's wife.

It was a different story for her, though. She had the hots for Joe. She dressed seductively—you know, in tight clothes with low necklines and high hemlines. Her hairstyle, perfume, winking eyes, and alluring body language were all designed to entice Joe. This didn't happen just once or twice either. The record shows that she flirted day after day, provocatively giving Joe the "come hither, let's get it on" look.

Although he was in the peak of his youthful virility, Joe remained committed to his God-given dreams and the ethics of his religious convictions. He was smart. He knew that "a whore is a deep ditch," as Proverbs 23:27a would later record. He also knew that:

> *"By means of a whorish woman a man is brought to a piece of bread: and the adultress will hunt for the precious life."* (Proverbs 6:26)

Nevertheless, she persisted.

What should a guy do in such a situation? The answer was stay away from her. And so, the ancient document reports,

> *"And it came to pass, as she spake to Joseph day by day, that he hearkened not unto her, to lie by her, or to be with her."* (Genesis 39:10)

The Scriptures teach us to:

> *"Flee also youthful lusts: but follow righteousness."* (2 Timothy 2:22)

That's exactly what Joe did. He had a greater destiny to pursue. Imagine! She was the boss's wife, good-looking and hot to trot.

She was lustful and sex-hungry. I'm sure she made Joe all kinds of promises of future rewards as well. In the natural, it must've seemed like Joe had everything to gain and nothing to lose by giving in to her temptations, but Joseph did what even David and Samson did not do years later. He said, "No!" and stayed away from her.

The story doesn't end there, however. One day, he went into the main house to take care of his responsibilities. Knowing he would be coming, Potiphar's wife was lying in wait. Catching him alone, she grabbed his garment, pulling him toward her. Rather than being trapped, he slipped out of the jacket and ran. She was furious. He had resisted her for the last time! She would show him!

After he was out of earshot, she messed up her hair, smeared her lipstick, and screamed at the top of her lungs, "Rape! Rape! Rape! Look what this Jew boy tried to do!" The servants who responded fell for the ruse, as would her husband. She showed Potiphar the garment Joe had left behind as proof of his attempt. The circumstantial evidence was all they needed. Joseph was sentenced to jail in an executive penitentiary reserved for the king's prisoners. Framed, he'd be there for seven years for something he did not do.

So, Joe, what of your dreams now? Where's your life going? Why were you born? To rot in a prison for something you didn't even do? Where's your God now? What of His promises to you? What of your dream? Why don't you just give up, enjoy your chains, or write a "crying in your beer" kind of song?

No! No such singing! No such songs! No such caving in! Forward instead, for direction is more important than speed! In fact, here's what happened.

> *"The Lord was with Joseph, and shewed him mercy, and gave him favour in the sight of the keeper of the prison.*
>
> *And the keeper of the prison committed to Joseph's hand all the prisoners that were in the prison; and whatsoever they did there, he was the doer of it.*

> *The keeper of the prison looked not to any thing that was under his hand; because the Lord was with him, and that which he did, the Lord made it to prosper."* (Genesis 39:21-23)

Now, this isn't in the text, but it makes perfect sense. If you had had a dream like Joe did, and then had so many things happen that seemed to contradict that dream, what would you pray for? I believe that in his situation, Joe prayed for more of an understanding of his dreams, and as a result, God gave him a gift—or maybe He just honed it—an ability for understanding dreams and interpreting them. Not only did this gift help him hang on to his dream, but it would also help him realize his dream. Just as Proverbs 18 tells us:

> *"A man's gift maketh room for him, and bringeth him before great men."* (Proverbs 18:16)

In going about his business helping other prisoners, Joseph met Pharaoh's butler and baker, who had each offended Pharaoh and been thrown into jail. Each of them had dreams that they did not understand, so Joseph, using his gift for interpreting dreams, explained the significance of their dreams to them. Joseph told the butler he would be restored and the baker that he would be executed. The following day, the baker was hung, and the butler was returned to service in Pharaoh's house. Though Joe had asked the butler to tell Pharaoh about his plight, the butler, despite the accuracy of Joe's interpretations, seemed to forget all about Joseph. (Or maybe it just wasn't God's timing yet—maybe God was waiting for a bigger occasion.)

Two more years went by. Out of the blue, Pharaoh had two disturbing dreams that he felt were important, so he started asking his advisors what they meant, but no one could tell him the meaning. Upon overhearing one of these conversations, the butler remembered the guy in prison who had interpreted his and the baker's dreams and had gotten both right. So, he told Pharaoh of Joseph's expertise.

Joseph was summoned from prison to the Egyptian version of the White House. Pharaoh recounted his dreams to Joe and then Joe explained the message God was trying to communicate to Pharaoh:

> *"Behold, there come seven years of great plenty throughout all the land of Egypt:*
>
> *and there shall arise after them seven years of famine; and all the plenty shall be forgotten in the land of Egypt; and the famine shall consume the land."* (Genesis 41:29-30)

Pharaoh was beside himself with concern. "What are we going to do?" he asked. Joe told him:

> *"Let Pharaoh look out a man discreet and wise, and set him over the land of Egypt.*
>
> *Let Pharaoh do this, and let him appoint officers over the land, and take up the fifth part of the land of Egypt in the seven plenteous years.*
>
> *And let them gather all the food of those good years that come, and lay up corn under the hand of Pharaoh, and let them keep food in the cities.*
>
> *And that food shall be for store to the land against the seven years of famine, which shall be in the land of Egypt; that the land perish not through the famine."* (Genesis 41:33-36)

Pharaoh said, "Joseph, you're that man! You're in charge! Nobody will do anything without your permission!"

That day, Joe went from the prison to the palace, from being a prisoner to prime minister. Joseph oversaw the buying and storing of a fifth of Egypt's produce over the next seven years. He also got married and had two sons. Things certainly took a turn for the better!

Then the famine began and spread throughout the entire Middle East. As the first years passed, other countries who hadn't stored up their surplus traveled to Egypt to plead for help. Eventually, (surprise! surprise!) ten of Joseph's eleven brothers showed up begging for food. Joseph recognized them, but they didn't recognize Joseph. He decided to see if they had changed. He spoke harshly to them through an interpreter (pretending he didn't speak their language) and even accused them of being spies. As he pressed them, they told him nothing but the truth, so Joe decided to put them to a further test. He told them they must bring him his younger brother, Benjamin, the baby of the family, to prove they were telling the truth. He would hold the oldest of them, Simeon, in captivity until they came back with the boy.

He then sent them away with the grain they had purchased, and he also returned the money they had given to buy it, by putting it back in their sacks. (Oh, the drama, the details! They are all revealed in Genesis chapters 39-50.) Imagine what finding that money must've been like for them! They were sure this was a setup, that they would be accused of being thieves as well if they went back, but they had to risk it. They had learned their lesson with the grief they had caused their father by selling Joseph into slavery. They wouldn't do it again by abandoning Simeon.

When the brothers returned and Joseph saw their sincerity, he couldn't maintain the ruse any longer. He revealed himself to his brothers, which only brought them greater fear at first, but he told them all was forgiven.

> *"'Ye thought evil against me,' he told them, 'but God meant it unto good.'"* (Genesis 50:20)

A grand reunion followed.

The God Who Works in Mysterious Ways

I can't help admitting that this is one of my favorite Bible stories, not just because of the intrigue and suspense, but because it so clearly shows how God can use our dreams and giftings, not only for our greatest benefit—despite the appearance of circumstances to the contrary many times—but also to accomplish great things.

Though Joseph spent thirteen years (from the time he was seventeen to the time he was summoned before Pharaoh) as a slave and a prisoner, what he learned in those years helped him save the entire Middle East from starving to death in the next fourteen years.

God had a purpose from the very beginning for Joseph's life. Even when others intended evil against him, God turned the tables on them and transformed it into good. Every bad thing that happened to Joseph, every time he did the right thing even though he wasn't being rewarded for it, every time he chose to honor others instead of giving in to satisfying his own base desires, God taught him something he would later need to save the world as he knew it.

A lot of people quote the saying, "God works in mysterious ways," as if it can be found, chapter and verse, in the Bible, but it is not there. What the Bible actually says is this:

> *"It is the glory of God to conceal a thing: but the honour of kings is to search out a matter."*
> (Proverbs 25:2)

While you might think, *I'm not a king*, I would answer, Neither was Joseph when he searched out the things God had hidden within him; but the day he was called upon for an answer, the day he was ready with that answer after all those years of searching out God's mysteries, he became a king.

In Revelation, John wrote,

> *"**(Jesus Christ) hath made us kings** and priests unto God and his Father."*
> (Revelation 1:6a, parentheses and emphasis mine)

Often the Bible speaks of things to come as if they are already true today. Abraham was commended because he believed the words of the God who:

> *"Calleth those things which be not as though they were."* (Romans 4:17b)

When I say there is greatness in you and that you are a king or queen in God, I'm not just blowing smoke. I'm agreeing with what God says about you. By sticking to his dream, Joseph did the same thing. Things may look bad now, but every story is defined more by the last chapter than it is by the first. Stories are defined more by triumph than by obstacles. In the now, we see the setbacks and difficulties, our handicaps and shortcomings, and so on, *but God.* (Never forget the God factor.)

That doesn't mean there won't be very real discouragements and tough times between where you are today and where you will be when you triumph. Think of everything that those in the previous chapters faced, or the problems that Joseph faced. I can't imagine anything worse than being sold into slavery (by his own brothers, no less) or being placed in an ancient Egyptian prison without any cause and having my freedom taken away like that. But Joseph endured, remained faithful, and was rewarded for it.

So, wherever you are in your life right now, I would encourage you to do the four things that Joseph did as you grab hold of your dreams in the same way:

1. Anchor Your Life to Sacred Truth

What is sacred? God is, and what He says is sacred truth. Life is sacred, too. Your life is sacred, as is the reason you were born. These are all truths. Despite the discouragements and hardships he faced, Joseph never let go.

What makes us sacred? The answer is in the Scriptures:

> *"Forasmuch then as we are the offspring of God."*
> (Acts 17:29a)

There it is. You are the offspring of God, a child of God, a son or daughter of the Most High. As a creature with free will, you are in the same category as God:

> *"God said, Let us make man in our image, after our likeness."* (Genesis 1:26)

Though we are far below Him, like a candle to the sun by comparison, nevertheless we, like Him, are light. We radiate with the same stuff; and like Him, what we decide matters.

To be *anchored* to the sacred also means to be attached to the truths we've been discussing. You anchor by accepting, believing, and vigorously adhering to the truth about God and about yourself and others. Whatever you have done in the past, whatever sins you have committed, whatever iniquities have consumed your life, there is a way back. Jesus came to provide the path back to our heavenly Father for all of us. We need a Savior. Really!

But Jesus has already done all that is needed for us to return to God—all we have to do is accept it. As Paul wrote to the Romans:

> *"That if thou shalt confess with thy mouth the Lord Jesus, and shalt believe in thine heart that God hath raised him from the dead, thou shalt be saved.*
>
> *For with the heart man believeth unto righteousness; and with the mouth confession is made unto salvation."* (Romans 10:9-10)

Imagine that you and I were walking along a railway track, balancing on those long pieces of steel that go on seemingly forever. If I started to lose my balance and you grabbed my hand so I didn't fall the six inches to the broken glass and cinders by the wooden ties, you would have saved me! (Thank you for that!) However, if we were on a train trestle traversing a canyon that was three hundred feet deep and you saved me from falling over the edge to be dashed upon the rocks below, then you would have *saved me indeed*! That is what Jesus offers each and every one of us.

Whatever you've done wrong, however many times you've done it, even if until now you damaged your real "self" which God made, there's forgiveness and the reestablishment of His divine aspirations for you. No matter what kind of reckless predicament you've gotten yourself into, Jesus has provided a way of rescue.

You see, in a very real sense, when you reject yourself, you reject God's work, and ultimately, it is a rejection of God Himself. Come back to yourself by coming back to Him. Learn how to love yourself by learning how to love Him. Come back to *you*, the *you* He made and planned and provided for. This is what He says about you:

> *"I have made the earth, and created man upon it: I, even my hands, have stretched out the heavens, and all their host have I commanded."* (Isaiah 45:12)

I'm going to print that verse again, leaving you a space to put your own name in it again. Ready? Read this again with your name in the blank:

> *"I have made the earth, and created _________ upon it: I, even my hands, have stretched out the heavens, and all their host have I commanded."*

God said He made you in the exact same breath with which He said He created the heavens. Get a picture of the stars. Google it. Stare at it. Realize that the God who created the stars is the same One who made you. In fact, He made them *for* you. Anchor yourself in such sacred truths.

2. Anchor Your Soul to the Sacred One

It is not enough to just be anchored to sacred truths, precious and wonderful as they are. *We must be anchored to God Himself.* Get connected if you are not. After getting connected, get attached.

Jesus is the connection and through Him we are attached. He put it this way:

> *"I am the way, the truth, and the life: no man cometh unto the Father, but by me."* (John 14:6)

He is the way; you'll never be lost. He is the truth; you will never be confused. He is the life; you will never be depressed. Be connected and attached to the eternal through Jesus!

But how? He will never fit into our lives just any old way; *we must fit into His*. He doesn't come under our direction; we must come under His. He is not ours to command; we must be His to command. Why? Because He is smarter or "wiser," as the Bible would say, and He loves us more than we love ourselves.

The cross is our proof. The cross is God's great "plus" sign. The center beam is vertical connecting earth to heaven. The horizontal beam is our life on the human plane elevated by the vertical. That's precisely what Jesus does: He lifts your life up to a richer, fuller plane of existence. It's no wonder the great blind Scottish preacher, George Matheson, penned these words:

> O Love that wilt not let me go,
> I rest my weary soul in thee;
> I give thee back the life I owe,
> that in thine ocean depths its flow
> May richer, fuller be.[14]

The issue is a simple one, though difficult for many to accept because it means giving up our own broken, corrupt lives for the life He has for us instead. I think the missionary Jim Elliot said it best: "He is no fool who gives up what he cannot keep to gain what he cannot lose."[15]

At the same time, the control thing throws a lot of people. They want to hold onto the mismanagement of their lives rather than giving it all up to bring their lives and every area in it under Christ's lordship and giving themselves over to Christ's proper management. It's difficult because most people do not want to give up the "god position" of their lives to God. They'd rather play god themselves. But we're not gods—at least not in that way. We only find our proper fulfillment when we step into our proper place. Jesus said it this way:

---

14 Edward Edwin Ryder, "The Story of Our Hymns: Matheson and His Song in the Night," Gutenberg (Project Gutenberg, September 29, 2010), http://www.gutenberg.org/files/33998/33998.txt)

15 Justin Taylor, "He Was No Fool," The Gospel Coalition (The Gospel Coalition, October 29, 2017), https://www.thegospelcoalition.org/blogs/justin-taylor/he-ws-no-fool/)

> *"If any man will come after me, let him deny himself, and take up his cross, and follow me.*
>
> *For whosoever will save his life shall lose it: and whosoever will lose his life for my sake shall find it."*
> (Matthew 16:24-25)

Instead we must realize that God's will for our lives is exactly what we would choose if we knew all the facts. So really, our lives are much better in His hands than they are in our own *because He knows all the facts*. You can trust your life in His hands, His care, His keeping, and His leading more than you can trust it in your own. Only when we realize and act upon this truth do we ever find the life we really wanted. And that only happens by anchoring our souls in the sacred One.

3. Remove All Unbiblical and Conflicting Data from Your Mind

Do not listen to any voice that contradicts the truths we have learned together. Accept no print, no music, no video, no information whatsoever, that does not agree with your sacred anchors. Let nothing break your anchor—*nothing!* No book, no lyric, no voice, no person, no devil, no demon, no foe, no friend, no circumstance, *no anything*—let nothing separate you from the love of God.

You can trust your life in His hands, His care, His keeping, and His leading more than you can trust it in your own.

Nothing can do so unless you allow it. As Paul, the converted Jewish jihadist, wrote to the Romans:

> *"Who shall separate us from the love of Christ? Shall tribulation, or distress, or persecution, or famine, or nakedness, or peril, or sword?*
>
> *As it is written, for thy sake we are killed all the day*

> *long; we are accounted as sheep for the slaughter.*
>
> *Nay, in all these things we are more than conquerors through him that loved us.*
>
> ***For I am persuaded, that neither death, nor life, nor angels, nor principalities, nor powers, nor things present, nor things to come,***
>
> ***nor height, nor depth, nor any other creature, shall be able to separate us from the love of God, which is in Christ Jesus our Lord.****"*
>
> (Romans 8:35-39, emphasis mine)

View all opposing thoughts as treasonous to your own well-being. Tolerate no opposition. This may seem like a daunting task at first—daunting because we are invaded by voices and advertisements and secular educationalists, billboards, newspapers, magazines, music, videos, and the Internet, which spout all kinds of anti-God propaganda. Instead, vet all the incoming data and reject what contradicts what the Bible teaches. We must.

> *"Let God be true, but every man a liar; as it is written, that thou mightest be justified in thy sayings, and mightest overcome when thou art judged."* (Romans 3:4)

4. Discover Your Gifting

This is the great deposit that God has invisibly and indivisibly bestowed upon you and placed within you. As I've been trying to show you up to this point, you are extraordinary, even if you do not know it yet. If you *like* your Creator, *you will like* yourself. If you learn to *love* Him, and understand how much He loves you, then *you will learn to properly love* yourself as well.

You are not an accident nor a mistake but the work of God's hands. You are magnificent and elegant, perfectly put together in a combination as different from others as your fingerprint. *Scientific American* reported, "Two like fingerprints would only be found in 10^{48} years."[16] (A quindecillionth is 1 followed by 48 zeroes, or 1 00000000 0000000000 0000000000 0000000000 0000000000 0000000000.) This time period is way beyond trillions and longer than we have been on the planet.

That's how unique you are! Biometric identification systems, whether referring to retinal scans, hand geometry, palm vein authentication, face recognition, or voice analysis *will never find another you*. And that's only your biometric uniqueness. What of your spiritual DNA? The answer is your *ENA,* your divinely ***E***mbedded ***N***atural ***A***bility.

Although it is often misattributed to Helen Keller because she quoted it so often and Edward Everett Hale, American author and chaplain, this was originally included in a collection written by Jeanie A. B. Greenough, so it is not known for sure who actually wrote it (see footnote):

I am only one, but I am one.
I cannot do everything,
But I can do something.
What I can do, I ought to do,
And what I ought to do,
By the grace of God, I will do.[17]

The author further proclaimed, "I will not let what I cannot do, interfere with what I can do." Why not memorize those lines and make them a personal motto? I've been saying them to myself for nearly forty years.

This is about you! You are not a copy, a duplicate, or a clone. You are an indispensable original, a first edition, made by and fathered by the great Creator, God Himself. Because He is our Creator, our *Father*, He is good and worthy of praise. We are made in His likeness and created in His image—and He's got big plans

---

16 *Scientific American,* 1911.

17 This first appeared in Jeanie A. B. Greenough's *Year of Beautiful Thoughts*, 1902, public domain. A few years later it was included in Edwin Osgood Grover, *The Book of Good Cheer*: "a Little Bundle of Cheery Thoughts" (New York: Algonquin Pub. Co., 1909), 28, and later still in James Dalton Morrison's *Masterpieces of Religious Verse* (New York: Harper & Row, 1948), 416, where it is titled "Lend a Hand."

for us, plans that will take eternity to fulfill. We have only to plug in to them through His Son, Jesus.

Before you and I begin this course of action, the discovery of the real *you* and talk about overcoming some of the hindrances, the barriers, and the obstacles that prevent self-discovery, let's deal with the gargantuan, herculean, titanic, monstrous social conditions of our day. We are embedded in a success cult; our culture actively practices the worship of success. How does that affect us? Read on.

Chapter Eight

Learning How To Be Ordinary

Twelve ordinary men changed the world. Maybe they were even below ordinary. Judas was financially insecure and ended up a thief. Simon was a rebel against Rome. Matthew held a job with the IRS. James and John were boisterous teenagers nicknamed the "Sons of Thunder" (Mark 3:17). Maybe they raced through the streets of Jerusalem on camels with racing stripes painted down their sides. Thomas was a doubter. Peter and his brother Andrew were fishermen. Those who saw Peter and John together observed how loud, dumb, and uneducated they were. Here's the report:

> *"Now when they saw the boldness of Peter and John, and perceived that they were unlearned and ignorant men, they marvelled."* (Acts 4:13)

They were "ignorant and unlearned"? Perhaps they were ignorant (they didn't know very much) and unlearned (they didn't know that they didn't know very much), so they got along okay.

What did these ordinary men do? What did they achieve? Here's what the news reporters of the day observed:

> *"These...have turned the world upside down."*
> (Acts 17:6)

And come to think of it, was probably right side up!

What's wrong with being ordinary? Moses, who led a million-plus people out of Egyptian captivity, wasn't a charismatic leader. He started off with an "OMG" and then confessed,

> *"O my Lord, I am not eloquent... I am slow of speech, and of a slow tongue."* (Exodus 4:10)

Gideon, a farmer's son, was threshing wheat when an angel dropped in on him and said,

> *"The Lord is with thee, thou mighty man of valor."*
> (Judges 6:12)

This was followed by another "OMG" and:

> *"Oh my Lord, if the Lord be with us, why then is all this befallen us?"* (Judges 6:13)

And the Lord replied to this whimpering weakling of a kid,

> *"Go in this thy might, and thou shalt save Israel."*
> (Judges 6:14)

Gideon replied, "Who, me?" followed by another "OMG":

> *"Oh my Lord, wherewith shall I save Israel? Behold, my family is poor in Manasseh, and I am the least in my father's house."* (Judges 6:15)

In essence, he said, "I'm a nothing; I'm a nobody. I'm just ordinary." But God said,

> *"Surely I will be with thee."* (Judges 6:16)

Perhaps we should pick up a clue here. God *with* you, Mr. or Mrs. or Ms. Ordinary, makes a difference, a big, big difference. Gideon ended up leading the vastly outnumbered Israelites to defeat their enemy. What can God do with you, Dear Ordinary?

David was a shepherd. Jesus was a carpenter. Paul, previously known as Saul, was a hypocrite, a tentmaker turned Jewish jihadist who was actively killing Christians, yet he ended up writing fourteen books of the New Testament. What's so wrong with being ordinary?

Why Is Ordinary So Scorned Today?

Everyone wants to be the hero, the head honcho, the leader, the champion, the one on top. "I'm the king of the castle and you're the dirty rascal" (an idiom of my day) has been replaced with other words, but the meaning has not changed. Everyone is trying to outdo, outshine, outclass, outthink, outstrip, and upstage everyone else. Stardom has taken over the culture. Narcissism rules.

> God with you, Mr. or Mrs. or Ms. Ordinary, makes a difference, a big, big difference.

We live in unusual surroundings, a culture in which success (or its view of success) has taken on almost cult-like traits. The success cult has taken over from ocean to ocean and border to border. Everyone, including the very young, live in a success pressure cooker. The world worships success and bows down to the gods of achievement. Young people are paralyzed by the fear of failure and the dread of being ordinary. Perceived mediocrity is scorned. Spirits of competitiveness have destroyed kindness, mercy, graciousness, love, and respect for others.

Trying to get ahead by pulling others down has become normal. Speech is cold unless fired by self-interest.

We live surrounded by superiority complexes: boasters, braggarts, and egotists. Multiply this with the exponential effects of popcorn-junk TV, gaming addictions, glossy-covered fashion magazines, Twitter feeds, pervasive social networking, a social media obsession, glamorized evil, smartphone addiction, and the oversexualization of our culture. As a result, we are now living in the real Great Repression.

The former (the Great Depression) was a time of economic stress and hardship, and one of the two worst events in our nation's history (the other being the Civil War). However, this present disaster rivals them both. The Great Repression is paralyzing, oppressive, depressive, coercive, and cruel, reflecting a culture that's harsh, severe, and demanding, one that has everyone marketing themselves. Being a winner in their own eyes and according to their own standards is everyone's primary goal. Everybody has to be omnipotent, but it's ordinary folks who make things happen.

Astronauts are the pop stars of science and technology, but for every astronaut we put in space, there are thousands upon thousands behind the scenes: engineers, medics, psychologists, technicians, trainers, controllers, scientists, manufacturers, accountants, administrators, and on and on the list goes. More than 17,000 people work with NASA. Even more work as government contractors that are not part of this number.[18] They are relatively unknown, uncelebrated, unseen, ordinary persons involved, but without them there would be no astronauts.

I was impressed with the last Christian movie I went to see. There were four or five lead actors. They were dynamic, meaningful, and demonstrative, moving one from laughter to tears and back again. The movie ended, and the credits began. The list seemed endless, but I stayed and watched them all (much to the chagrin of my friends who were ready to leave). The rolling credits began by listing the supporting actors, then they moved on to producers galore, scriptwriters, music writers, set designers, wardrobe designers, and on and on and on.

These were the ordinary people, the invisible people. But without them, there would have been no successful lead actors, no movie, no show, no audience, no box office, no money, no profits,

18 Brian Dunbar, "What Is NASA?," NASA (NASA, June 16, 2015), https://www.nasa.gov/audience/forstudents/5-8/features/nasa-knows/what-is-nasa-58.html)

and zero notoriety. In truth, it's extraordinary to be ordinary, not driven, not manipulated, unpretentious, just real and meaningful, without being anxious or a workaholic, not fueled by depression or perfectionism, and without the rat race or driving demons. These days, it takes courage to be one's own self, but that is the place of peace.

In the meantime, we simply must consider the dangers of falling victim to the success cult. Sometimes the smart thing to do in life is to think backward, that is, to think the opposite from the culturally dictated norms and notions. The majority can take leave of their senses and be wrong, dead wrong, and I mean *dead!*

With the increase of juvenile access to social media has come a thirty-five percent increase in teen suicide. Even suicide rates among preteen children are skyrocketing. Cyber-bullicide (online bullying-provoked suicide) stats are also up. The victims of cyberbullying are twice as likely to commit suicide as those who are not exposed to this. It may be a surprise to know that cyberbullying offenders are themselves one and a half times more likely to commit suicide than the average child. However, this is only one aspect of the negative influence of social media exposure on the young.

Suicide pacts, which are agreements between two or more people to die by suicide, are formed on the Internet and often among complete strangers. In some countries, cyber-suicides account for one-third of all suicides. Children are exposed to message boards, video-sharing websites, chat rooms, discussion forums, and supposed "support groups" that often spawn whimsical notions of self-injury as an effective coping measure. Suicide is the second leading cause of death for young people between the ages of 10 and 34, according to the Centers for Disease Control and Prevention, which track the leading causes of death in the United States, and twice as prevalent as homicides.[19] But it gets worse.

Pro-suicide groups are springing up at an alarming rate. In these groups, suicide methods are explicitly detailed. Young

19 "Suicide," National Institute of Mental Health (U.S. Department of Health and Human Services), accessed January 16, 2020, https://www.nimh.nih.gov/health/statistics/suicide.shtml)

minds, yet untrained by their fathers (forty-two percent of which are absent altogether), are unprotected, unfortified, and unarmed against this death propaganda.

There is another prevalent style of self-murder. It's suicide on an installment plan. No rope, no knife, no gun, but the gradual and less detectable form of self-mutilation that begins with self-rejection and increases over time. Nail after nail is driven into the coffin before the body finally arrives. It's not just drink after drink or drug after drug, but damning thought after damning thought, and why?

It is a result of the success cult, a misplaced or excessive admiration for a particular person or thing. It usually surrounds leaders and causes an obsession, a fixation, a mania, an absurd devotion to an unfeasible end. Tragically, much of Christendom has taken up the success mantra too, but it is an ungodly and unChristlike incantation. Didn't Jesus say:

> God's not into showmanship.

> *"Learn of me; for I am meek and lowly in heart: and ye shall find rest unto your souls."*
> (Matthew 11:29)

Would-be saviors would come riding in on white stallions with flags flying, bands playing, confetti falling, and crowds cheering, but not Jesus. As foretold, Jesus came "lowly, and riding upon an ass" (Zechariah 9:9). God's not into showmanship. He doesn't have to make any Hollywood appearances. And neither do you.

> *"When pride cometh, then cometh shame: but with the lowly is wisdom."* (Proverbs 11:2)

> *"Though the Lord be high, yet hath he respect unto the lowly: but the proud he knoweth afar off."*
> (Psalm 138:6)

> *"Better it is to be of an humble spirit with the lowly, than to divide the spoil with the proud."*
> (Proverbs 16:19)

> *"Most men will proclaim every one his own goodness: but a faithful man who can find?"*
> (Proverbs 20:6)

One day the disciples were arguing about who was the greatest. Jesus shocked them by saying, "Whoever wants to be first shall be last" (Mark 9:35).

On another occasion, Jesus reported on the issue of everyone wanting to be the boss. The KJV called it to exercise "lordship over the people." Then Jesus declared,

> *"But so shall it not be among you: but whosoever will be great among you, shall be your minister,*
>
> *and whosever of you will be the chiefest, shall be servant of all.*
>
> *For even the Son of man came not to be ministered unto, but to minister, and to give his life a ransom for many."* (Mark 10:43-45)

Who's going to sit in the highest position? Who is going to be the greatest? The answer is the non-highfalutin', non-pompous, non-self-promoting, ordinary person, that's who.

Children and teens alike live surrounded by a success cult in which everyone is boasting and bragging, showing off, competing and contending, claiming and crowing, declaring themselves to be better than everyone else. This is wickedness. Here's how the Bible puts it:

> *"Lord, how long shall the wicked, how long shall the wicked triumph?*
>
> *How long shall they utter and speak hard things? And all the workers of iniquity boast themselves?*

> *They break in pieces thy people, O Lord, and afflict thine heritage."* (Psalm 94:3-5)

Notice that boasting breaks other people into pieces and afflicts them. It's brutish:

> *"Understand, ye brutish among the people: and ye fools, when will ye be wise?*
>
> *...The Lord knoweth the thoughts of man, that they are vanity."* (Psalm 94:8,11)

In our culture, we treat one another offensively and rudely. How so? By the perpetual one-upmanship, the "I am better than you" posturing of our culture. Over and over and over again, young people are exposed to this on the Internet, where everyone else is a hero, a star, a champion, a paragon, a winner, a superstar, a celebrity, a demigod, a leader, on top of the pile, and either openly or by implication, worthy of being worshiped.

Here's the trap: In comparing oneself with all the boasters, I simply must repeat the Scriptures again. This kind of comparison to others is such a life-destroying practice that I will emphasize it several times during this chapter. The warning that follows is very clear:

> *"For we dare not make ourselves of the number, or compare ourselves with some that commend themselves: but they measuring themselves by themselves, and comparing themselves among themselves, are not wise.*
>
> *But we will not boast of things without our measure, but according to the measure of the rule which God hath distributed to us.*
>
> *For we stretch not ourselves beyond our measure."*
>
> (2 Corinthians 10:12-14a)

We dare not…
We dare not compare ourselves!

We dare not compare ourselves with those that commend themselves!

They "are not wise" *who do this.* This is a polite and respectful (which the Bible always is) way of saying that to do this is to be an idiot, a fool, a moron, a stupid blockhead, a nincompoop, an ignoramus, a dunce, and a dumbbell. Have you got the idea?

You are not comparable to anyone else! And if you make this serious blunder of comparing yourself with others, you will either have an inferiority complex or a superiority complex, depending on with whom you compare yourself. An inferiority complex is an unrealistic feeling of general inadequacy caused by a supposed inferiority to one's peers and is usually marked by aggressive behavior in an effort to compensate. And by the way, a superiority complex is usually a cover-up for actual feelings of inferiority and failure.

In a culture where everyone is trying to be a genius, young people (and I hope not you, dear reader) become conflicted as to their identity, and worse, they experience discouragement, depression, and then despair.

The self-help sections in a bookstore are some of the largest, with titles about how to rise to the top, how to be successful, how to outdo your competition, how to be rich, how to dress for success, how to have influence, and on and on the list goes. I'm not against reading a self-improvement book or two (the Bible is the greatest of them all). I'm merely trying to point out the obsessive, all- consuming pathology of the success cult.

Whatever happened to being ordinary? A quote attributed to Abraham Lincoln sums it up: "God must love the common man; He made so many of them."

Learn How to Be Ordinary

To be ordinary is to be normal, settled, established, and self-accepting, aware of one's strengths and weaknesses, with a realistic appraisal of one's talents, capabilities, and worth. The primary essence of this book is the real self-discovery of the real you. But as long as we are trying to be like someone else, we will not have self-love (which, by the way, has nothing to do with being selfish). How does God view ordinary people? What kind of people is He looking for? Brace yourself!

> *"For ye see your calling, brethren, how that not many wise men after the flesh, not many mighty, not many noble, are called:*
>
> *But God hath chosen the foolish things of the world to confound the wise; and God hath chosen the weak things of the world to confound the things which are mighty;*
>
> *and base things of the world, and things which are despised, hath God chosen, yea, and things which are not, to bring to nought things that are.*
>
> (1 Corinthians 1:26-28)

Here's the list:

- Not many wise
- Not many mighty
- Not many noble
- Those who are foolish
- Those who are weak
- Those who are base
- Those who are nobodies

God is not looking for smarty-pants, bodybuilders, or the elite. He likes the simple, the weak, the ridiculed, and the unimportant. He is not looking for show-offs, but for humility, meekness, and a willingness to be used. In a moment I'll show you why, but first, let's look at these same verses in the *Message* translation:

> *"Take a good look, friends, at who you were when you got called into this life. I don't see many of 'the brightest and the best' among you, not many influential, not many from high-society families. Isn't it obvious that God deliberately chose men*

> *and women that the culture overlooks and exploits and abuses, chose these 'nobodies' to expose the hollow pretensions of the 'somebodies'? That makes it quite clear that none of you can get by with blowing your own horn before God."*
>
> (1 Corinthians 1:26-29 MSG)

There is no need to blow your own horn. Why is that? Because there is a divine life principle that compensates for any of us, and for anything we or others think we might lack. Here's the simple formula: You plus God are more than equal to any life task that you may be called upon to meet. And what you are (authentically) will affect your children. Notice:

> *"Most men will proclaim every one his own goodness: but a faithful man who can find?*
>
> *The just man walketh in his integrity: his children are blessed after him."* (Proverbs 20:6-7)

Conversely, if parents are egocentric, self-centered, selfish, and narcissistic, those traits will be passed on to the children. The Bible term for this narcissistic condition is *iniquity*. Note the clarity of Scripture:

> *"The Lord is longsuffering..., and by no means clearing the guilty, visiting the iniquity of the fathers upon the children unto the third and fourth generation."*
>
> (Numbers 14:18)

You plus God are more than equal to any life task that you may be called upon to meet.

This is one of the reasons we are graciously warned:

> *"For I say, through the grace given unto me, to every man that is among you, not to think of himself more highly than he ought to think; but to think*

soberly, according as God hath dealt to every man." (Romans 12:3)

What God, your Creator, has dealt to you is remarkably wonderful. This is a joy that is set before you as you continue this book and discover the gift God has placed within you. In the meantime, don't reject being ordinary. Instead, celebrate what God has given to you personally, your personal gifting.

"For what shall it profit a man, if he shall gain the whole world, and lose his soul? Or what shall a man give in exchange for ***his*** *soul?"*
(Mark 8:36-37, emphasis mine)

The Message says this:

"What kind of deal is it to get everything you want but lose yourself?" (Matthew 16:26 MSG)

Love doesn't have a "swelled head" (1 Corinthians 13:4 MSG). It "is not puffed up" (1 Corinthians 13:4). There is no need to boast:

"But we will not boast of things without our measure, but according to the measure of the rule which God hath distributed to us."
(2 Corinthians 10:13)

Watch out for boasters. They will tend to make you compare yourself with them, and they intend for you to lose and be less than them. They want to put you down. Don't listen to them. The Scriptures describe how they enjoy this evil:

"But now ye rejoice in your boastings: all such rejoicing is evil." (James 4:16)

"As it is, you are full of your grandiose selves. All such vaunting self-importance is evil."
(James 4:16 MSG)

Chapter Nine

How to Live in a God-Rejecting Culture

(Or under a God-Rejecting Government)

Angela Peters was born in Flint, Michigan, three months early, and with cerebral palsy. Cerebral palsy is a condition that forces your muscles to contract constantly unless you are sleeping. As a teen, Angela was confined to a wheelchair and had to deal with mountains of depression.

According to her own words, she didn't like herself, and in high school, most people were mean to her. She says, "Since I didn't like myself, I thought that if only I had a boyfriend, my wheelchair would somehow disappear and I would be like any other teenage girl: accepted. That didn't happen."

Angela's thoughts ran very deep. She thought about life and its meaning. She reports, "Over the years, I slowly had to learn that Jesus accepts me, wheelchair and all." Angela spent much time alone, in silence, in contemplation, and we know that "still waters run deep." She began to write down her insights. She has published at least three books that are now available on Amazon. I have read some of her writings. Everyone should. You can go to her website at www.heavenlypoems.com and read what she has there, and learn what kind of a life she now lives. What an influence she has today. I recall several of her insights. Here's a part of one she called "Living in a Never-Ending Nightmare":

Every day we are living in a nightmare
This world took Jesus out of our society
We took out what is right
By bringing in what is wrong.[20]

Angela now knows why she was born. Her life has meaning and purpose. With enthusiasm, she cites this Scripture:

> *"Thou has turned for me my mourning into dancing: Thou hast put off my sackcloth, and girded me with gladness;*
>
> *To the end that my glory may sing praise to thee, and not be silent. O Lord my God, I will give thanks unto thee for ever."* (Psalm 30:11-12)

Angela said it as accurately as any brilliant sociologist could have described it: "If a culture takes Jesus out of a society, they take out what is right and bring in the wrong." For example, wherever genuine (and I do mean *genuine*) Christianity has influence in a country, the value of human life goes up, esteem for womanhood is high, and respect for legitimate authority is honored. Take Jesus out and the value of human life goes down—way down. They even kill their own babies. I'm not sure there is anything sadder than to see women marching for the right to kill their own babies.

In any culture, there are three kinds of people: those who live under God's management; those who do not live under God's management; and those who claim to be under God's management but are not. Societies ebb and flow between good and evil, true right and wrong, love and selfishness. There is a moral ebb and flow. In William Shakespeare's *Julius Caesar*, Act IV, Scene III, we are treated to a profound metaphorical insight:

---

20 Angela Peters, "Living in a Never Ending Nightmare," Heavenly Poems by Angela Peters | Poetry About My Life, accessed January 31, 2020, http://www.heavenlypoems.com/)

There is a tide in the affairs of men.
Which taken at the flood leads on to fortune;
Omitted, all the voyage of their life
Is bound in shallows and in miseries.
On such a full sea are we now afloat,
And we must take the current when it serves,
Or lose our ventures.[21]

We learn that we must recognize this ebb and flow, and avail ourselves of an opportunity or a warning. We live in a time of moral ebb, of impending danger, in which "truth is fallen in the street" (Isaiah 59:14). In fact, we are surrounded by false politicians, false leaders, and false teachers. Of them, the Scriptures say that they shall bring in damnable ideas and many shall follow their pernicious ways. *Pernicious* means "causing insidious harm, ruinous, injurious, and hurtful.[22] But it gets worse:

> *"The way of truth shall be evil spoken of."*
>
> (2 Peter 2:2b)

> *"They've put themselves on a fast downhill slide to destruction, but not before they recruit a crowd of mixed-up followers who can't tell right from wrong. They give the way of truth a bad name."*
>
> (2 Peter 2:1b-2a MSG)

How do nations get in this condition? Why is America near the tipping point and reaching critical mass, where the truth of the truth is rarely followed and where high-level decisions are made,

---

21 William Shakespeare, *Julius Caesar*, Full Text - Act IV - Scene III - Owl Eyes, accessed January 31, 2020, https://www.owleyes.org/text/julius-caesar/read/act-iv-scene-iii#root-71646-111)

22 "Pernicious," Dictionary.com (Dictionary.com), accessed January 31, 2020, https://www.dictionary.com/browse/pernicious)

not in the loving interest of the people but for self-interest? Here's the Bible's answer:

> *"Why do the heathen rage, and the people imagine a vain thing?*
>
> *The kings of the earth set themselves, and the rulers take counsel together, against the Lord, and against his anointed, saying,*
>
> *Let us break their bands asunder, and cast away their cords from us.* (Psalm 2:1-3)

There you have it. The kings, presidents, senators, and congressmen have collectively decided against the Lord and His ways. They want no restraint by principles. And all hell will break out because nations have forgotten God (Psalm 9:17). Here is the above verse again:

> *"Why the big noise, nations? Why the mean plots, peoples? Earth-leaders push for position, demagogues and delegates meet for summit talks, the God-deniers, the Messiah-defiers: 'Let's get free of God! Cast loose from Messiah!'"*
>
> (Psalm 2:1-3 MSG)

So what do we do in the midst of a God-rejecting culture? How can we avoid being sucked in, sold out, conned, bamboozled, victimized, deceived, duped, and cheated? Here's my best advice:

Keep your life under and accountable to God: Remember that being a genuine Christian is a change of government, from self-rule to God's rule.

> *"The government shall be upon his shoulder: and his name shall be called Wonderful, Counsellor, The mighty God, the everlasting Father, the Prince of Peace. Of the increase of his government and peace there shall be no end."* (Isaiah 9:6b-7a)

Avoid defilement by vetting all thoughts and incoming data: Think about what you think about. To muse means to think. *Amusement* comes from the word *amuse*, which means "not thinking." Avoid distractions.

> *"Be not conformed to the world: but be ye*
> *transformed by the renewing of your mind."*
> (Romans 12:2)

Stay addicted to the use of your gifting, your endowment, deposited in you by God:

> *"Neglect not the gift that is in thee."*
> (1 Timothy 4:14)

> *"Stir up the gift of God, which is in thee."*
> (2 Timothy 1:6)

Your gifting, your Embedded Natural Ability, is your ministry: Your gifting, your Embedded Natural Ability, is your true vocation, your holy endeavor, your greatest fulfillment. It is intrinsically and indivisibly a part of you. As you'll see later, it's your *thing* in life. It's the light you shine in life. And this is a great addiction.

> *"They have addicted themselves to the ministry."*
> (1 Corinthians 16:15)

We are encouraged to be:

> *"Not slothful in (the) business (of the ministry);*
> *fervent in spirit; serving the Lord."*
> (Romans 12:11, additions mine)

Stay unoffendable: If anyone can provoke you, they win. Blaise Pascal wrote, "All of our reasoning ends in surrender to feeling."[23] Maturity can be evaluated by how difficult it is to offend us.

> *"Great peace have they which love thy law: and nothing shall offend them."* (Psalm 119:165)

Loving the laws of God makes us impossible to offend. Here a few laws of God from which you can clearly understand this:

> *"Love your enemies, bless them that curse you, do good to them that hate you."* (Matthew 5:44)

Keep in fellowship with like-minded followers: Remember some of the basic truths about friendships and companionship:

> *"He that walketh with wise men shall be wise: but a companion of fools shall be destroyed."*
> (Proverbs 13:20)

> *"Make no friendship with an angry man; and with a furious man thou shalt not go: lest thou learn his ways, and get a snare to thy soul."*
> (Proverbs 22:24-25)

Stay with those you can encourage and those who will encourage you.

Learn to stand (alone, if necessary): In a world of compromise, there are some who don't. Be one of them. Years ago, I memorized what is sometimes called the "Warrior's Creed." It was found among the papers of a young African pastor who was martyred for his faith in Zimbabwe in the twentieth century. Here it is for you:

---

23 Blaise Pascal, "Blaise Pascal Quotes," BrainyQuote (Xplore), accessed February 1, 2020, https://www.brainyquote.com/quotes/blaise_pascal_379447)

I'm a part of the fellowship of the unashamed! The die has been cast.

I have stepped over the line. The decision has been made. I'm a disciple of His and I won't look back, let up, slow down, back away, or be still. My past is redeemed. My present makes sense. My future is secure. I'm done and finished with low-living, sight-walking, small planning, smooth knees, colorless dreams, tamed visions, mundane talking, cheap living, and dwarfed goals.

I no longer need preeminence, prosperity, position, promotions, or popularity. I don't have to be right, or first, or tops, or recognized, or praised, or rewarded. I live by faith, lean on His presence, walk by patience, lift by prayer, and labor by Holy Spirit power.

My face is set. My gate is fast. My goal is heaven. My road may be narrow, my way rough, my companions few, but my guide is reliable and my mission is clear.

I will not be bought, compromised, detoured, lured away, turned back, deluded or delayed.

I will not flinch in the face of sacrifice or hesitate in the presence of the adversary. I will not negotiate at the table of the enemy, ponder at the pool of popularity, or meander in the maze of mediocrity.

I won't give up, shut up, or let up until I have stayed up, stored up, prayed up, paid up, and preached up for the cause of Christ.

> I am a disciple of Jesus. I must give until I drop, preach until all know, and work until He comes. And when He does come for His own, He'll have no problems recognizing me. My colors will be clear![24]

Live love: Don't let anyone keep you from loving, for this is the ultimate achievement in life.

> *"Above all things have fervent charity among yourselves: for charity shall cover the multitude of sins."* (1 Peter 4:8)

24 ——, "African Martyr's Statement," Missions: An African martyr's statement about his level of commitment, accessed February 1, 2020, http://home.snu.edu/~hculbert/commit.htm)

Chapter Ten

How 2 B U

Your gifting is not going to show up in your deoxyribonucleic acid (DNA) report because DNA only contains biological instructions called its genome. These chemical building blocks are termed nuclear, half of which come your father and half of which come from your mother, but all of the mitochondrial DNA comes from your mother only. It is certainly an interesting study; however, spiritual gifts are not biometric. Neither are they passed on genetically. Instead, they are conferred by the Creator and deposited, not in the chemistry of your earth home, your body, but into you, your spirit. That's why they are called *spiritual* gifts. They were deposited into your spirit, the real you—the you that will live long after your body perishes from the earth.

So? Aside from DNA, how shall you discover your spiritual gifts, the real you? The answer lies in understanding your **ENA**, your divinely **E**MBEDDED **N**ATURAL **A**BILITY!

You Have a Divinely Embedded Natural Ability!

The first step is to know and understand each of the gifts—each of the ENA options.

I have included the details of each of the spiritual gifts in seven chapters of Part 2. There, I will attempt to give you as thorough an understanding of each of them as possible, dedicating a chapter to each one of them. In each chapter and for each gift, each ENA, I will outline the following:

1. The name of the gift (the Embedded Natural Ability or ENA)

2. A detailed description of the gift
3. Biblical examples of the gift
4. The "focus" of the gift (its way of looking at life situations)
5. The dangers inherent in it (built-in risks that must be overcome by specific disciplines)
6. How each gift relates to the others

As you come to recognize and understand each of these gifts, you will probably *see yourself* in one of the descriptions. Or you may vacillate back and forth between two of them. Relax. Don't be uptight about it. God is as zealous for you to know the great riches and treasures He has placed within you as you are—probably more so.

As you read the descriptions, you will recognize features in other people whom you know well. You will also learn how your gifting could relate to your vocational effectiveness, and how it affects marriage and the raising of children. You'll be able to identify the giftings of others, which will translate into a new respect for others by comprehending the unique treasures God has deposited in them as well as yourself.

Please suffer me a bit of poetic license, which refers to the freedom to depart from the conventional rules of language when writing, in order to bring you a more effective understanding. You will get the actual Bible terms, but in my words, the seven ENAs are as follows:

1. The Messenger: one who is designed to carry the message of the Maker to humanity. (I also call this a Proclaimer, though the word used in Romans 12:6 is "prophet.")
2. The Helper: one who sees the needs of others and offers assistance, support, advice, and aid; translated "ministry" in Romans 12:7.
3. The Explainer: one who explains and conveys knowledge, understanding, and wisdom to others, "he that teacheth."

4. The Encourager: one who uplifts, inspires, and motivates others toward functioning successfully, "he that exhorteth."
5. The Provider: one who discreetly gives resources to others to enable and improve their ability to function, "he that giveth."
6. The Organizer: one who sees the big picture and administrates to provide creative opportunities so other giftings can function well, "he that ruleth."
7. The Caregiver: one who mercifully comforts the distressed, so they can recover to their functionality, "he that sheweth mercy."

The second step is to understand the benefits of discovering the real you, your gifting, your Embedded Natural Ability. The third step is to realize the hindrances to self-discovery. The fourth step is to be properly motivated. The fifth step is to discover which of the seven is *you*.

You will grasp all this as you read and study the last chapters of this book. In the meantime, we first need to see the benefits, understand the hindrances, and settle our ultimate motivation in life, so here we go!

God made a stunning, staggering, startling decision.

A Word about Creativity

Animals are ruled by instinct. That's why beavers build dams, cats meow, dogs bark, and horses neigh. Animals are preprogrammed to certain innate behaviors. No animals build cars or airplanes. They are locked in, but you are not!

You, like all of mankind, were made "in the image of God." You were not preprogrammed (although you should beware of some silly theologians who teach that you are). God is sovereign. Of that, there is no doubt or dispute. However, God made a stunning, staggering, startling decision. He decided to give you a piece of His sovereignty. He put you in charge of you. You are a decision-maker. He intended you to have protection in your younger years through your parents, a father and a mother who would teach you until you were well-enough advised to take over your own life and from then on, do as *you* will.

You are not a robot, an automaton, or a machine that performs functions according to predetermined coded instructions, nor are you an imitation of a human being. The crazy notion proposed by some theologians that God preprogrammed everybody, even predetermining some to be evil and hell-bent, is preposterous and certainly out of character (His character, which is love).

You were created to create.

God placed you in charge of you. You are not merely a pawn on some celestial chessboard, where God is the only player and makes all the moves. You were created to create. Creativity is an instinctive part of your personhood. Beware of it being stifled.

Now, it's true that your gifting somewhat defines you because you didn't choose your gift. The Giver decides the gift, your gift, your ENA. But within each gifting lies a vast opportunity for creativity.

- The **Messenger** is created to create clear communications of truth.
- The **Helper** creates good works to help others along their life path.
- The **Explainer** creates understanding, so others can live a successful life path.
- The **Encourager** creates inspiration and incentives to empower others on their life path.
- The **Provider** creates assets beyond their own living expenses, which they responsibly share with others to enable them to function on their life paths.
- The **Organizer** oversees and creates opportunities for others.

- The **Caregiver** creates help and helping processes so others can recover and pursue their life paths.

Within your gifting, there are immense and vast opportunities for your creativity. You were created to create.

Chapter Eleven

The Benefits of Discovering Your Endowments

(Your ENA)

The word *endowment* means a gift. In our case, it is a divinely Embedded Natural Ability. Theologians describe this as a "spiritual gift." What is meant by this phrase is simply that God has deposited natural ability in your spirit. You are a spirit. That's the part of you that God personally created. Remember, He is called "the Father of spirits" (Hebrews 12:9). You are a spirit, you live in a body, and your soul possesses the attributes of mind and emotion. Here are some of the benefits of discovering your spiritual gifts:

You Will Know God's Will for Your Life

God's will for your life is exactly what you would choose if you knew all the facts. Paul, the apostle and teacher, warned us to be careful that we don't think too highly of ourselves but to think soberly (Romans 12:3). He was writing about being serious about discovering our gifts. Just before this, he wrote that we can "prove what is that good, and acceptable, and perfect, will of God" (Romans 12:2). Imagine that! You can have proof of God's will for your life. And look at that description of God's proven will for your life: It is good. It is acceptable. It is perfect. In other words, it's so good that you will accept it. It will fit you perfectly. Synonyms for *perfect* include faultless, flawless, consummate, ultimate, complete, total, unmitigated, quintessential, unequalled, unrivaled, unexcelled, unparalleled, unsurpassed, inimitable, and peerless.[25] (Check your thesaurus for more!) The point is that the will of God you will discover by identifying your endowed gifting will be *perfect*—perfect for you! Kiss your fingertips. That means it's delicious!

God's will for your life is exactly what you would choose if you knew all the facts.

A word of caution here: Paul pleads with us to first do *three* things so that we can discover the perfect will of God for our lives. Here they are:

1. **Your body must be under the control of God.**

Otherwise, your body will control you. Pity the person who is managed and manipulated by his or her body. They are like zombies, walking around mindlessly, with their brain deadened, enslaved robotically to whatever bodily appetite rules them each moment. Our bodies as well as our spirits are the Lord's. Check this out:

> *"What? know ye not that your body is the temple of the Holy Ghost which is in you, which ye have of God, and ye are not your own?*
>
> *For ye are bought with a price: therefore glorify God in your body, and in your spirit, which are God's."* (1 Corinthians 6:19-20)

25 "Perfect: Synonyms of Perfect by Lexico," Lexico Dictionaries | English (Lexico Dictionaries), accessed February 1, 2020, https://www.lexico.com/synonym/perfect)

The question now is this: What step or steps should we take to ensure our bodies are the Lord's? The answer is this:

> *"That ye present your bodies a living sacrifice, holy, acceptable unto God, which is your reasonable service."* (Romans 12:1b)

When I was a new Christian, I did this every morning. I stood in front of the mirror (and, mind you, on some days I wasn't all that easy to look at!). Looking in the mirror, I would say, "Here are my hands, God. I present them to You today. May I use them to help others." Then I would present my eyes and say, "God, I give You my eyes. Today, I will look on that which is pure. Lord, these are Your eyes, given to me, so may I see others as You see them. May I see the needs of others just like Jesus would; because God, I present my eyes to You." In like manner, I presented my ears, my feet, my lips, my tongue, and every other part of me. This was an everyday routine for me. To this day, I'm grateful to the young man who taught me to present my body to the Lord every day.

In the Old Testament, the people were forever offering dead sacrifices to God. Now we offer a *living* sacrifice—ourselves. This is the sacrifice that is holy and acceptable to God. One more thing: The Scripture says that this is our "reasonable service." *Reasonable* means logical, sensible, rational, practical, and appropriate.[26]

2. Be not conformed to the world.

This is the second step necessary to discover the will of God for your life. The world's way of thinking is generally the opposite of God's. Though this world is loved by God (and oh, how it is loved), it is at enmity with Him. It is philosophically and diametrically opposed to godliness. That is why John the Beloved warned us,

> *"Love not the world, neither the things that are in*

26 "Reasonable," Dictionary.com (Dictionary.com), accessed February 7, 2020, https://www.dictionary.com/browse/reasonable?s=t)

> *the world. If any man love the world, the love of the Father is not in him.*
>
> *For all that is in the world, the lust of the flesh, and the lust of the eyes, and the pride of life, is not of the Father, but is of the world.*
>
> *And the world passeth away, and the lust thereof: but he that doeth the will of God abideth for ever."* (1 John 2:15-17)

Notice that the context of Romans 12 is "the will of God." To know the will of God, you and I must refuse to comply with the world's philosophy, values, or influences. J.B. Phillips renders Romans 12:1 this way:

> *"Don't let the world around you squeeze you into its own mould, but let God re-mould your minds from within."* (Romans 12:2 PHILLIPS)

3. **Get your mind under control and think correctly—so utterly so that you will be transformed.**

> *"And be not conformed to this world: but be ye transformed by the renewing of your mind."*
> (Romans 12:2)

Are you ready for transformation? Transformation is like a metamorphosis, a transfiguration, a transmutation. It's a total makeover, an overhaul, a reconstruction. It's radical and revolutionary. God formed us. Sin deformed us. Others try to reform us, but God transforms us. We are utterly reconstructed, renewed, and revamped. How does it happen? By the renewing of our minds!

The verb "renewing" here is in the present passive progressive tense.[27] (You do remember that from your ninth-grade English class, right?) It means that the action is ongoing, both in the present and

---

27 James Strong, "341. Anakainoó," Strong's Greek: 341. ἀνακαινόω (anakainoó) -- to make new (Biblehub), accessed February 7, 2020, https://biblehub.com/greek/341.htm)

into the future. It is a discipline that we never stop practicing. Why must it be a perpetual discipline? Because you can have your mind brought up to speed, so to speak, and then along comes an influence to un-renew you (to change your mind). It could be an acquaintance (that's why you need to be careful of who your friends are). It could be a movie, a song, a book, an advertisement, and goodness knows what else in the world that has the capacity to tear down our built-up thinking. It could be an accumulation of all of the above. Thus, we need to renew our minds and keep them in this renewed condition. How do we do that?

The answer is by nonstop, day and night meditation on Scripture (God's words, thoughts, and ideas). (More details on this are found in Supplement 1.) Let's get back to the benefits of knowing your gifting.

You Will Know Your Purpose in Life

What God has given you, deposited in you, and planted, *embedded in you,* is now *in your possession.* It is your personal equipment. You have been furnished, supplied, and suited for your life task. You are prepared and qualified by His endowment to you (and it is actually *in* you). You have definition and directions that are distinct and clear. Let me illustrate.

Vocationally speaking, when a man is trained to weld, what should he do? He should weld. The plumber plumbs, the sower sows, the cook cooks, the builder builds, and so on. People do what they are vocationally trained to do. In a similar, yet much more profound way, the discovery of your endowed gifting, your ENA, is a clear indication of what you should do. You will have an undeniable inborn energy that will be focused toward a given achievement. You will know from your gifting exactly what your purpose in life should be: accomplishing your gifting!

You Will Have Energy

When you are operating in your ENA, or should I say, *when your gift is functioning through you*, you can do it tirelessly.

It's easy. I call this the "no pressure" principle. I'll never forget listening to the great evangelist David Wilkerson in Midland, Texas. His crusade meeting was over, and we had retired to his bus in the parking lot.

Whenever I was with David, I was like a sponge, absorbing every word I could. That night he told me one of his secrets. After passionately preaching for over an hour, as he often did, you would think he'd be tired. Add to that the fact that he would give an altar call and basically begin a second meeting with the hundreds who responded. I've seen him praying from person to person in the "after service" for long periods of time. You'd think he'd be tired, like a cloth that has just been wrung out.

Here's what he told me. He said, "David, when you are operating in your gifting, you do so tirelessly. In fact, you come out of the meeting stronger than you were when you went in." The reason he gave was this: When God is working through you, actually *through your gift*, there's no effort. It just flows from God through you and your gift to others.

You Will Be Relaxed Just Being Your Real Self

We can all do a lot of things, and we should. But when we are functioning in our gift, it is natural, with no pretense and no extra labor required. For example, I happen to be a teacher, an explainer of truth, but I spent years doing evangelism. I travelled with teams from college to college, high school to high school, beach to beach, park to park, street to street. I built an open-air stage, and we went wherever the crowds were, set up, dropped our stage (actually the hinged sidewall), turned on the generator, powered up the sound system, sang, gathered a crowd, and testified; and then I'd preach. I did it. But it was a lot of pressure.

On the other hand, I could get in front of a group with a blackboard (I'm showing my age now!), later a whiteboard, and then an overhead projector, and now a computer-fed video-wall, and go for hours. I mean it. I could get a thousand people to testify to this. I often taught discipleship camps from morning to night with only short breaks for lunch and dinner. No glory be to me. It's just that when you operate in your gifting, or should I say when your gifting is operating in you, you can function tirelessly with no pressure—none!

You Will Have Fulfillment in Life

True joy and fulfillment in life comes from discovering your gift, developing it, and using it for the highest good of God and others. What you can authentically offer to others becomes a joy. You give what you've got. You sow out of your gifting. You know it. You feel it. You let it flow. It reaches and changes others. You bear fruit. Your fruit remains. People grow, develop, think, and mature because you let divine stuff flow out of you to them. And, my friend, you've got the stuff.

Love will be manifested through your gifting to others.

Nicky Cruz, the author of *Run, Baby, Run*, and a hero in David Wilkerson's book *The Cross and the Switchblade*, was a onetime gangster, leader of the Mau Mau gang, in New York City. Now he runs his own outreach ministry. I heard this story about him: Converted and now working the streets of NYC with Wilkerson, he came in to Wilkerson's office, plopped himself down in a chair, and complained, "I'm all dried up, weary." Wilkerson said, "No, you just don't have enough victims to let your love out on. Go find somebody who needs your love." The story has it that Nicky went out, did what he was told, and came back shouting, "I got it back."

People grow, develop, think, and mature because you let divine stuff flow out of you to them.

Sometimes we just require exposure to those who need what we've got. Almost magically our gift goes into operation. Out it comes. People are blessed, and we get the refreshment. Nothing makes one feel so strong as the call for help.

God will be working ***through*** you.

"We then, as workers together with him."
(2 Corinthians 6:1)

Imagine that! God is working with you. And you are working with God. Together! Take a hallelujah break if you wish. What could be more glorious than that? ENA plus God! When you are functioning in your gifting, you discover (sometimes with utter amazement) that something divine is happening. Something of God, something of the Holy Spirit, is seeping out of you, sometimes rushing out of you. Old-timers call it the anointing. What is that?

"But the anointing which ye have received of him abideth in you, and ye need not that any man teach you." (1 John 2:27)

It's a God-empowerment. You got it from God Himself. And it's *inside* of you. This empowerment abides, adheres, and dwells in you. It teaches you. The Bible calls it *unction.*

"Ye have an unction from the Holy One."
(1 John 2:20)

God will work through what you are.

This is an amazing benefit. God is working through you and your gift. That's the principle of how divine gifting works. It is *from God, through you and your gifting, to others.* You can expect the supernatural. God will work through what you are. How wonderful to experience the outflow and overflow of the inflowing of God's Holy Spirit.

You will understand your personal worth and value.

Do you have any idea, even a slight notion, of how valuable you are to the kingdom of God? To the church? To the world? To others? Without knowing, developing, and functioning in your gift, you are left unquantifiable. You cannot measure your worth because you don't know it. Although this verse refers primarily to our possessing the "light of the gospel," it can have a noncontextual meaning, too.

> *"We have this treasure in earthen vessels."*
> (2 Corinthians 4:7)

"Earthen vessels" is a term referring to our bodies. There is a treasure in you. Upon its discovery, you will see your personal value and worth. It's in your ENA.

Through Discovering Your ENA, You Will Know What Member of the Body of Christ You Are

Everyone needs to know why they were born.

So, what's this "body of Christ" idea? It's simply this. We are to Jesus today what His body was to Him when He was here. He used His body to go places, meet people, encourage, correct, deliver, proclaim, teach, explain, heal, salvage, and even reprove. When He left here (and He's coming back), He said, "Now you are My body." He presented this analogy of all of us doing what He did. Each of us is a part, a significant part. Jesus now sees through our eyes, listens for the call for help through our ears, speaks through our lips, walks on our feet, thinks through our minds, and loves through our hearts.

We are to Jesus today what His body was to Him when He was here.

The gifts are analogous to the various members of the body of Christ. There are only seven kinds of members in the body of

Christ, seven differing ENAs. You are one of them. Here's the proof:

> *"For as we have many members in one body, and all members have not the same office:*
>
> *So we, being many, are one body in Christ, and every one members one of another.*
>
> *Having then gifts differing according to the grace that is given to us."* (Romans 12:4-6)

Notice the following in reference to the body of Christ:

- There are many members.
- All members don't have the same function (The Greek word translated "office" in KJV is *praxis*, and means function.)[28]
- We are united as one body.
- We are connected, "members one of another."
- What makes us different from one another is our ENA: "having then gifts differing."

When you discover your gift, you will know what member you are, and thus how you fit into the larger scheme of things, which is to be the representation of Christ today (what His literal body was to Him when He was here 2,000-plus years ago).

When Christ was here physically, He personified perfection. He performed all of these seven functions flawlessly, faultlessly, and fully. Now each of us is a part of His body, and we are to function together according to the gift we have been given to use toward others "having then gifts differing."

Annie Johnson Flint wrote the following poem. I include it here in the hopes of clarifying this body concept:

---

28 James Strong, "4234. Praxis," Strong's Greek: 4234. πρᾶξις (praxis) -- a deed, function (Biblehub), accessed February 1, 2020, https://biblehub.com/greek/4234.htm)

Christ has no hands but our hands
To do His work today;
He has no feet but our feet
To lead men in the way;
He has no tongues but our tongues
To tell men how He died;
He has no help but our help
To bring them to His side.

We are the only Bible
The careless world will read;
We are the sinner's Gospel,
We are the scoffer's creed;
We are the Lord's last message,
Given in deed and word;
What if the type is crooked?
What if the print is blurred?

What if our hands are busy
With other work than His?
What if our feet are walking
Where sin's allurement is?
What if our tongues are speaking
Of things His lips would spurn?
How can we hope to help Him
Or welcome His return?[29]

You will joyfully accept and appreciate the other members and their giftings, those with different and similar Embedded

29 Annie Johnson Flint, "The World's Bible," Poem: The World's Bible by Annie Johnson Flint, accessed February 1, 2020, https://www.poetrynook.com/poem/worlds-bible)

Natural Abilities.

The body of Christ works as one but has many members:

> *"For by one Spirit are we all baptized into one body."* (1 Corinthians 12:13)
>
> *"For the body is not one member, but many."* (1 Corinthians 12:14)

God Himself determines not only the giftings, but according to the analogy, the various members of the body.

> *"But now hath God set the members every one of them in the body, as it hath pleased him."* (1 Corinthians 12:18)

There is to be no division, and members are to have the same care and respect for one another.

> *"That there should be no schism in the body; but that the members should have the same care one for another."* (1 Corinthians 12:25)

The entire twelfth chapter of 1 Corinthians should be read. For the sake of brevity, I have extracted various points. Here is one more: We cannot, we must not, reject any member, but instead recognize our personal need for one another:

> *"And the eye cannot say unto the hand, I have no need of thee: nor again the head to the feet, I have no need of you."* (1 Corinthians 12:21)

The gifts, the ENA, are not only different, but given by different measures.

One of the highest compliments ever paid to me by a friend was from a colleague who said, "Johnston, you don't have much talent but what you've got, you use."

There are ten-talent teachers, five-talent teachers, and one-talent teachers like me. The gifts and ENA are given by measure. To be frank, I've seen some five-talent-gifted persons do more than ten-talent versions of the same. Why? Because one discovered his gift, developed it, and was using it, and the other was not.

You and I have been given stewardship of our ENA. Shall we disrespect one-talent-level people? No. Never. We need them. Some would give them less honor, but heaven forbids doing so. What we find in the Scriptures is totally out of character with our iniquitous, competitive culture. It staggers the unsanctified thinking of our day.

> *"And those members of the body, which we think to be less honourable, upon these we bestow more abundant honour; and our uncomely parts have more abundant comeliness.*
>
> *For our comely parts have no need: but God hath tempered the body together, having given more abundant honour to that part which lacked."*
>
> (1 Corinthians 12:23-24)

My armpit is not a very honorable member of my body, but I need it, and I give it special attention. I check it, wash it, deodorize it, and check it again. And if I get a sore under there, I give it lots of attention. In the body of Christ, God has "tempered" us, which means combined all the parts together, and He tells us to pay special attention to the parts that we think are lacking and show them more respect.

We are very, very connected.

In fact, we are so connected that if:

> *"One member suffer, all the members suffer with it; or one member be honoured, all the members rejoice with it."* (1 Corinthians 12:26)

Oh, how we love one another. And if the world sees our love for one another, they will know we are Christians because of it.

In fact, immediately after the listing of the seven kinds of members, the seven kinds of giftings, the final statements are about love, and it gets to this singular evidence of genuine love:

> *"Rejoice with them that do rejoice, and weep with them that weep."* (Romans 12:15)

You don't have to do it all—you are only one member.

This should be comforting to you. No one is the whole body of Christ, and no one is more than one member of it. Ego and pride attempt to make us think otherwise. I'm only a part, but I am a part!

> *"Now ye are the body of Christ, and members in particular."* (1 Corinthians 12:27)

We are particular members. That means that we are specific, distinct, and individual members. It means we only have to do our part.

You will be stable for the rest of your life.

Your gift will not change or get swapped out from under you at any time in this life. We can't trade them in, trade them out, dismiss them, or annihilate them. They are attached to the real us.

> *"For the gifts and calling of God are without*

> *repentance."* (Romans 11:29)

It is also translated this way:

> *"God's gifts and God's call are under full warranty—never canceled, never rescinded."*
> (Romans 11:29 MSG)

(We will cover callings later.)

You will have direction for development.

Once we know our gift, we are able to nurture it, develop it, keep it alive and functional, and apply creative elements to enhance and further what we have been given. We assume full responsibility now, not in a nebulous, hazy, vague, blurry, or generalized way. We become the caretakers and developers and operators of what we have been given. Sometimes it must be stirred up and certainly it must never be neglected.

> *"Wherefore I put thee in remembrance that thou stir up the gift of God, which is in thee."*
> (2 Timothy 1:6)

> *"Neglect not the gift that is in thee, which was given thee."* (1 Timothy 4:14)

You will be not only successful but rewarded by God.

You will automatically achieve as you allow what you are gifted at to function. What you have in you just needs to get out. And when it does, look at the promise:

> *"A man's gift maketh room for him, and bringeth him before great men."* (Proverbs 18:16)

Your Embedded Natural Ability will bring you before eminent

people and situations. That is success. Yet there is more because God promises you that He will remember and reward you.

> *"For God is not unrighteous to forget your work and labour of love, which ye have shewed toward his name, in that ye have ministered to the saints, and do minister."* (Hebrews 6:10)

The rewards promised to us by God are so great and so numerous that they require this life and the next life to enjoy them.

Chapter Twelve

Hindrances to Discovering Your Endowment

The Opinions of Others

The search for your real self is simple, but it is not easy. It is not easy because from our birth, throughout our childhood, and even into our adult years, we have been subjected to uninformed feedback from others who have no idea who we really are. Unfortunately, we tend to believe we are what others have told us we are. And some of us have been told some pretty nasty things. Few, if any at all, have done anything more than guess. Little or no diligence has been exercised in our direction, so we are now a conglomeration of conflicting (and ill-informed) opinions.

It's not that the opinions of others do not have value. Some do. But both those opinions and those persons must be vetted. All opinions must be carefully and critically examined. They must be scrutinized, inspected and investigated, assessed and appraised. The counsel we get can be either beneficial or damning. For this reason, our loving Father warns, advises, and encourages us in written form:

> *"Blessed is the man that walketh not in the counsel of the ungodly, nor standeth in the way of sinners, nor sitteth in the seat of the scornful."* (Psalm 1:1)

This is how we vet the people giving us advice. Do not take counsel from the ungodly, who do not display or convey the character of God. Do not take recommendations from sinners. Do not take advisement from scorners, those who mock, belittle, or display contempt or disdain for others anywhere. Consider *all* advice in the light of God's Word.

We must intentionally remove all unbiblical feedback that has been inputted into our lives from others. The Bible tells us how to do that. In Isaiah, we learn that there will be people and opinions that will "be gathered against us." In actual fact, those persons are in trouble with God. Here's what God says:

> *"Behold, they shall surely gather together, but not by me: whosoever shall gather together against thee shall fall for thy sake."* (Isaiah 54:15)

It's true that those gathered against you might be doing so in ignorance and without any evil intent. Albert Einstein said, "Only two things are infinite, the universe and human stupidity, and I'm not sure about the former."[30] You really do not want to be ill-advised.

The question is this: How do we remove the unbiblical data, the opinions that are like weapons that are formed against us? Here, embedded in this verse is the secret:

> *"No weapon that is formed against thee shall prosper; and every tongue that shall rise against thee in judgment thou shalt condemn."*
> (Isaiah 54:17)

The weapons formed against you are the words from the

30 Albert Einstein, "Albert Einstein Quotes," BrainyQuote (Xplore), accessed February 7, 2020, https://www.brainyquote.com/quotes/albert_einstein_100015)

tongues that give their judgment or opinions against you. So, what do we do? We are to condemn those tongues, those words, those wrong (and sometimes devious) opinions, wherever we find them. However, *we don't condemn people*. We condemn the ideas, the opinions, the messages, and the tongues. To condemn means to proclaim and express complete disapproval. In essence, we denounce and censure the wrong and misinformed opinions. In so doing, we remove this unbiblical data from our thinking. One last word: Don't miss the word "every" in the Scripture. This means we must have *zero tolerance* for unbiblical ideas. And be warned that they can be found within the churc as well as in the world. The devil loves to infiltrate church circles, so accept only those ideas and message that agree with God's Word and His message, and refuse all else.

Comparing Ourselves with Others

Repetition is the classic method of learning, so here I go again. I simply *must* repeat this grave danger, this warning. I am referring to the Scripture that warns us about comparing ourselves with others and solemnly begins with, "We dare not…."

Yikes! We learned to do this very thing at a very young age. Parents and peers did it to us. We were "rated" according to how we performed in comparison to other children. Government schools specialized in and emphasized pitting us one against the other. We were measured by appearances, our grades, size and weight, athletic ability, and the list goes on *ad nauseum*. And it never quits. It escalates in the teen years. The older we got, the more we had to compete with others. Through college and into the business world, we lived perpetually on a measuring scale. We were on one side of the scale and a constant parade of others were on the other side, always being contrasted against one another. Sometimes we thought we won. Many times, we lost. We usually won or lost depending on the person with whom we were compared. Inferiority (and superiority) complexes lived and died and lived again. Competition was deemed healthy. Really? In what universe?

Mental health, emotional strength, and social stability have been entirely destroyed because of this heathen practice. Everyone is forced to live as a gladiator in an arena of life in which the crowds roar gleefully at the victor whose heel is on the throat of the defeated underling. Who cares about the little boy who didn't pass?

A sad-faced little fellow sits alone in deep disgrace,
There's a lump arising in his throat, tears streaming down his face.
He wandered from his playmates, for he doesn't want to hear
Their shouts of merry laughter, since the world has lost its cheer;
He has sipped the cup of sorrow, he has drained the bitter glass,
And his heart is fairly breaking: he's the boy who didn't pass.

In the apple tree the robin sings a cheery little song,
But he doesn't seem to hear it, showing plainly something's wrong.
Comes his faithful little spaniel for a romp and a bit of play,
But the troubled little fellow sternly bids him go away.
All alone he sits in sorrow, with his hair a tangled mess,
And his eyes are red with weeping; he's the boy who didn't pass.

How he hates himself for failing, he can hear his playmates jeer,
For they've left him with the dullards – gone ahead a half of year;
And he tried so hard to conquer, oh, he tried to do his best,
But now he knows he's weaker, yes, and duller than the rest.
He's ashamed to tell his mother, for he thinks she'll hate him too—
The little boy who didn't pass, who failed at getting through.

Oh, you who boast a laughing son and speak of him as bright,
And you who love a little girl who comes to you tonight
With smiling eyes and dancing feet, with honors from her school,
Turn to that lonely little boy who thinks he's a fool
And take him kindly by the hand, the dullest in his class,
He's the one that most needs love, the boy who didn't pass.

—Anonymous[31]

---

31 "Poems About Failure," (https://newspaperarchive.com/burlington-hawk-eye-jan-30-1909-p-7/)

Through our comparison, we destroy the dignity of persons for whom Christ died. Imagine the evil of this. Clearly, we are instructed to "honour all men" (1 Peter 2:17). No one should be dishonored; no one should be left behind; no one should be rejected or unloved; no one should be disdained. No, not one. How savage have we become?

Rugged individualism is destroyed by irrational conformity to the opinions and comparisons of others. We need to return to the dictum, "This above all- to thine own self be true, and it must follow, as the night the day, thou canst not then be false to any man."[32] Or as we render it today: "Be true to thine own self, for only then can we be true to others." If not, we will be forever presenting a "fake" us to others.

No running with the pack, no swimming with the stream, no going with the flow, no acquiescing to public opinion, and no going along to get along. *If we care too much for what others think, we become their prisoners*. We lose any distinction by surrendering to the pressure of the masses, or our immediate sphere of associates. We get lost in the sea of indistinct vagueness and tragically, lost to the excellence that sets us apart in society. We become a part of the blur of mediocrity. Suddenly we are just run of the mill, all because of our false fear of being freaky or unaccepted.

We must march on, oblivious to the praise or blame of others. Our quest for acceptance has inadvertently led to varying degrees of self-rejection, a miserable and unhappy state of being. We lose our personal identity, and that means we end up *not knowing who we are*. The resultant identity crisis eventually shows itself, but worse yet, it can become a regular, everyday psychological crisis. There is no needle, no compass, to accurately point us to self-realization. A "midlife crisis" is simply the result of having lived years without knowing why we were born. It's a long time from the cradle to the grave. Life should be more than the meaningless passage of time. Instead of happiness and healthiness, we feel out of place in the world. Why you were born is about identity achievement.

---

32 William Shakespeare, *Hamlet*, Act I, Scene 3, Open Source Shakespeare, accessed February 7, 2020, https://www.opensourceshakespeare.org/views/plays/play_view.php?WorkID=hamlet&Act=1&Scene=3&Scope=scene), 565.

Frederick Douglass said it this way: "I prefer to be true to myself, even at the hazard of incurring ridicule of others, rather than to be false, and to incur my own abhorrence."[33] Steve Jobs said, "Your time is limited, so don't waste it living someone else's life."[34]

Iniquity

Iniquity is the Bible's word for narcissism, the motivation and attempt to create an inequality, play god, set up ego in the god position, and be something we are not. Iniquity is a two-edged sword, cutting both ways. For some, iniquity consists of trying to be above God and others. Some attempt to be lower than they were designed to be. Some even vacillate between these two extremes. On the one hand, they are really trying to get themselves above others. If they fail to realize those dreams, they may give up and settle for much less. This is a far too important and exhaustive subject to be covered here. However, it is so crucial to your success that I have written an entire book on the subject. It was originally published as *How to Conquer Iniquity*, but is now updated and available as *How You See Yourself.* In case you had not noticed, narcissism is the plague of our day. Everybody is playing god and doing what seems right in their own eyes.

Limited Experience with Others

People are most important. People are the ones for whom God has eternal intentions. Our cars and trucks and homes and toys will not last forever, but people will. And your value is directly related to people. The ultimate achievement in this life is affecting forever-living persons. When you, by your treasured endowment, your gifting God put inside you, affect a person, you affect eternity in countless ways. How infinite is that! Imagine, little ol' you and

---

33 Frederick Douglass, "A Quote by Frederick Douglass," Goodreads (Goodreads), accessed February 7, 2020, https://www.goodreads.com/quotes/82354-i-prefer-to-be-true-to-myself-even-at-the)

34 Steve Jobs, "Steve Jobs Quotes," BrainyQuote (Xplore), accessed February 7, 2020, https://www.brainyquote.com/quotes/steve_jobs_416854)

me having an *infinite* effect.

The danger for most is that we have been too distracted with things and ambitions and schedules and so many lesser achievements that we haven't learned how we best relate to others. It's possible to be a hermit, living in self-absolved isolation, even in the middle of the crowds around us. Thus, the energies and abilities that we have been given are largely ignored because of the distractions and amusements of life. Remember, to "muse" means to think, ponder, contemplate, mull over, and reflect deeply on. "*A*muse" means the opposite. It means to divert or distract. Thus, amusement becomes the murderer of thought.

The ultimate achievement in this life is affecting forever-living persons.

Your gifting or endowment (at the most fundamental level) determines how you relate to others. There are seven biblically defined ways, seven giftings, and you have been given one that is predominate. Your endowment is how you think, how you relate, how you are motivated and fulfilled. It's your spiritual DNA.

1. Attempting to Choose One's Own Endowment or Divinely Embedded Natural Ability

The giver decides the gift that will be given. I know what you're thinking. At Christmastime, you got what you wanted because you dropped enough hints. Maybe you even outright asked. My wife used to be good at this, and if I told the whole truth right now (and I guess I'd better!), I've been pretty good at it myself.

The truth is that we were given these great deposits of God before we even had understanding or self-awareness, when we were still in our mother's womb during the process in which we were created. We had no choice. Even if we did, do we really think we could make better decisions than God did about us? *We don't get to choose. We get to discover.*

2. Wrong Value System

When you see God's endowment options and giftings, you may think that some of them are better than the others. Wrong! They are all *equal in value*. They are just different in function. Each of them is of inestimable value and worthy of the highest respect.

In fact, the attempt to choose can actually prevent you from discovering your God-given endowment. And this choice would be wrong because it is based on a false evaluation of the worth of each gift. So, relax, and let's walk down some paths together. These trails will lead you around obstacles and roadblocks, and in the end, you will discover you and your real value and intrinsic worth. Nothing is more important than that to your actual success.

3. Assuming the Gifts and Embedded Natural Abilities Are Personality Types

They are not. Neither your gift nor any of your ENA has to do with being an introvert or an extrovert. They are not about psychometrics or temperament. Proto-psychological theory breaks temperaments down into the sanguine, who are optimistic and social; the choleric, who are short-tempered and irritable; the melancholy, analytical and quiet; and the phlegmatic, relaxed and peaceful. These should not be construed as having anything to do with discovering your endowment.

The sixteen Myers-Briggs Personality Types were extrapolated from the MBTI Theory from Jung's book on psychological types. Isabel Briggs Myers and Katharine Cook Briggs developed the Myers-Briggs Temperament Indicators (MBTI) as an introspective self-report questionnaire designed to indicate psychological preferences on how people perceive the world and make decisions.[35]

However, our source of determining the differentiations between persons is based on the ancient, but vetted and verified, documents compiled in the biblical canon. In a word, our understanding

35 "Myers–Briggs Type Indicator," Wikipedia (Wikimedia Foundation, January 29, 2020), https://en.wikipedia.org/wiki/Myers–Briggs_Type_Indicator)

comes from the inspired, inerrant, infallible, and irrevocable Word of God. God, being the Chief and only Designer of Humanity (and of each person specifically) is the only authoritative expert on the matter. Be careful not to confuse psychological theory with this divine system.

And now we must address motive, the basic fundamental and structural intent and reason that governs everything we do or say.

Chapter Thirteen

Born to Love

You were *not* born to raise hell. No one was born to raise hell—not even the devil! Satan's original name was Lucifer. Although he wasn't "born" but "created," he was created to bring beauty into the universe of God. He did this for eons of time until he became narcissistic, the contemporary word for the biblical word "iniquity." Here's the Scripture that describes this:

> *"Thou wast perfect in thy ways from the day that thou wast created, till iniquity was found in thee."*
> (Ezekiel 28:15)

Lucifer became selfish and self-dedicated. He had not been created that way. He chose to be that way. God made this statement:

> *"How art thou fallen from heaven, O Lucifer, son of the morning! How art thou cut down."*
> (Isaiah 14:12)

Then he indicates five reasons for what happened:

> *"For thou hast said in thine heart, **I will** ascend into heaven, **I will** exalt my throne above the stars of God: **I will** sit also upon the mount of the congregation, in the sides of the north:*

> ***I will*** *ascend above the heights of the clouds;* ***I will*** *be like the most High."* (Isaiah 14:13-14)

No one has been created to raise hell. *We were born to love.* You were born to love. How? By using your gifting for the Lord and for the good of His universe and all who live in it. That is why you were born. But let's back up a bit and talk about love, for love is the essence of God.

When I was a boy, I was given a large plastic replica of a walnut. When I cracked it open, a long narrow scroll of paper rolled out with one end staying attached to the inside of the walnut. The title at the top of the paper said, "The Gospel in a Nutshell." It read:

For God (the greatest Giver)
So loved (the greatest motive)
The world (the greatest need)
That He gave (the greatest act)
His only begotten Son (the greatest gift)
That whosoever (the greatest invitation)
Believeth (the greatest simplicity)
In Him (the greatest person)
Should not perish (the greatest deliverance)
But (the greatest exception)
Have (the greatest certainty)
Everlasting life (the greatest possession).

> Love is God's philosophy—and it must become ours.

Both life and eternity are about love because God is about love. Love is God's philosophy—and it must become ours. Love is the opposite of selfishness, the opposite of being self-absorbed, self-obsessed, conceited, boastful, pretentious, self-centered, and self-regarding. Such attitudes make a person unable to deal with criticism and they are often accompanied by feelings of insecurity, shame, and vulnerability. Humiliation of any kind can make them angry, depressed, or moody.

That doesn't sound like the grounds for much happiness, does it? People who are self-centered are considered narcissistic.

Love is exactly the opposite. It is choosing the highest good of God, His universe, and others, without personal benefit or self-gratification as a motive. The endowment we received from God is not for personal consumption. It is our inbred means of blessing others: the Messenger by delivering his message, the Helper through service to others, the Teacher by clarifying truth, the Exhorter by encouraging others, the Provider by funding others, the Organizer by overseeing the total well-being of the community, and the Caregiver by bringing mercy and healing to the hurting. This is how each of us loves in our own unique way.

But love is not a natural inclination. It must be learned, and then it must be exercised. It is not our default mode. Each time a choice is presented to us, we have to reject selfishness and opt to love instead. It's an everyday, every-situation choice.

> *"If I could speak all the languages of earth and of angels, but didn't love others, I would only be a noisy gong or a clanging cymbal.*
>
> *If I had the gift of prophecy, and if I understood all of God's secret plans and possessed all knowledge, and if I had such faith that I could move mountains, but didn't love others, I would be nothing.*
>
> *If I gave everything I have to the poor and even sacrificed my body, I could boast about it; but if I didn't love others, I would have gained nothing."*
>
> *(1 Corinthians 13:1-3 NLT)*

Let me illustrate this "must be done in love" principle further. Let's say Mary is a Helper. She bakes an apple pie for a new neighbor. How nice! How thoughtful! How Christlike! But the neighbor doesn't so much as say, "Thank you." In response, Mary gets upset and says to herself, *If that's all the thanks I get, see if I ever do that again!* Who was she really making the pie for? *Herself.* And when she did not get back at least the "thanks" that she thought was her due, she got angry.

That's not an example of doing something in love, and that's why it doesn't count.

Now let's assume, for the sake of illustration, that Mary gets converted to Jesus and begins to live *for* the Lord. Now she bakes and delivers the same apple pie. No thank you? *No problem.* She didn't do it for thanks. She did it for the Lord—she did it to love God. And she'll just keep on doing that, no matter how others react.

What Paul is saying in 1 Corinthians 13 is that you could have the most wonderful gift in the world, be the most eloquent Messenger, the most proficient Helper, the most sought-after Teacher, the most motivational Encourager, the most generous Provider, the most meticulous Organizer, or the most longsuffering Caregiver, but *if you don't have love, it doesn't matter.*

Your great gift would be wasted, for all of your aims would be selfish rather than selfless. You wouldn't be doing things "as unto the Lord" but unto yourself. You'd just be going through the motions and, in the end, do more harm than good. This is why the Scriptures tell us:

> *"He died for all, that they which live* ***should not henceforth live unto themselves****, but unto him which died for them, and rose again."*
> (2 Corinthians 5:15, emphasis mine)

> *"If any man will come after me,* ***let him deny himself****, and take up his cross, and follow me."*
> (Matthew 16:24, emphasis mine)

What is this cross that we are to carry? It is the cross upon which our dominating ego is crucified. We must carry this cross daily:

> *"If any man will come after me, let him deny himself, and* ***take up his cross daily, and follow me****."* (Luke 9:23, emphasis mine)

Paul further testified,

> *"I die daily."* (1 Corinthians 15:31b)

He did not mean that he was constantly at the point of death, but that he had to give up his selfishness daily, his right to live for his own desires. Instead, he chose to serve God and others, regardless of the troubles it caused him. (And it caused him many troubles! Just read through 2 Corinthians 11:23-29!) He died daily to his right to a selfish disposition.

A selfish disposition is the deterrent to love. Love and selfishness are polar opposites. Jesus came to set us free from selfishness. How? By His death and a resurrection! Paul makes it clear:

> *"I am crucified with Christ: nevertheless I live; yet not I, but Christ liveth in me: and the life which I now live in the flesh I live by the faith of the Son of God, who loved me, and gave himself for me."*
> (Galatians 2:20)

Notice the clarity provided in *The Message* translation:

> *"Indeed, I have been crucified with Christ. My ego is no longer central...The life you see me living is not 'mine,' but it is lived by faith in the Son of God, who loved me and gave himself for me. I am not going to go back on that."* (Galatians 2:20 MSG)

The cross, our cross, is the one upon which our old selfish ways are crucified, so that the new loving us can emerge. Only then can we truly be free to live—free to "do good." Only then can we live by faith as we have been instructed. You have been given a measured faith to use your gift.

> *"According as God hath dealt to every man the measure of faith...*
> *having then gifts differing according to the grace that is given to us."* (Romans 12:3,6)

> *"You have faith to walk in your gift. And faith, according to Galatians, 'worketh by love.'"*
>
> (Galatians 5:6)

Everything God does is birthed by love, giving way to the highest good. So it is with us. Everything we truly do in His name must be birthed by love. It is carried out in love. Love is God's philosophy; and so, love must be our philosophy. It is what propels us forward and powers our gifting. In this way, others become the object of our affections, that they may benefit from our gifting.

But what if the others are obnoxious, selfish, unworthy, and ungrateful?

Then we do it anyway because we're not doing it to please them, *but to please God.* We don't love because others deserve it; we love because God loved us when we *didn't* deserve it.

> *"We love him, because he first loved us.*
>
> *If a man say, I love God, and hateth his brother, he is a liar: for he that loveth not his brother whom he hath seen, how can he love God whom he hath not seen?*
>
> *And this commandment have we from him, that he who loveth God love his brother also."*
>
> (1 John 4:19-21)

Professor Austin O'Malley wrote, "Those that deserve love the least, need it the most."[36] The secret is knowing that what we do for others, we are really doing for God. It may look like we are doing things for others, but we are doing them because we love Him. We see this in Jesus' own words:

---

36 Austin O'Malley, "Austin O'Malley Quote: 'Those Who Deserve Love the Least Need It the Most," Quotefancy, accessed February 7, 2020, https://quotefancy.com/quote/1709298/Austin-O-Malley-Those-who-deserve-love-the-least-need-it-the-most)

> *"For I was an hungred, and ye gave me meat: I was thirsty, and ye gave me drink: I was a stranger, and ye took me in:*
>
> *naked, and ye clothed me: I was sick, and ye visited me: I was in prison, and ye came unto me.*
>
> *Then shall the righteous answer him, saying, Lord, when saw we thee an hungred, and fed thee? Or thirsty, and gave thee drink?*
>
> *When saw we thee a stranger, and took thee in? Or naked, and clothed thee?*
>
> *Or when saw we thee sick, or in prison, and came unto thee?*
>
> *And the King shall answer and say unto them, Verily I say unto you, inasmuch as ye have done it unto one of the least of these my brethren,* ***ye have done it unto me****."*
>
> (Matthew 25:35-40, emphasis mine)

Think about it. They asked, "Visited You in prison? Fed You? When did that happen?"

Jesus responded, "Every time you did it to someone who couldn't pay you back, it was the same as doing it to Me." This is quite a lesson!

We actually serve the Lord by serving others. He wants the others to see our "good works, and glorify your Father which is in heaven" (Matthew 5:16). We need nothing back from others; thus, there are no disappointments.

> *"My soul, wait thou only upon God; for my expectation is from him...*
>
> *I shall not be moved."* (Psalm 62:5-6)

Expect nothing from others and you will not be disappointed—and *no disappointment means no resentment, no bitterness, and no anger*. We will not be affected (or infected) by others. We can live oblivious to the praise or blame of human beings. Only of the

Pharisees and hypocrites was it said,

> *"They loved the praise of men more than the praise of God."* (John 12:43)

What an awful state of affairs that would be!

To lock this principle into my brain when I was a boy, my father taught me this song:

Lord, help me live from day to day

In such a self-forgetful way
That even when I kneel to pray
My prayer shall be for others.

Chorus:

Yes, others, Lord, yes others;
Let this my motto be;
Help me to live for others
That I may live like Thee.

Help me in all the work I do
To ever be sincere and true,
And know that all I'd do for You
Must needs be done for others.

Let "Self" be crucified and slain
And Buried deep: and all in vain
May efforts be to rise again,
Except to live for others.

So when my work on earth is done,
And my new work in heav'n's begun,
I'll praise You for the crown I've won,
But praise You more for others.[37]

37 Written by Charles D. Meigs in 1902, public domain.

Chapter Fourteen

Why You Were Born to Live Forever

"O death, where is thy sting? O grave, where is thy victory?"
(1 Corinthians 15:55)

None of us is getting out of here alive.

But we are getting out of here. I am, and you are. The exit door is called death. You and I, like everyone else, will one day exit this life. This reason alone should be sufficient for us to seek a proper understanding of *why we were born*.

Peter Marshall was twice appointed as chaplain to the United States Senate. His life was memorialized in the 1955 Academy Award-nominated movie *A Man Called Peter*. On December 7, 1941, when Japan was attacking Pearl Harbor in Hawaii, Pastor Marshall was speaking in the chapel of the United States Naval Academy. His text was from the letter of James:

> *"For what is your life. It is even a vapor that appeareth for awhile, then vanisheth away."*
> (James 4:14)

He asked the following:

> "But what is death? Is it to be blown out, like a candle in the wind? Is it a shivering void in which there is nothing that lives? Is it a cold space into which we are launched to be evaporated, or to disappear? Are we to believe that a half-mad eternal humorist tossed the worlds aloft and left their destiny to chance? That a man's life is the development of a nameless vagrancy? That a hole in the ground six feet deep is his final heritage? There are a thousand insane things easier to believe than these! How can we believe that human personality will not survive when One who went into the grave and beyond came back to say, 'Whosoever believeth in me shall not perish, but have eternal life.'"[38]

Real Christians never die. Here's what Jesus said:

> *"Whosoever liveth and believeth in me shall never die."* (John 11:26)

Jesus then asked this question: "Do you believe this?" We had better believe it because He was giving us the facts. He had prefaced this statement by saying,

> *"I am the resurrection, and the life: he that believeth in me, though he were dead, yet shall he live."* (John 11:25)

And for you, dear follower of the Lord, your death is a graduation, a promotion.

You are invited by God to sign up for eternity with Him. You were "so loved" by Him that He made a way, the acceptance of

---

38 Peter Marshall, "December 7, 1941 Sermon," Facebook, accessed February 1, 2020, https://www.facebook.com/notes/terry-michael-hestilow/dr-peter-marshalls-message-to-the-midshipmen-chapel-service-usna-december-7-1941/10152135784748869)

which puts you into the category of "never perishing…but having eternal life" (John 3:16). No one else but God could give you this. No one else but God has it to give. That is the provision He made. That is the offer He extends to you. The terms are simple:

Believe sufficiently to forsake all wrong, all others, and believe sufficiently to follow Him forever.

"To follow Him" means to travel in the same direction. Live like He lives. Adopt without compromise His philosophy of love, the eternal way of life to be pursued without regret or remorse—always, always choosing the highest good in every situation and for everyone in the universe without personal benefit or personal profit as a motive. (Not that you won't be rewarded, but it's God's place to do that, not others.)

This philosophy of love is not a mere ideology. It is an energy, a life force, focused in the direction of benevolence toward all. When God, with your consent, in your longing for Him, enters your life, He brings His life to you *and through you* to others. When He fills you with His Spirit, He fills you with His love as well:

When He fills you with His Spirit, He fills you with His love as well.

> *"The love of God is shed abroad in our hearts by the Holy Ghost which is given unto us."*
>
> (Romans 5:5)

This love is not only the essence of God, but the irrevocable evidence that we are His and that we have indeed been recipients of His grace and entered into the "Christ life."

> *"By this shall all men know that ye are my disciples, if ye have love one to another."*
>
> (John 13:35)

> *"Beloved, let us love one another: for love is of God; and every one that loveth is born of God, and knoweth God.*

> *He that loveth not knoweth not God; for God is love."* (1 John 4:7-8)

Love is the nature of God as well as the philosophy of God. Only love is capable of sustaining life. Selfishness, the opposite of love, is unsustainable. Selfishness is the primary destructive motive behind all evil. It is iniquity, that very thing that separates human beings from our Father in heaven.

God intends for you and me to live as He lives—*loving*ly. What will it be like? For starters, He intends to bless you unimaginably.

> *"That in the ages to come he might shew the exceeding riches of his grace in his kindness toward us through Christ Jesus."* (Ephesians 2:7)

You will be blessed, but will you have non-boring, meaningful employment? Most assuredly!

Take a look at the promises of God. Here is just one of many:

> *"Well done, thou good and faithful servant: thou hast been faithful over a few things, I will make thee ruler over many things: enter thou into the joy of thy lord."* (Matthew 25:21)

Note the following:

- You will be commended for being good.
- You will be commended for being faithful.
- You will be promoted.
- Your role will be administrative.
- You will be given entry into the joy of God.

What is of vital importance is to note that your new assignments will be based on how well you handled the few things in front of you in this life. Note the verse right before it:

> *"He that had received five talents came and brought other five talents, saying, Lord, thou deliveredst unto me five talents: behold, I have gained beside them five talents more."*
>
> (Matthew 25:20)

What have you been given in this life? Your gifting! Jesus says that the kingdom of heaven works like this. A man called his servants and gave them some of his goods. One got five talents, another two talents, and another one talent. They were given these talents according to their abilities. Note that some were given more than others. How is that fair? The answer lies in understanding that it is not how much ability you have been given, but what you do with that ability.

> *"For unto whomsoever much is given, of him shall be much required: and to whom men have committed much, of him they will ask the more."*
>
> (Luke 12:48)

You and I are only responsible for what we have been given. That's another reason we are not to compare ourselves with others. We just have to be faithful with what we've been given. That's all. It certainly appears that the distribution of roles in God's kingdom and in eternity will be determined by our faithfulness here.

> Character becomes the basis of proper praise of others.

We all know that the will of God for each and every one of us is Christlikeness, right? This can only be quantified by listing, defining, and assimilating each of His character qualities into our lives so that they are entrenched so thoroughly in us that they automatically control our attitudes, thoughts, words, and behaviors. What a great family project! Character then becomes the basis of proper praise of others. It enables us to see the great attributes of our

Savior in one another, as well as enhances the effectiveness of each gift.

And there is no greater attribute of God than His love.

"Do Unto Others"

Look for opportunity. Discover needs. Set aside blocks of time. Be accountable to the administrators in your church. Be available. Take your assignments seriously. Report back. Practice your gift with all of your might.

> *"Whatsoever thy hand findeth to do, do it with thy might; for there is no work, nor device, nor knowledge, nor wisdom, in the grave, whither thou goest."* (Ecclesiastes 9:10)

The *Message* says it this way:

> *"Whatever turns up, grab it and do it. And heartily! This is your last and only chance at it, for there's neither work to do nor thoughts to think in the company of the dead, where you're most certainly headed."* (Ecclesiastes 9:10, MSG)

Most of all, remember to give God the glory.

> *"For it is God which worketh in you both to will and to do of his good pleasure."* (Philippians 2:13)

This is your time. This is your opportunity to use your God-given ability to influence eternity. The time is now. To quote Jesus one more time,

> *"I must work the works of him that sent me, while it is day: the night cometh, when no man can work."* (John 9:4)

You are here on planet Earth because you were sent for a purpose. You were not merely sent but equipped. Your time, just like my time, is limited. It is time to apply ourselves. The urgency of application is based on this realization. We ask God in the same manner as the wise men of old who prayed,

> *"So teach us to number our days, that we may apply our hearts unto wisdom."* (Psalm 90:12)

Perhaps the best way to summarize this chapter is by citing just two lines of a poem written by C.T. (Charles Thomas) Studd, a rugged follower of the Lord, who believed that it was worthwhile to lose all this world can offer and stake everything on the world to come. (Norman Grubb's biography of his life is a must-read.) Here is what C.T. wrote:

Only one life, 'twill soon be past,
Only what's done for Christ will last.[39]

Let's go back to the basics, to God: the Creator, the Sustainer of Life, the *Numero Uno* of the universe, the Designer of Life, affectionately and accurately referred to as our heavenly Father, the Originator of you. This wonderful Being has great plans for you and for your life. He is the One who has endowed you with supernatural gifts.

Our life philosophy must be based on Him, His character, and His nature. What is that? I repeat, if you could only use one word to describe Him, it would have to be the word L-O-V-E! *Love* is God summed up. Exercise your gifts in that love.

Free to Be You

You are about to experience freedom, if you will *see*, *remember*, and *live* according to the counsel, the "perfect law":

39 "Charles Studd," Wikipedia (Wikimedia Foundation, September 16, 2019), https://en.wikipedia.org/wiki/Charles_Studd)

"But if you look carefully into the perfect law that sets you free." (James 1:25 NLT)

The perfect law that produces liberty is love. Love is the perfect law and God's philosophy of life. Love is the authoritative standard and the rule of human conduct designed by God.

"God is love." (1 John 4:8)

And everything He does, He does out of the essential nature of His great being, which is love. Not only do others need you, but you need the *real* you. We all search for fulfillment in life, but so few seem to look in the right places. The wrong places range from materialism to popularity, from position and rank to illicit relationships, from alcohol to drugs, from stress-free jobs to high-rise office buildings. Where can joy, true happiness, and fulfillment be found?

They are found in meaning. Life must have meaning to even make sense—and meaning is found in discovering *why you were born.*

Strange! You don't have to cross the widest ocean or scale the highest mountain. You don't have to consult a psychiatrist or visit a priest. You have only to look inside you. It is in you—that gift, an inclination, an energy, a motivation, a deposit placed there by omnipotence and omniscience, by divinity Himself, and it will show you the way to *you*. Let me help you look inside of you. It is there. It is resident. It hasn't left. It is waiting. It's a gift waiting to be unwrapped. It's a treasure waiting to be unearthed. It is a joy unspeakable!

"Thanks be unto God for his unspeakable gift!"
(2 Corinthians 9:15)

Do you remember Jesus' parable?

"The kingdom of heaven is like unto treasure hid in a field; the which when a man hath found, he

> *hideth, and for joy thereof goeth and selleth all that he hath, and buyeth that field."*
>
> (Matthew 13:44)

What is it worth to you to discover this treasure? What are you willing to invest to take hold of this piece of God's kingdom that until now has been hidden in the field of your life? Will you search it out? Will you investigate? Will you consult with others to see how they see you? Will you pray to God to reveal it to you?

When you find this treasure, I assure you, joy will be yours forever. Joy is the exaltation of your inward spirit that comes from harmony with God and His gifting to you. All that remains after you discover why you were born is to develop what you've been given and use it for the rest of your life on this earth.

Joy is the exaltation of your inward spirit that comes from harmony with God and His gifting to you.

If you look constantly into the mirror of God's Word, you will see love looking back at you. You will see what love sees in you. You will see yourself through the eyes of love, the eyes of God. There is no other accurate way to see you! If you have not looked into this mirror, you haven't seen the real, wonderful you.

Dearest reader, I implore you to know and believe what this mirror shows you.

> *"We have known and believed the love that God hath to us. God is love; and he that dwelleth in love dwelleth in God, and God in him."*
>
> (1 John 4:16)

Embrace what you see in His Word! Hold it closely. Hug it. Cuddle up to it. Clutch it. Clasp it. Grasp it! Enthusiastically wrap your arms around it and never let it go. Here's a brief summary of what we've seen looking into the mirror of God's Word, and we've been seeing it together since you first started reading this book:

1. You were planned. You were not an accident. *Love designed you.*
2. You were known 270 days before you were born by God—*personally.*
3. You were *designed and crafted by an Artist* who makes no mistakes.
4. You were *placed* in a baby's body.
5. You were *discovered* by your parents.
6. Nine months later*, they saw you for the first time.*
7. You were *never* really alone.
8. You were born for *a reason, a purpose.*
9. You were *designed to love.*
10. You were endowed with a gifting, an Embedded Natural Ability, that is *specific to you.*
11. You have been *given opportunity* to *lovingly use* your ENA.
12. No tragedy or interruption *can thwart your purpose* in life.
13. You have been given the opportunity *to marry and have children.*
14. You have been given the opportunity *to point those children in right directions.*
15. You have been given the opportunity *to be employed or in business.*
16. You will never really die*, but transition to be with God.*
17. You will be with your Creator *in person forever,* living in a place prepared for *you.*
18. You will live forever *engaged in the greatest enterprises in the universe.*
19. There will be no *end* of you.
20. You will forever *love and be loved.*

No one, including me, is capable of calculating your value. You and I are now complete with giftings that, when properly used, will impact eternity. Imagine that! As God reaches through us to others, those others may well be part of a changed forever. This is remarkable. It is serious, even epoch-making. You are influencing eternity. It's simply incalculable.

Since starting this book, we've come a long way together, you and I. What comes to my mind as we draw to the close of this chapter is a poem I learned in my teen years. Written as a song in 1936, it's called "Mizpah," and is based on this Scripture:

> *"Therefore was the name of it called...Mizpah;*
> *for he said, 'The Lord watch between me and thee,*
> *when we are absent one from another.'"*
>
> (Genesis 31:48-49)

Mizpah is the Hebrew word for a watchtower, and often refers to an agreement between people with the understanding that God is watching over them as a witness, as in the case of Laban and Jacob referred to in the verse above.[40]

"Mizpah" by Julia A. Baker

Go thou thy way and I go mine,
Apart, yet not afar,
Only a thin veil hangs between
The pathways where we are;
And "God keep watch
'tween me and thee,"
This is my prayer;
He looks my way, He looketh mine,
And keeps us near.

I know not where thy road will lie,
Or which way mine will be,
If mine will lead through parching sands,
And thine beside the sea;
But God will watch 'tween me and thee,

40 GotQuestions.org, "What Is the Importance of Mizpah in the Bible?" GotQuestions.org, December 19, 2018, https://www.gotquestions.org/Mizpah-in-the-Bible.html)

So never fear,
He holds thy hand, He holdeth mine,
And keeps us near.

Should wealth and fame perchance be thine,
And my lot lonely be,
Or you be sad and sorrowful
And glory be for me,
Yet God will watch ’tween me and thee;
We are His care.
One arm ’round thee and one ’round me
Will keep us near.

I sigh ofttimes to see thy face,
But if this may not be,
I’ll leave thee to the care of Him
Who cares for thee and me;
He keeps us both beneath His wings,
This comfort’s dear;
One wing o’er thee, and one o’er me,
So we are near.

So while our paths are separate,
And thy way is not mine,
Yet coming to the Mercy Seat
My soul will meet with thine,
And “God keep watch ’tween me and thee,”
I’ll whisper there;
He blesseth thee, He blesseth me,
And we are near.[41]

Godspeed on your journey! I can’t wait to hear what you accomplish as you lovingly put your gifting into action! Keep me posted. And don’t forget: Love is the measure by which life is assessed!

---

41 Julia Aldrich Baker, “Mizpah,” Poem: Mizpah by Julia Aldrich Baker, accessed February 4, 2020, https://www.poetrynook.com/poem/mizpah)

Part Two

How to Discover Your ENA

Chapter Fifteen

Seven Steps to Discovering Your Giftedness

(Your ENA, Your Endowment)

1. Know and understand each of the seven ENAs.
2. Compare the focus and perspective of each gifting.
3. Identify yourself by understanding the characteristics of each gifting.
4. Observe the weaknesses inherent in each gifting. (You just might reverse identify.)
5. Compare yourself with the biographies of biblical characters.
6. Get the opinions from gift-informed friends, family, or ministers.
7. Try each of them out and see what "fits" you.

Then get involved and enjoy personal fulfillment the rest of your life. Celebrate as you see God Himself working through you to bless others. Attach yourself to a local group of Christians (a church) in order to allow the administrative gifts God gave the body the opportunity to help you develop and perfect your personal gifting (Ephesians 4:11-12). If they happen not to understand what you have learned here, get them a copy and let the discussion and the development of a biblical church agenda begin. You and they will find the Big Picture details in Appendix Two.

By reading the remaining chapters, you will understand why others differ from you, the benefits of your spouse's point of view, why your gifted children are as they are, and how to avoid unnecessary conflicts that are merely differences of opinion based on the differences of our ENA's focus and characteristics. Each of the subsequent chapters describe an ENA and contain the following components for that gifting:

Introductory Story: These illustrate the ENA and help us gain a frame of reference for understanding what this gifting looks like.

Its Focus: This sentence pinpoints the primary target of this ENA.

Its Vocational Application: Each gifting from God, each Embedded Natural Ability, enables us to perform our vocation naturally, without pressure, almost intuitively. This section covers the marketplace, and lists the many jobs in which this ENA is most often found.

God has invested a particular gifting in you, not only for your own benefit, but for that of others.

Its Altruistic Application: This section covers the way this ENA is a specialist equipped to serve mankind in distinct and determined ways. God has gifted you for the benefit of others as well as yourself. God is interested in everybody. He loves everybody.

Altruism is the belief that the well-being of others is equally, if not *more* important, than the well-being or even the survival of self. It refers to behavior that is selfless, self-sacrificing, noble, considerate, charitable and loving. God has invested a particular gifting in you, not only for your own benefit, but for that of others. Your gifting has spiritual intentions. The narcissist can't relate here. The narcissist merely (and only) sees his or her gifting as a means of selfish gain.

Its Top Characteristics: This part lists the primary qualities of this ENA to help the reader identify it. These often include a description of what motivates this person to do what he or she does, and how those motivations serve the body of Christ.

A Biblical Example: Multiple examples of every gift can be found in the Bible, so they are outlined here. Studying these stories rounds out our understanding of this ENA and how it was used by God historically and operates in the body of Christ today.

Its Inherent Weaknesses: Every personality has its qualities and weaknesses. In like manner, each ENA has its own peculiar strengths and weaknesses. Considering our incredible ability to deceive ourselves, *forewarned is forearmed*, so it makes sense for us to explore the possible failings of our ENA. Then we will not be taken unawares by our own propensities. In fact, it is sometimes through seeing them that we can identify most strongly with our ENA. No one knows our failings better than we do.

Take the first five steps outlined at the top of the page by studying the next seven chapters. God be with you!

Chapter Sixteen

Are You A Messenger?

The American condition in 1963 was not unlike Charles Dickens's first lines of *A Tale of Two Cities*: "It was the best of times, it was the worst of times, it was the age of wisdom, it was the age of foolishness, it was the epoch of belief, it was the epoch of incredulity, it was the season of Light, it was the season of Darkness, it was the spring of hope, it was the winter of despair, we had everything before us, we had nothing before us, we were all going direct to Heaven, we were all going direct the other way."[42] Dickens described an age of opposite situations in two countries: England and France on the eve of the French Revolution. In 1960s America, Jim Crow laws held the South in the grip of institutionalized discrimination and segregation, while the North considered those laws a moral and national disgrace.

Change was desperately needed, but that change would never come without a Messenger. Dr. Martin Luther King, Jr. was that Messenger. On August 23, 1963, 250,000 people assembled to hear his remarkable message, "I Have a Dream" from the steps of the Lincoln Memorial. Passion infused his every word, as he quoted the Declaration of Independence and Abraham Lincoln's Gettysburg Address and Emancipation Proclamation. Dr. King's message still lives today. It changed America for God and for good. Consequently, in 1964 President Lyndon B. Johnson signed the Civil Rights Act, which legally ended discrimination and

---

42 Charles Dickens, *A Tale of Two Cities*, public domain.

segregation in the nation. No Messenger would have meant no message, which would have meant no change.

The importance of a Messenger and his or her message must not be underestimated. We're not talking about spam; these are not fake messages. A message may be life-and-death critical. In fact, the Message may well be eternal-life and eternal-death critical. Although some important messages may not be esteemed as they ought, the truth is that without Messengers, nations and people perish.

We've come a long way since the days of the Pony Express. Messages—good and evil—now travel at virtually the speed of light.

Focus

Messengers represent God through communicating the gospel, rightly handling His truth.

Vocational Application

Messengers make great salespeople or marketers. They have a product. They've studied it well and have prepared a sales pitch. Now their task is to get exposure to as many prospects as possible and make their case for a purchase. They demonstrate the need and demand for the product.

Obviously, a large part of their gift is their ability to speak. They may use diagrams to illustrate their points or testimonials from others who verify the benefits of the product(s) they sell. The Messenger, Marketer, and Salesperson need to have *closing skills* so that the transaction takes place

Their gifting from God, their Embedded Natural Ability, enables them to perform their vocation naturally, without pressure, almost intuitively. They've got talent (on loan from God).

The Messenger/Marketer may also communicate using technology in assorted ways: anything from audio to video to social media, e-mail, voice mail messaging, networking conversations, blogs, brochures, websites, TV, radio, advertising, and more. He or she may not have the technical skills but they have the message, the pitch, the selling technique, the presentation, and the strategy.

Lacking personal skills in technology, the Messenger/Marketer will employ the skills of the Helper to get the job done, but he or she is a master of the message, a natural persuader. Their faith in their product spurs them on. If they lose motivation, they need to hear from the Encourager, an Exhorter who will "fire them up" and get them going again. Can you see how each of us as gifted individuals needs other gifted persons?

Altruistic Application

The altruistic application of the Messenger makes you a *Messenger of God.* Imagine the import of that! So here we go. The Messenger is representing God and speaking for Him, so he or she must be wholeheartedly connected and submitted to God, or they will not be able to carry out this task successfully. When they are, they lay down their lives for their hearers, as they walk in this ENA which not only compels them to speak, but also grants them an innate sensitivity to the plight of those around them. Seeing the true spiritual condition of another, mingled with the compassion of God Himself, makes them both powerful and formidable.

The Messenger

A Messenger is a communicator, a proclaimer, an articulator of a specific message, a declarer, a transmitter. He or she is a person who is gifted in speaking and/or writing with the intent to persuade others to act and live according to truth. In the Old Testament, these were referred to as "prophets," messengers of God with a sensitivity to right and wrong, true and false, authentic and fake. To the Proclaimer, alias the Messenger, there are no grays.

The Messenger/Proclaimer/Prophet is often an uncomfortable person to be around because they brook no compromise, make no concessions, and accept nothing substandard when it comes to vital truths. They are consistently "straight up," resolute, and determined to present the facts of the case. They determine the facts of the case by having an extraordinary sensitivity to the spiritual condition or the needs of their listener or audience.

The Messenger is not just an academic dealing in cold facts. There is a sense of deep grief over the hurting conditions of others, even as God does. Did you know that about God? Did you know He experiences unfathomable grief over the condition of wayward man? In Genesis 6:5-6 when God saw the greatness of man's wickedness it says, "It grieved him at His heart." Imagine God experiencing grief in His heart. He has great feelings towards us.

The Messenger/Cmmunicator/Proclaimer/Prophet Ezekiel gives us a profound, incomprehensible insight into the heart of God. After describing the judgment that must fall on the wickedness of man, Ezekiel pulls back a curtain to briefly show us what few ever know about God. Here is what God said:

> *"I am broken with their whorish heart, which hath departed from me, and with their eyes, which go a whoring after their idols."* (Ezekiel 6:9)

God broken? God brokenhearted? Who would have guessed?

Other Bible Messengers knew the grief of God and felt it themselves. Imagine Micah's disclosure of God's humility. Here's what God said:

> *"O my people, what have I done unto thee? And wherein have I wearied thee? Testify against me."*
> (Micah 6:3)

Does anybody want to stand up and tell God where He has gone wrong? Somewhere our theologians seem to have lost track of the real character and nature of God. Dear Reader, God is not some austere, removed, off-in-space, cold, calculated, know-it-all being. Instead He is exactly like Christ: Christ, the visible image of the invisible God; Christ, in whom dwells all the fullness of God; Christ, of whom it is accurately reported that He is "touched with the feeling of our infirmities" (Hebrews 4:15).

Messengers, in a very real sense, represent God accurately. Their understanding of the wickedness of man and the great love of God for sinful man makes them impassioned in their quest to communicate, be heard, and receive a response.

My father represented God to me very well when I was a rebellious teenager. I remember the night he loaned me his car, which was unusual. It wasn't that he was stingy; it was that I wasn't too smart. My father told me I was to meet him back at the church on a Wednesday night to pick him and mom up after a prayer meeting. It was the dead of winter. I thought, *Well, maybe if I get back on time—or better yet early!—I'll get the car again.* So I was parked a couple of parking spots away from the side door of the church. I remember thinking how warm the pool of light from the bare bulb looked that encircled the door, even though I knew it was below freezing outside.

> Messengers, in a very real sense, represent God accurately.

Rather than go in, I sat and waited. When I got cold, I'd run the car a little bit to heat it up, but I didn't want to go in. I fought everything my parents stood for because I didn't understand them, and at the time, was rebellious against God. Instead of joining them, I listened to the radio to pass the time.

Eventually, the door opened, and my dad walked out in his shirt sleeves. He looked up and down the street, saw me in the car, and walked towards me. Rather than getting out, I just put the window down. As he came near, I saw my dad had tears in his eyes and perspiration on his brow. When he got to the car, he asked, "Son, why don't you come into the church and pray with me?"

Next came one of the moments I've regretted the most in my life.

I looked into his eyes and cracked. "Take your religion and go to hell."

My dad just looked at me, tears making his eyes shine in the dim light. He calmly turned and walked back into the church. Twenty minutes or so later, he and mom came out and we rode home in silence.

The next day, probably after some other thoughtless comment I'd made, he stopped me and said, "Son, you can walk all over the top of me—I'll get down on the floor if you want me to and you can stomp on me—but son, you will never stop me from loving you."

Those words broke my heart. As I have thought back over the years to that time, I realize that no one has ever represented God to me as clearly as my father did over a lifetime of loving me, often despite myself.

That's exactly what God is like: You can ignore Him, ridicule Him, mock Him, despise Him, and reject Him, and do you know what He does? *He just keeps on loving you.*

Imagine God's humility. He doesn't walk away or pout. He just keeps on gently knocking, asking permission to come into your life.

> *"Behold, I stand at the door, and knock: if any man hear my voice, and open the door, I will come in to him, and will sup with him and he with me."* (Revelation 3:20)

This is how Messengers represent God and His message. The preaching of repentance without love is condemnation, but those with the gift of proclamation can't help but tell others of the God who:

> *"Sent not his Son into the world to condemn the world; but that the world through him might be saved."* (John 3:17)

A Focus on the Message, the Truth

> *"This then is the message which we have heard of him, and declare unto you, that God is light, and in him is no darkness at all."* (1 John 1:5)

The Greek word used in Romans 12:6 is *propheteia*, which signifies "the speaking forth of the mind and counsel of God."[43]

43 W. E. Vine, Merrill F. Unger, and William White Jr., *Vine's Complete Expository Dictionary of Old and New Testament Words* (Nashville: Nelson, 1996), 492.

Another word you could use is proclaim or "to deliver a message." Thus, the person could be called a prophet, an evangelist, a proclaimer, or a messenger. (There are also the offices of prophet and evangelist which are administrative positions in a local church and are different than this, so let's just use the words Messenger or Proclaimer to avoid confusion. You can get up to speed on the Big Picture later in the Appendix entitled, "The Theological Context of Spiritual Gifts.")

When we hear the word *prophecy,* most acquaint it with the foretelling of future events, and that is a big part of what prophets did in the Bible. But the actual meaning of the word *to prophesy* means "to speak forth, to forthtell,"[44] so it is much more than just speaking of the future. Messengers are people who carry a message, and that message is primarily the one the people they speak with need to hear most. Messengers are those who have a natural inclination to speak out and bring an important message to others.

> The Messenger is obsessed with communicating the gospel.

What is that message? (I'm glad you asked!) While it will take different forms in different circumstances, spiritually it is whatever is needed to bring the person they are speaking to closer to God. So, in essence, the Messenger is obsessed with communicating the gospel—*the good news*—that Jesus came, died, and rose again, so that each of us could be reconciled with God and know Him personally.

Human beings cannot save themselves. We cannot pull ourselves up by our own bootstraps. We need a Savior. Something has to happen inside—and that something is really a Someone! That "Someone" has to be bigger, better, stronger, and wiser than all others, capable of accomplishing two things: a) the getting rid of our old condition and b) producing a new, better condition. We find that in one Person alone.

---

44 "KJV Dictionary Definition: Prophesied," AV1611.com, accessed February 4, 2020, https://av1611.com/kjbp/kjv-dictionary/prophesied.html)

> *"**Therefore if any man be in Christ,** he is a new creature: old things are passed away; behold, all things are become new. "*
>
> (2 Corinthians 5:17, emphasis mine)

The Messenger presents the Jesus of the cross and the cross of Jesus, the offer of God's grace extended because of Christ's loving accomplishment. Just as a salesman must set forth the terms of a purchase contract, so must also the terms of the gospel be made clear. There are four conditions, which we will cover more about later, for genuine conversion to Christ:

1. Repentance
2. Faith
3. Baptism
4. Continuance

Be assured that the message of the Messenger is *love,* and God intends that it be delivered in a loving, grace-filled manner, just as Jesus Himself showed us.

Jesus, God's Messenger

Jesus perfectly illustrated the Embedded Natural Ability of being a Messenger to the woman at the well in John 4. Look briefly at the story:

> *"Jesus therefore, being wearied with his journey, sat thus on the well: and it was about the sixth hour.*
>
> *There cometh a woman of Samaria to draw water: Jesus saith unto her, Give me to drink.*
>
> *(For his disciples were gone away unto the city to buy meat.)*
>
> *Then saith the woman of Samaria unto him, How is it that thou, being a Jew, askest drink of me, which am a woman of Samaria? For the Jews have no dealings with the Samaritans.*

> *Jesus answered and said unto her, If thou knewest the gift of God, and who it is that saith to thee, Give me to drink; thou wouldest have asked of him, and he would have given thee living water.*
>
> *The woman saith unto him, Sir, thou hast nothing to draw with, and the well is deep: from whence then hast thou that living water?*
>
> *Art thou greater than our father Jacob, which gave us the well, and drank thereof himself, and his children, and his cattle?*
>
> *Jesus answered and said unto her, Whosoever drinketh of this water shall thirst again:*
>
> *But whosoever drinketh of the water that I shall give him shall never thirst; but the water that I shall give him shall be in him a well of water springing up into everlasting life."* (John 4:6-14)

Do you see how precious this seemingly random woman was to Jesus? He was hot, thirsty, tired, and perhaps thinking of jumping into the well to cool off (okay, probably not that), but He was less concerned about actually getting a drink than He was about talking to this woman about God and seeing if He could bring her closer to the Father. That is the heart of a true Messenger!

The Characteristics of a Messenger

Messengers are all about communicating the messages of God and truth, so that others will hear it and respond. Here are the top five attributes of being a Messenger:

Messengers Are Communicating the Message of God

Near the beginning of His ministry, Jesus went into a synagogue and read from Isaiah 61:

> *"The Spirit of the Lord is upon me, for he has anointed me to bring Good News to the poor. He has sent me to proclaim that captives will be released, that the blind will see, that the oppressed will be set free, and that the time of the Lord's favor has come."* (Luke 4:18-19 NLT)

When He was finished, He gave the scroll back to the minister and said,

> *"The Scripture you've just heard has been fulfilled this very day!"* (Luke 4:21 NLT)

Jesus had no doubt about His mission in life from that day forward. He was going to proclaim the good news of the kingdom.

Messengers Are Uncompromising about the Message

Messengers can seem intolerant because they're not willing to compromise the truth. They have a black-and-white point of view. Because of this, they can seem blunt. Though we know He was all about love, even Jesus Himself sounded harsh at times:

> *"He that believeth and is baptized shall be saved; but he that believeth not shall be damned."*
> (Mark 16:16)

To the Messenger, each person is either in or out, saved or damned. The stakes are so high, have such an eternal dimension to them, that Messengers are compelled by an embedded urgency that humanity is in big trouble, but that there is a solution.

The Messenger wants to be clear, crystal clear. God is light and in Him is no darkness at all—zero, zilch, zip, nil, nix, nada (1 John 1:5). Peter clearly articulates that a Christian, every Christian, is "called out of darkness into His marvelous light" (1 Peter 2:9). In Colossians, it is declared that He has "delivered us from the power of darkness" (Colossians 1:13).

Messengers Will Pay Any Price to Make Sure People Hear the Message

Nothing, absolutely nothing, could be more important. Eternity is at stake. But not only eternity, but true success in this life as well. Because of this accurate understanding of the risk and the immense potential loss to every human being, the Messenger is galvanized into action. They know no embarrassment and overcome every barrier to communication. This verse is their mantra:

> *"For I am not ashamed of the gospel of Christ: for it is the power of God unto salvation to every one that believeth."* (Romans 1:16)

Messengers know the high risks, the danger; and thus, the supreme importance that each person hears the message in a clear, uncompromising way, so that they can then call upon the Lord for His "so great a salvation" (Hebrews 2:3).

Messengers Communicate a Message of Grace

Notwithstanding a holy hatred for evil (because the Messenger knows both the temporal and eternal destructive power of evil), the Messenger's message is always one of grace. Grace is the unearned activity of God in us, delivering us from all known sin and iniquity, and progressively making us like the Lord Jesus Christ. Grace is not God pretending we are not sinful when we still are. Grace is not a cover-up. Grace doesn't cover; it cleanses. This grace, the power of change, is not passive or docile. Grace is actually God doing supernatural transformational work in us, as we properly respond to His message of love.

Grace was provided for us by the death, burial, and resurrection of Jesus. Oh, what a Savior! Unlike all the dead religious leaders, Jesus is alive, and He comes walking out of the pages of the Bible right into our lives today. His touch still has its ancient power. As the Word states:

> *"Jesus Christ the same yesterday, to day and for ever."* (Hebrews 13:8)

His grace is available to everyone.

> *"For the grace of God that bringeth salvation hath appeared to all men."* (Titus 2:11)

> *"The Lord...is not willing that any should perish, but that all should come to repentance."* (2 Peter 3:9)

God is sincere in His offer to all mankind.

Messengers Are Motivated by Love

The ultimate message of God is *love*. If we had to define God in just one word, that word would have to be *love* as the Scriptures tell us: "God is love" (1 John 4:8). This verse also tells us, "He that loveth not knoweth not God." This is why the Messenger's message is love because they know God.

> Grace is actually God doing supernatural transformational work in us, as we properly respond to His message of love.

Love must be the motive and the manner of the Messenger. True, the sinful person must be confronted, but certainly not in an angry, bitter, and officious manner. Jesus didn't do that, and He is our example in all things. Why would we ever think we could do it better than He did?

Biblical Examples of Messengers

Jesus isn't the only example of a proclaimer in the Bible. Virtually every prophet in the Old Testament was gifted to communicate both the good news and the bad news (that people were distancing themselves from God) to entire nations. In the New Testament, I'd choose Peter as a stand-out example of a Messenger. He proclaimed God's message both publicly to large audiences and privately to individuals like we saw Jesus do with the woman at the well. Peter was the one that "stood up" on the day of Pentecost, a Jewish celebration, to preach the gospel of God for the first time (Acts 2:14). Jerusalem was jammed with tourists and devout Jews from all parts of the world. Meanwhile, the Holy Spirit had fallen like fire on the 120 God-seekers who then took to the streets, speaking multiple languages in the midst of the multicultural, multilingual crowds. There was a lot of confusion. Some even accused the God-seekers of being drunk.

But then Peter, that paragon of messengers, stepped up to the podium, proclaiming exactly what they should do. He said,

> *"Repent, and be baptized every one of you in the name of Jesus Christ for the remission of sins, and ye shall receive the gift of the Holy Ghost."*
> (Acts 2:38)

The Message paraphrases his words:

> *"Change your life. Turn to God and be baptized, each of you, in the name of Jesus Christ, so your sins are forgiven. Receive the gift of the Holy Spirit."* (Acts 2:38 MSG)

The results? Three thousand took him at his word, were baptized, and signed up to follow Jesus. (You can read the entire narrative for yourself in Acts 2.)

Peter well illustrates the Messenger (or Proclaiming) gift on the individual level as well. When a new convert named Simon wanted to buy the gifts of the Spirit he saw demonstrated by Philip, Peter, like all Messengers, demonstrated his commitment to the truth and his loyalty to the things of God without deference to the opinions of others. Peter wasted no time proclaiming to him,

> *"Thy money perish with thee, because thou has thought that the gift of God may be purchased with money."* (Acts 8:20)

To really grasp the unvarnished reality disguised by the kind dignity of King James English, here are Peter's words in *The Message*:

> *"To hell with your money! And you along with it. Why, that's unthinkable—trying to buy God's gift! You'll never be part of what God is doing by striking bargains and offering bribes. Change your ways—and now! Ask the Master to forgive you for trying to use God to make money. I can see this is an old habit with you; you reek with money-lust."* (Acts 8:20 MSG)

Simon's response? Repentance.

> *"Pray ye to the Lord for me, that none of these things which ye have spoken come upon me."* (Acts 8:24)

The Top Weaknesses and Dangers for Messengers

The gift of being a Messenger is not without its weaknesses. One must be careful to overcome weaknesses by staying linked closely with other gifted persons. Mouths don't work as well as they ought if the ears are not also employed. As the Scriptures tell us:

> *"A wicked messenger falleth into mischief: but a faithful ambassador is health."* (Proverbs 13:17)

The word *wicked* here comes from the same root[45] as the word

45 James Strong, "7563. Rasha," Strong's Hebrew: 7563. רָשָׁע (rasha) -- wicked, criminal (Biblehub), accessed February 7, 2020, https://biblehub.com/hebrew/7563.htm)

iniquity, which means "not being equal to."[46] In this case, it is a Messenger who *is not equal* to what a true and faithful Messenger should be. It is possible to be endowed by God but pay no attention to God's investment in you, apply no diligence to discovering the right way to operate in His Embedded Natural Ability, and then use this inborn energy and predisposition in selfish, unholy ways—thus getting into all kinds of mischief. But a *faithful* Messenger or Ambassador is *healthy*. The word *ambassador* is another word for *messenger* and is also used in the New Testament:

> *"Now then we are ambassadors for Christ, as though God did beseech you by us: we pray you in Christ's stead, be ye reconciled to God."*
> (2 Corinthians 5:20)

Note the specific elements in this passage which reaffirm the Proclaimer's mission:

The ambassador represents Christ.

- God is reaching out to others through the ambassador.
- The ambassador's message is, "Be reconciled to God!"

What other intrinsic dangers and/or weaknesses do Messengers face?

Messengers Can Grow Prideful, Thinking the Crowds Gather for Them

Pride is a root issue with which all must deal. When we speak of pride, we are not referring to a proper sense of satisfaction from one's achievement, but the self-exaltation of ego that results in boasting, exaggerating, overstating, and long-windedness. (As we will see, pride is the first and foremost risk for each and all the giftings.)

It's amazing to me that Jesus spent most of His time speaking

46 Bill Parker, *What Is Salvation? A Biblical Study of God's Greatest Gift*, Morrisville, NC: Lulu Publishing, 2014, 48.

to one person at a time while many Messengers today only want to speak from pulpits and stages. Yes, Jesus did speak to crowds of five to ten thousand at a time sometimes, but there was also the woman at the well, blind Bartimaeus, the widow with the issue of blood, and many others He ministered to one-on-one.

Messengers Can Be Harsh When They Should Be Compassionate

Harshness is an attitude, a demeanor that is not only unbecoming, but also unfit for a Messenger. Like God, it is the place of Messengers to say some weighty things, but when God says such things, He has tears in His eyes. Correction and compassion cannot be separated if the words are to be effective.

Fathers often tell their children during a spanking that "this hurts me more than it hurts you. I'm doing this because I love you." One little guy looked up at his father and said, "Dad, I can hardly wait till I grow up, so I can show you how much I love you." While we all get a snicker out of anecdotes like this, it is true that refusing to chasten a child is a refusal to love him. As Proverbs 13 tells us,

> *"He that spareth his rod hateth his son: But he that loveth him chasteneth him betimes."*
>
> (Proverbs 13:24)

But correction must only be done in compassion and not anger. The correction of a child done in anger will not correct. It's as the Bible affirms,

> *"The rod of his anger shall fail."* (Proverbs 22:8)

When there is only harsh correction and no love, rebellion is only driven deeper in and not given room to repent.

Messengers Can Fail to Balance Mercy and Truth

Mercy and truth are eternal companions. One might even think of them as a married couple that are better together than apart. We see this clearly indicated in Psalm 85:10:

> *"Mercy and truth are met together; righteousness and peace have kissed each other."* (Psalm 85:10)

This psalm speaks of the nearness of salvation to those that have the fear of the Lord.

Mercy is love stooping down in disregard of the strictness and severity of justice in order to meet truth, redemptive truth, the truth that the war is ended, that the sinners can cast their hope upon the grace of God, and give themselves up to being and doing right, so they may have peace. Thus:

> *"Righteousness and peace have kissed each other."* (Psalm 85:10)

Letting Self-examination Lead to Self-condemnation Rather than Repentance

Satan is called "the accuser of our brethren" (Revelation 12:10). The devil is a finger-pointing, condemning agitator and **he is a liar**. He seeks to "devour" people (1 Peter 5:8-9) and uses an array of tactics to do so. We are all well-advised *not* to believe him. He will load you up with false guilt, if he can. Never side with him against yourself. He is into the blame-and-shame game. Believing him will produce a root of bitterness and self-destruction. We should all memorize the following verse and recite it to ourselves often:

> *"There is therefore now no condemnation to them which are in Christ Jesus, who walk not after the flesh, but after the Spirit."* (Romans 8:1)

No condemnation! Get it? None! Counteract, thwart, and defeat Satan's attacks by using the "sword of the Spirit, which is the word of God" (Ephesians 6:17). Of course, if you are still walking after the flesh, then you need to quit that to discover the joy of condemnation-free living.

Messengers Must Be Careful Not to Water Down the Requirements of Accepting the Gospel

In the same light, messengers must be careful not to fail in articulating the full conditions of salvation: repentance, confession of faith, baptism, and continuance.

Repentance is a willingness to have a change of heart—to convert from self-rule to Christ-rule.

Repentance is not the giving up of one or more known sins. That would be like cutting off a limb of the tree when the whole tree needs to come down. Repentance is a willingness to have a change of heart—to convert from self-rule to Christ-rule. It is the giving up of the rebellious heart condition that has enthroned the ego and usurped the rightful place of God in one's heart.

Faith is the casting of oneself on the gracious work of Jesus, the Son of God, who died and gave Himself for us,

> *"That He might redeem us from all iniquity, and purify unto Himself a peculiar people, zealous of good works."* (Titus 2:14)

The grace of God draws all men to respond in repentance. Faith does a supernatural thing. God, by His Holy Spirit, enters into that person's life and transforms him or her, taking over His rightful place, and making the old pass away. Everything becomes new. We are now under new management and we confess that Jesus is our new Lord and new Master.

Continuance is also essential. Our relationship with the Lord is not a start and stop, start again, stop again thing. The Lord Himself made it clear.

> *"Then said Jesus to those Jews which believed on him, 'If ye continue in my word, then are ye my disciples indeed; and ye shall know the truth, and the truth shall make you free.'"*
>
> (John 8:31-32)

Some extra dangers should be noted, so here's a quick list. Messengers can:

- Be critical, negative, and judgmental
- Expose the issues without proposing solutions
- Be impulsive, jumping to conclusions rather than appraising a situation correctly
- Be blunt instead of tactful
- Oppose wrong*doers* instead of opposing the *wrongs*
- Show disrespect for the giftings of others

Wrapping It Up

Are you a Messenger? As you read the above descriptions, did you identify with them? When you reviewed the weakness and dangers listed, did they remind you of you? It may seem strange, but I have known people who discovered their personal gifting by recognizing and identifying with the weaknesses more than the positive characteristics of their gift. All of the above should be viewed as indicators.

But don't jump to a conclusion yet. We have six more Embedded Natural Abilities to understand before attempting to absolutely judge our own. Come, read on with me!

Chapter Seventeen

Are You a Helper?

It was the early 1930s—some of the worst days of the Great Depression. Money was scarce. A lot of people were out of work. There were also a lot of fathers who hadn't come back from the War to End All Wars—World War I. At least, that was the case for this little boy. Now there was just he and his mother trying to make ends meet and keep food on the table.

The boy's mother scrubbed floors for a pittance. It was never enough. Missing his father and loving his mother, the little guy wanted to help. Once a week he would get a few apples, shine them up, and put them in a little basket on top of a piece of white tissue paper which made the apples all the more attractive. He made a little sign for the basket that said, "Apples - 5 Cents." On Saturday mornings, he would go down to the train station in their remote Midwestern town to sell them.

On this particular Friday night, he had gotten ready as usual. The apples were polished. He carefully placed the tissue paper on the bottom of the basket and the apples almost sparkled. His sign was stuck neatly to the side of the basket. The excitement of making some money the next morning to help his mother made his heart pound and his mind wander to the train station all through the night. He couldn't sleep. It was some time before he was able to doze off. The next morning, the alarm clock sounded and he jumped out of bed. He washed his face, brushed his teeth, and scrubbed his fingernails. He didn't want to lose any time getting sent back to clean again because he failed to pass his mother's inspection. Then a quick last polish of the apples, breakfast, and he was off to the train station.

He arrived early. He was a lone figure on the platform waiting for the first train of the day: the great Chicago Flyer. Then he felt it. The first few tremors, then the slight quivering, then the shaking. Suddenly there it was. The train came steaming and screaming and screeching into the station. When it finally stopped, several conductors stepped out at various points along its length. They set steps in front of each door and then seemingly hundreds of people poured out and down the platform towards the little boy waiting to sell his apples. He proudly held up the basket as they approached.

Not paying attention, a big man bumped into the little boy knocking him down. His basket flew sending the apples in every direction. Others, in just as much of a rush, kicked or stepped on them, without noticing. Just as quickly as it had appeared, the crowd was gone. The train began pulling out. In a matter of mere seconds, he was all alone on the platform again, only this time with no apples and not a nickel in his pocket. All his chances to help his mother were gone.

> What we do, sometimes without even speaking a word, should help people see Jesus.

A tear forming at the corner of his eye, the little boy picked up his basket and turned to leave. He nearly ran into a tall stranger he hadn't noticed standing there. The man picked the little boy up, took a white silken handkerchief from his pocket, and wiped the tears from his face. What apples were left undamaged, he helped picked up, one by one. He jumped down to the tracks where some of the apples had fallen off the platform. They lay by the broken glass and cinders near the tracks. The man picked them up and with the same handkerchief, he polished each of the apples as best he could and placed them back in the basket. He walked over and picked up the "Apples - 5 Cents" sign, wiped the footprints off of it, and placed it back on the basket as well. Then he reached into his pocket and pulled out a handful of loose change: quarters, dimes, and nickels. He told the little boy to hold out his hand and placed the money in them.

Fresh tears in the boy's eyes, he looked up and asked, "Sir, are you Jesus?"

This is the best story I've ever heard to illustrate both the function and importance of the gift of being a Helper of others, a servant of God. I've asked myself: *How often have other persons been able to see Jesus in my actions?*

What we do, sometimes without even speaking a word, should help people see Jesus.

Focus

Meeting needs by doing deeds.

Vocational Application

Helpers have a multitude of occupational options. They perform work for the benefit of their clients and customers across a vast field of service industries, providing intangible products such as accounting, cleaning, landscaping, deliveries, transportation, food preparation, construction, hospitality, photography, design, personal assistance, auto detailing, laundry and grocery, painting, repair, companionship for the elderly, even dog walking. And there are many, many more. They don't need to sell or market products.

Skill development is essential, but once in their helper and serving groove, they can function tirelessly, joyfully meeting the needs of others.

Altruistic Application

Since God is love, He is focused on doing good. The Helper shows God's love through their awareness of the needs of those around them, and the effort they put forth in meeting those needs. Since they naturally *see* what should happen and how to help another, they are the ones who jump up to take care of others with joy, finding personal satisfaction in the act of helping without any fanfare. They literally love doing good works.

> *"The Lord is good to all: and His tender mercies are over all his works."* *(Psalm 145:9)*

For this reason, it should not be surprising to learn the following about ourselves:

> *"Created in Christ Jesus unto good works."*
> (Ephesians 2:10)

> *"He creates each of us by Christ Jesus to join him in the work he does, the good work he has gotten ready for us to do, work we had better be doing."*
> (Ephesians 2:10 MSG)

The Helper

The Messenger proclaims the love of God. The Helper *demonstrates* the love of God through the doing of good deeds. Helpers exemplify the love of God by responding to the needs of those around them, by caring for people as if they were part of their own families—by giving *handouts* to those in dire emergencies and *hand ups* to those who need to be pulled out of lifestyles that are dragging them—and often those closest to them—down.

The gift, the ENA, of being a Helper, is not only found in Romans 12. It is mentioned in 1 Corinthians:

> *"And God hath set some in the church, first apostles, secondarily prophets, thirdly teachers, after that miracles, then gifts of healings,* ***helps****, governments, diversities of tongues."*
> (1 Corinthians 12:28, emphasis mine)

The Helper is a hands-on person. They are get-things-done people. They are the types you can rely on not only to finish their tasks but to do them with excellence.

> *"As unto Christ;*
>
> *not with eyeservice, as menpleasers; but as the servants of Christ, doing the will of God from the heart;*
>
> *with good will doing service, as to the Lord, and not to men."* (Ephesians 6:5b-7)

Helpers are committed to joyfully meeting the practical needs of others without concern for receiving praise or appreciation. Their joy is to answer the call in their own hearts, which, of course, doesn't mean we should take such people for granted, but they are not doing it to receive a Nobel Prize or some kind of grandiose recognition. While we should all perform good deeds, those gifted with serving are specialists. Note that being a specialist in one area doesn't preclude us from our responsibilities in other areas. We all proclaim, we all encourage, we all teach, we all give, we all care for others, we all lead, we all serve but, *in particular*, each of us has one of these gifts that are *embedded* in us. This is what 1 Corinthians 12:27 means when it says, "members in particular."

> We don't do good works to become Christians but because we are Christians, we do good works.

Standing in the place of safety and stability as we are in Christ, we can throw lifelines to others. We don't do good works to become Christians but because we *are* Christians, we do good works. This is the proper representation—think "*re*-presentation"—of Jesus because Jesus was known for doing good. As the Scriptures tells us,

> *"**Jesus** of Nazareth... **went about doing good**, and healing all that were oppressed of the devil; for God was with him."* (Acts 10:38)

"Doing good": that's what occupied Jesus's time and efforts. It is interesting to note that He did that because "God was with

Him." God accompanies Helpers in all their endeavors. When Jesus ascended, He left this work to His followers on the earth— the church— or more specifically, *you and me.*

Jesus as a Servant

I had a team travelling with me for a number of years when I went different places to preach. On one occasion, while we were standing at the back of a church just talking, a janitor came in the door on the far side of the auditorium, struggling with a long ladder. I just watched. It never occurred to me to help him. (Shame on me.) But one of my team members—a Helper—hurried to the other side of the church without hesitation, helped the janitor get the ladder in, helped him set it up, and steadied it as he climbed to change a bulb in the ceiling. Helpers see needs and respond with deeds. It's instinctual, embedded in them by God.

In His Olivet Discourse (the Inaugural Address That Changed the World), Jesus said,

> *"Let your light so shine before men, that they may see your good works, and glorify your Father which is in heaven."* (Matthew 5:16)

Notice the nature of our shining light: doing good deeds! Good works are important because they reveal the kindhearted nature, the caring disposition, and the humility of our Father.

On one occasion the disciples were doing what our culture has perfected. They were comparing themselves to one another in an attempt to establish who was the top dog, the king of the castle, the dominant disciple, the superior one. Here's the text:

> *"And there was also a strife among them, which of them should be accounted the greatest."*
> (Luke 22:24)

Another translation says they were bickering about which of them would be the greatest. It's not very unlike today. Everyone wants to outdo the other, show off their superiority. This fundamental flaw is what has turned our culture, yeah, the cultures of the world into unresolvable conflict. The egalitarian conviction that all persons are created equal has been, at best, turned into an academic quotation from the second paragraph of the Declaration of Independence which says,

> "We hold these truths to be self-evident, that all men are created equal, that they are endowed by their Creator with certain unalienable Rights."[47]

But generally speaking, we do not treat others as equals. We suppose them to be inferior and we, superior. This is the very fountain of racial and gender strife. We've got it now: nation rising against nation, ethnos against ethnos, rich against the poor *ad infinitum*!

The disciples were quarreling among themselves about who was better and who was the greatest. Here's Jesus' answer. In Luke 22:23-27, Jesus says the Gentiles wanted to be bosses, exercising lordship over the people.

> *"But ye shall not be so: but he that is greatest among you, let him be as the younger; and he that is chief, as he that doth serve."* (Luke 22:26)

And then Jesus reveals a staggering truth about Himself:

> *"I am among you as he that serveth."* (Luke 22:27)

To most of us, this is an astonishing idea. God, a servant! Yet it is said of Him, that He:

> *"Made himself of no reputation, and took upon him the form of a servant."* (Philippians 2:7)

---

47 Thomas Jefferson et al., "The Declaration of Independence: Full Text," ushistory.org (Independence Hall Association), accessed January 15, 2020, https://www.ushistory.org/declaration/document/)

Watch how clear the Master made this truth:

> *"Having loved his own which were in the world, he loved them unto the end.*
>
> *And supper being ended...*
>
> *He (Jesus) riseth from supper, and laid aside his garments; and took a towel, and girded himself.*
>
> *After that he poureth water into a basin, and began to wash the disciples' feet, and to wipe them with the towel wherewith he was girded...*
>
> *So after he had washed their feet, and had taken his garments, and was set down again, he said unto them, Know ye what I have done to you?*
>
> *Ye call me Master and Lord: and ye say well; for so I am.*
>
> *If I then, your Lord and Master, have washed your feet; ye also ought to wash one another's feet.*
>
> *For I have given you an example, that ye should do as I have done to you.*
>
> *Verily, verily, I say unto you, the servant is not greater than his lord; neither he that is sent greater than he that sent him.*
>
> *If ye know these things, happy are ye if ye do them."* (John 13:1-2, 4-5, 12-17)

Imagine: God on the planet proclaiming Himself to be a servant—and washing stinky, filthy feet. Dear reader, do we want to be Christlike? Really? Jesus told us this:

> *"Neither be ye called masters: for one is your Master, even Christ.*
>
> *But he that is greatest among you shall be your servant.*

> *And whosoever shall exalt himself shall be abased; and he that shall humble himself shall be exalted."*
> (Matthew 23:10-12)

Greatness is not identified by how many serve us, but by how many we serve.

The Five Top Characteristics of a Helper

Helper are the personifications of Jesus, and just like Him, they have the following attributes.

1. They Help Without Strife or Showing Off

Servers don't show off. They're not pompous. They're humble. They're not haughty. Just as Jesus acted when He was with His disciple, it wasn't a big show. He just got the job done. As Scripture tells us:

> *"Let nothing be done through strife or vainglory, but in lowliness of mind let each esteem other better than themselves."* (Philippians 2:3)

2. They Esteem Others

Notice the rest of that above, "let each esteem other better than themselves." To *esteem* means "to think very highly or favorably of."[48] This does not mean others *are* better than you— they are not—but we are to lift them up and hold them in esteem *as if they were*.

Greatness is not identified by how many serve us, but by how many we serve.

To most of us, this seems novel if not absurd but remember,

48 "Esteem," Merriam-Webster (Merriam-Webster), accessed February 8, 2020, https://www.merriam-webster.com/dictionary/esteem)

the whole point of serving someone is to help them experience the love of God, for them to get a glimpse of how special they are in His eyes. Jesus came with a radical new approach to life. It was the antithesis of what every self-seeking person was doing: to be a giver, not a taker; to give up Himself for others; to hold every human in high regard and dignity. (Don't you love Him?) This is affirmed and confirmed in the next verse:

> *"Look not every man on his own things, but every man also on the things of others."* (Philippians 2:4)

To "look on the things of others" simply means to consider others and evaluate their needs in a situation *before* you do anything for yourself. That's not the typical *What's in it for me?* we are so used to hearing today, is it?

3. They Adopt the Mental Disposition of Christ

Philippians continues this thread, telling us:

> *"Let this mind be in you, which was also in Christ Jesus."* (Philippians 2:5)

Following Jesus, the Model, means having the same thinking, the same mental disposition, the same attitude, being of the same mind. Helpers take the pressure off others, have no problem playing "second fiddle," or rolling up their sleeves to produce visible results. Let us now venture on some uncharted waters of truth.

4. They're Not in It to Build Some Kind of Personal Reputation

> *"Who, being in the form of God, thought it not robbery to be equal with God:*
>
> *but made himself of no reputation, and took upon him the form of a servant, and was made in the likeness of men."* (Philippians 2:6-7)

Jesus was God come to planet Earth, right? He is God. He didn't steal the title of God. When He got to Earth He became one of us and took our form. Now that is a serious example of humbling oneself: to come from a high state to a low state *voluntarily*, from being the Creator to being one of the created.

We learn from Him that Helpers (or Servers) must be oblivious to building their own reputation—their own little empires. It will interfere with the pure and correct motive for serving others and building the kingdom of heaven.

5. Helpers Serve to Please God Alone

If the others we serve are not grateful, we tend to be resentful or even bitter and think, *If that's all the thanks I get, see if I ever do that again.* But not the Server who is doing what they do for the Lord. Note this:

> *"With good will* ***doing service, as to the Lord, and not to men****:*
>
> *knowing that whatsoever good thing any man doeth, the same shall he receive of the Lord."*
>
> (Ephesians 6:7-8)

The Server's expectations are only from the Lord, not other people. This is one of their great secrets of sustainability: They have the capacity to carry on, oblivious to the praise or blame or ingratitude of others.

Biblical Examples of Helpers

While the perfect example is Jesus, He's not the only example in the Bible. Here are a handful of others with the same ENA whose lives you can study for the traits mentioned above:

- As we saw in Chapter Seven, Joseph was a servant in the house of Potiphar (Genesis 39:1-6), and then in prison

(Genesis 39:21-23). He was then raised to be a public servant as Prime Minister of Egypt (Genesis 41:37-42).
- Aaron and Hur served Moses, holding up his hands, so that Joshua would succeed in leading Israel against the Amalekites (Exodus 17:8-13).
- Joshua was "minister" (personal assistant) to Moses (Exodus 24:13).
- Elisha served Elijah (1 Kings 19:19-21).
- David served King Saul (1 Samuel 16:15-23), and even though Saul tried to kill him, David refused to ever raise his hand against his former master and king (1 Samuel 18:6-16).
- Esther saved the Jews by serving her husband, King Ahasuerus (Esther 5-6).
- Daniel served in the government of King Darius (Daniel 6:1).
- Stephen and Philip were appointed to serve tables, so the disciples could remain in the Word and prayer (Acts 6:1-6).
- John Mark recorded the sermons of Peter which become the gospel of Mark, and then was later deemed "useful" to Paul (2 Timothy 4:11).

While there are certainly others, these should each show you the value of having a servant's heart.

Weaknesses and Dangers for Helpers

The Helper, just like each of the giftings, is not without weaknesses. Here are the top five I've noticed:

Pride Over Their Good Deeds

Pride's always the number one issue, right? It's the attitude of ego. The Messenger is proud of his speaking ability, and—as you'll see in the next chapter—the temptation of Explainers is to be proud of their knowledge. For the Server, it's, "Look at what I've done!" and "What have you done for others? Not much, heh?" It's easy to become judgmental towards those not as gifted to serve.

Becoming Bitter or Resentful

We all like kudos and praise. If we do not get them or don't get them to the level we deem sufficient, we tend to become bitter for not being appreciated. It's like a person who says, "If that's all the thanks I get, see if I ever do that again." Bitterness is a great danger; and according to Scripture, it's contagious. When we get bitter, we often spread it to others:

> *"Follow peace with all men, and holiness, without which no man shall see the Lord:*
>
> *looking diligently lest any man fail of the grace of God; lest any root of bitterness springing up trouble you, and thereby many be defiled."*
> (Hebrews 12:14-15)

The solution to bitterness is twofold:

1. The Helper must always act out of love which, by definition, is choosing and doing what is best for others without personal profit or benefit or self-adulation as a motive.
2. The Helper should realize that they are not really doing what they do for the other person *but for the Lord Himself.*

> *"Whatsoever ye do, do it heartily, as unto the Lord, and not unto men."* (Colossians 3:23)

Here is a fascinating insight (allow me some poetic license here). Jesus, if you can imagine, says, "I was hungry and you gave me your hamburger; I was thirsty and you bought me a soda; I was lonely and you hung out with me; I had no clothes and you bought me a pair of jeans and a T-shirt; I was vomiting and sick and you held my head; I had to do prison time and you checked in on me."

I'm sure the disciples thought Jesus had lost it when He said all this, but they played along and said, "Come on, Jesus. Stop joking. Stop pulling our legs. Be serious! When did we ever see you hungry, thirsty, or OMG, naked? When were you ever sick? In prison, Jesus? Really?"

Here's King Jesus' shocking illumination of truth.

> *"Whenever you did any of these things to overlooked, forgotten, and suffering persons, you were doing it for Me."*
>
> (Matthew 25:40, my paraphrase)

Becoming Overbearing and Overreaching One's Authority

The Server must not be pushy, trying to meet people's needs when they may not even know they have a need or when not invited to do so. The Helper should seek permission—both to help and get others to help. Servers shouldn't expect everyone around them to have the same level of determination and commitment that they do. It's easy to become impatient with others when they aren't as willing and eager to step in and take part of the load.

The Helper should let people ask for help. A Helper can be so zealous that it's like they want to pick up a person's pencil before they've even dropped it. That can feel obnoxious and invasive. The motivation may be right, but the method is overbearing. To coin a biblical phrase Paul used in reference to his fellow Israelites, they can have "zeal…but not according to knowledge" (Romans 10:2). This problem can happen to anyone. The danger is that the Helper could become pushy, insistent, intrusive, and overreaching, trying to help somebody who may not even know he or she needs help. Having the proverbial cart before the horse, they can blunder through and "help" people who may not even want their help.

Enabling Self-destructive Behavior

We all want to see people's lives change for the better, but a lot of people need heart changes before real change can occur. *Helpers should never do for others what they can and should do for themselves.* Doing this carries the risk of letting those people become irresponsible, entitled, and can even prevent them from doing what they should do when the burden is on them to do it.

There are real needs in which a handout can be an incredible blessing to help someone get through a rough patch, but we don't want to give a handout as much as we want to provide a hand-up, a hand to pull someone up out of their dilemma. Servers must consider the consequences as well as the benefits of giving their help.

Love isn't codependent. Helpers must seek not to enable bad behavior and be conned by sad stories based on lies. Servers have open hearts and open hands to help, but also need to be discerning about what is really helping versus what enables further poor lifestyle choices.

Assuming Those with Different Gifts Are Lazy

It can be easy to oversimplify things and look at the Proclaimer or the Teacher, and think, *Wow! Their gift is so easy! All they have to do is get up in front of people and talk!* Helpers could easily see themselves as the ones who *really* carry the burden for people and do the "real work." Remember, each gifting sees through his or her personal gift perspective. Others may not be lazy or insensitive, just focused differently. The Server must be careful not to be so focused as to overlook the spiritual and emotional needs of the one being served.

> Helpers are the restorers of the grace we were all created to carry.

Here are a few miscellaneous extras in the weakness category of the Helper:

- Bitterness, if not appreciated
- Resentful of being looked down upon as a mere Helper
- Minimizing the value of one's own gift of serving
- Neglect of one's own spouse and family in helping others
- Inability to say "no" when it is prudent to do so
- Overlooking spiritual needs to meet only the practical
- Failing to realize that some people are reaping what they have sown
- Interfering with God's discipline on, or God's reproof, of others
- Overextending one's self

Wrapping It Up

Even if we are not a Helper, this is the one in which we should most participate. Of all the giftings, it is the one through which it is easiest to *see* the heart of God. It is the most visible place where the hands and feet of God can be seen loving the world. I included a poem called "The World's Bible" in chapter 11. It might be a good idea to reread it now.

What if our hands are busy
  With other work than His?
What if our feet are walking
  Where sin's allurement is?
What if our tongues are speaking
  Of things His lips would spurn?
How can we hope to help Him
  Or welcome His return?

Our service is exclusively for God, even while we are serving others. This creates in the Helper an internal joy factor and a motivation that cannot be deterred. We do everything in His name!

> *"For God is not unrighteous to forget your work and labour of love, which ye have shewed toward his name, in that ye have ministered to the saints, and do minister."* (Hebrews 6:10)

Helpers are the restorers of the grace we were all created to carry. Helpers are the "lights that shine before men" that "they may see your good works, and glorify your father which is in heaven" (Matthew 5:16). They are also the people many will accuse to "have turned the world upside down" (Acts 17:6), even though what they are doing is really turning it upside right.

May we all be accused of such things because of our zeal for doing His good works!

Chapter Eighteen

Are You an Explainer?

Many years ago in a Swiss village, there lived a schoolmaster named Pestalozzi. He was greatly loved and esteemed by the community because he had taught most of them at some age or another. He was the type of teacher who didn't just educate minds, but helped mold the character and souls of his students. He opened up to them the magnificent world God created with all of its possibilities.

When he passed on, because of his selfless service for so many years, the community decided to commemorate his contribution with a statue. A sculptor was found and commissioned to do the work. The day of unveiling came amidst great expectation. The work was indeed magnificent, and the likeness was incredibly exact. It was met with hushed reverence and admiration. Before them stood the likeness of Pestalozzi with a young student kneeling before him with uplifted gaze focused upon the face of the teacher.

In the days and weeks following the unveiling, many who knew Pestalozzi found that something about the monument disturbed them at a very deep level. Though the statue was an excellent replica of their beloved schoolmaster, something about the presentation betrayed the values that made him the great man he was. He'd never taught that his students might look up to him in awe, but that they would look out into their world in amazement of all that it held, revere God, and be inspired to try to accomplish all that was in their hearts.

They called the sculptor back to them, and, with new instructions, he recast the statue.

The second unveiling showed the same kneeling child, but this time not looking at the face of the teacher, but out into the beckoning world beyond with Pestalozzi standing behind and pointing toward the horizon. Everyone was pleased with the new depiction because they knew it honored who Pestalozzi was as much as what he looked like.[49]

Focus

Explaining truth in order to bring understanding.

Vocational Application

Explainers make good teachers at all levels of academics. They make good automobile service managers, helping others understand the why of their situation in vehicle repair or other areas. If the whole truth be told, parents need to explain much to their children, stuff beyond the facts of life (but that, too).

Counselling, psychology, mediation, special education, science, languages, sociology, law, paralegal, writing, human resources, social work, guidance counselling, consulting, coaching, tutoring, and, of course, many, many more areas require Explainers.

Their skill development usually centers around research, fact finding, vetting, and communication skills ranging from speaking to writing with the purpose of bringing understanding to others.

Altruistic Application

Spiritual, moral and ethical truths seem to have vastly disappeared, given the present narcissistic culture and world condition. The demand for truth teaching is immense. It is predicted that in the latter days there will be,

---

49 Paul Lee Tan, *Encyclopedia of 7700 Illustrations: Signs of the Times* (Garland, TX: Bible Communications, Inc., 1996), 1427.

*"A **famine** in the land, not a famine of bread, nor a thirst for water, but of **hearing the words of the Lord**:*

and they shall wander from sea to sea, and from the north even to the east, they shall run to and fro to seek the word of the Lord, and shall not find it."

(Amos 8:11-12)

*"Judgment is turned away backward, and justice standeth afar off: for **truth is fallen in the street**, and equity cannot enter.*

*Yea, **truth faileth**; and he that departeth from evil maketh himself a prey: and the Lord saw it, and it displeased him that there was no judgment."*

(Isaiah 59:14-15)

*"Justice is beaten back, righteousness is banished to the sidelines, **truth staggers** down the street, honesty is nowhere to be found, good is missing in action. Anyone renouncing evil is beaten and robbed.*

God looked and saw evil looming on the horizon—so much evil and no sign of Justice. He couldn't believe what he saw: not a soul around to correct this awful situation." (Isaiah 59:14-15 MSG)

"As I urged you upon my departure for Macedonia, remain on at Ephesus so that you may instruct certain men not to teach strange doctrines,

nor to pay attention to myths and endless genealogies, which give rise to mere speculation rather than furthering the administration of God which is by faith.

> *But the **goal of our instruction is love from a pure heart and a good conscience and a sincere faith**."*
> (1 Timothy 1:3-5 NASB, emphasis mine)

The Explainer–The Teacher

The Messenger proclaims the love of God. The Helper demonstrates the love of God by doing good deeds. The Teacher explains the love of God and instructs us how to walk in it.

In the *King James Version*, the Explainer is called a teacher, a *didaskalos* in Greek.[50] Proclaimers proclaim. Teachers explain. It is the difference between preaching and teaching. Preaching is done to excite the soul towards salvation or godly action. It is primarily concerned with proclaiming the gospel and inspiring the hearers to act on it. Teaching is more how-to. It is not as much to instigate action as to instruct, so that action is taken properly and effectively. The Messenger proclaims, "This is the truth! Respond to God's love!" The Teacher explains, "This is the Truth, and let me break down why it is true and what it means. Then you will be able to love like God loves. Let me show you how to do this."

In order to appreciate the Explainer, we must have a good grasp on the importance of understanding and wisdom. Wisdom and understanding are coupled together in fifty-three different verses in the Bible. For example, they are both mentioned in Proverbs 4:

> *"Wisdom is the principal thing; therefore get wisdom: and with all thy getting get understanding."* (Proverbs 4:7)

Understanding is referred to 156 times in Scripture. (Don't worry, I'm not going to list them all.) Understanding is the comprehension of the dynamics and the mental grasp of the cause-and-effect relationships in all aspects of life. It means to have an

---

50 James Strong, "1320. Didaskalos," Strong's Greek: 1320. διδάσκαλος (didaskalos) -- an instructor (Biblehub), accessed February 8, 2020, https://biblehub.com/greek/1320.htm)

intelligible concept, to know the facts of what is really going on in any given situation.

Teachers are also focused on communicating wisdom. Wisdom is *knowing what to do* with knowledge, when to apply it and how to use it effectively, what knowledge to apply in which circumstances, and so on. Wisdom is the ability to see and respond to life situations from God's point of view; He is right, always right, dead right.

So just where does the Explainer/Teacher get their understanding? The answer is twofold. He or she must get it from God. Job asked the question twice:

> *"But where shall wisdom be found? and where is the place of understanding?...*
>
> *Whence then cometh wisdom? and where is the place of understanding?"* (Job 28:12, 20)

And Job found the answer to his own question. First, man doesn't know it. It's not found in the land of the living. It is hidden from the eyes of all living, and after a litany of other vain, empty sources, Job concluded,

> *"God understandeth the way thereof, and he knoweth the place thereof."* (Job 28:23)

So understanding is only found in God. That means that first and foremost, the Explainer must know God. The Teacher must be in relationship with God. The second source is God's Word.

> *"The entrance of thy words giveth light; it giveth understanding unto the simple."* (Psalm 119:130)

So, in essence, the Explainer of truth must know God and must know and understand God's Word—the laws, the principles, the statutes God wrote to us by His Spirit that are collected in the Bible. Who could be a better example of that than Jesus?

Jesus the Teacher

Jesus is the personification of each and all of these seven gifts. He performed each gift perfectly, and Explaining was no exception. It was said of Him,

> *"Then opened he their understanding, that they might understand the scriptures."* (Luke 24:45)

This is what Explainers do. They open people's understanding so that more people can understand the truths of God. Here is what Jesus said about Himself:

> *"To this end was I born, and for this cause came I into the world, that I should bear witness unto the truth. Every one that is of the truth heareth my voice."* (John 18:37)

Jesus came to explain truth. In fact, He came to be the personification of truth, as we are told by the Apostle John, who quoted Jesus as saying,

> *"I am the way, the* ***truth, and the life****."*
> (John 14:6, emphasis mine)

In the Sermon on the Mount, which I have referred to earlier as *The Inaugural Address That Changed the World* (and I've written a book by that title), Jesus taught.

> *"And seeing the multitudes, he went up into a mountain: and when he was set, his disciples came unto him:*
>
> *and he opened his mouth, and taught them."*
> (Matthew 5:1-2)

For the next *three chapters*, Jesus explains the principles of God to the people, returning them to the way God intended things originally, as opposed to how they had been distorted through years of tradition and human justification. He told them things like,

> *"You know the next commandment pretty well, too: 'Don't go to bed with another's spouse.'*
>
> *But don't think you've preserved your virtue simply by staying out of bed. Your heart can be corrupted by lust even quicker than your body. Those leering looks you think nobody notices—they also corrupt."* (Matthew 5:27-28 MSG)

> *"Ye have heard that it hath been said, Thou shalt love thy neighbour, and hate thine enemy.*
>
> *But I say unto you, Love your enemies, bless them that curse you, do good to them that hate you, and pray for them which despitefully use you, and persecute you;*
>
> *that ye may be the children of your Father which is in heaven."* (Matthew 5:43-45)

He was correcting the false traditions they had been taught and returning their understanding to God's truth. Today, it often seems the truth isn't that popular. People want to *choose* and *speak* their "own truth." The implications of this are severe. The ability to make wise judgments or arbitrate fairly on matters is impaired; justice is corrupted, and right versus wrong "has become a matter of opinion." Isaiah spoke about the same thing when it happened in ancient Israel:

> *"Judgment is turned away backward, and justice standeth afar off: for* ***truth is fallen in the street, and equity cannot enter***."
> (Isaiah 59:14, emphasis mine)

> *"Woe unto them that call evil good, and good evil; that put darkness for light, and light for darkness;*

that put bitter for sweet, and sweet for bitter!

Woe unto them that are wise in their own eyes,
and prudent in their own sight!" (Isaiah 5:20-21)

Right and wrong are absolutes and facts are actualities, but when "every man did that which was right in his own eyes" (Judges 17:6), reality is lost. Today, our culture today is jammed with people that are like a pair of spectacles behind which there are no eyes. There has never been a time that needed more people willing to teach and explain the truth. As Proverbs advises, we need to seek wisdom from God's Word and not let our own thinking and emotions rule us.

"The way of the fool is right in his own eyes, but he that hearkeneth unto counsel is wise."
(Proverbs 12:15)

"There is a generation that are pure in their own eyes, and yet is not washed from their filthiness."
(Proverbs 30:12)

Truth must be established and everyone but God has a bias and sees through their own filters and opinions. Thus, is the necessity for godly teachers: impartial, unprejudiced, nonpartisan, equitable, and objective. Jesus, God here among us, came to accomplish two objectives:

1. Affirm the Scripture as the absolute truth (see Luke 24:45 again).
2. Bring understanding.

We need people in this culture to take up the same mission.

The Characteristics of an Explainer

What are the characteristics of the Explainer or Teacher? Here are the ones I've found stand out the most:

Explainers Love to Study and Think

Explainers are first learners and researchers. They hunger to pray, study Scripture, research facts, think through issues, unsort complexities, find solutions, stick to the truth, honor God, care about people, organize thoughts and arguments sequentially, capture interest, explain in detail, prepare others for eternity, develop character, be trustworthy, and above all, be true to the truth. All of these are in the nature of the true Teacher. Many aspire to be teachers but love of studying is one of the things that distinguish the true teacher from the wannabes.

The Explainer is a Bible researcher, an accumulator of truth. The Teacher craves accuracy and precision and goes to great depths to properly interpret Scripture. It frustrates the Explainer to hear someone misuse, misquote, or misapply Scripture. The Explainer searches out the truth, all the truth, and wants nothing but the truth.[51] This is what everyone should demand, even as the king did with Micaiah,

> *"How many times shall I adjure thee that thou say* ***nothing but the truth*** *to me in the name of the Lord?"* (2 Chronicles 18:15)

Explainers Desire to be Thorough, Accurate, and Practical

Explainers must resolve each issue of life to their own mental satisfaction. They are never comfortable with conflicting views. They want the facts, all the facts. Therefore, they vet, verify, and validate all data. Doctor Luke said it this way in his gospel,

> *"That thou mightest know the certainty of those things, wherein thou hast been instructed."*
> (Luke 1:4)

To Teacher/Explainers, there is no room for error. No casual

51 By the way and for your information, we got the name of our website: NothingButTheTruth.org from 2 Chronicles 18:15.

approach to the truth is acceptable—no guessing, no triviality, no philosophizing, no assumptions, no vagueness, no blurring, no distortion, no confusion, no partial truths, no incompleteness, no subjectivity, no imbalance, no presumptions, and no trust in information simply because it is stated by a famous expert. They want the truth on every issue and they want it to be easily understood and functional. They check everything, and really care about context in presenting the Word of God. Anything less than these is regarded as careless at best.

Explainers Are Aware of the Severity of Error

Explainers are uneasy until they have personally made a thorough investigation of all the facts. This is because Teachers must answer to God, as James warned us:

> *"My brethren, be not many masters (teachers), knowing that we shall receive the greater condemnation."* (James 3:1, parenthesis added)

(We'll look more at this warning later.) They know someday they will be judged for the accuracy of what they teach for, in essence, they are directing the lives of others.

They need the approval of God and so they must study. That is the essence of the Scripture,

> *"Study to shew thyself approved unto God, a workman that needeth not to be ashamed, rightly dividing the word of truth."* (2 Timothy 2:15)

The task is dividing all the truths of Scripture into categories so that they can offer biblical solutions to each and all of life's situations. Teachers are not content to dabble in mere surface symptoms. Explainers immerse themselves, so they can grasp and then communicate a deep understanding of the truths revealed in the Scriptures, so that people know how to live and be successful in their life endeavors.

Explainers Settle for Nothing but the Truth

Each gifting has a perspective of its own, a way of looking, a focus. The Messenger's focus is on the message, the gospel. The Helper's focus is on meeting needs through doing deeds. The Explainer focuses on communicating the truth.

What is the truth? Horatius Bonar (1808–1889), a Scottish poet, forever influenced my life with these lines:

> Thou must be true thyself,
> If thou the truth wouldst teach;
> Thy soul must overflow, if thou
> Another's soul would'st reach!
> It needs the overflow of heart
> To give the lips full speech.
>
> Think truly, and thy thoughts
> Shall the world's famine feed;
> Speak truly, and each word of thine
> Shall be a fruitful seed;
> Live truly, and thy life shall be
> A great and noble creed.[52]

I drastically failed in my younger years to grasp truth. I had to go back to the beginning and learn about repentance and redemption, forgiveness and cleansing. Oh, beloved, there is no sin He will not forgive. There is no sinfulness He cannot cleanse. There is no brokenness that He cannot repair. There is no condemnation that He cannot remove. There is no disorder He cannot heal. That's why He is called Savior and Redeemer.

Of all the truths an Explainer must master, the character of God, the love of God, and the great principles of redemption are the most vital.

---

52 Horatius Bonar, "Be True," Be true (Bonar, set by Eleanor Everest Freer) (The LiederNet Archive: Texts and Translations to Lieder, mélodies, canzoni, and other classical vocal music), accessed February 9, 2020, https://www.lieder.net/lieder/get_text.html?TextId=53847)

The Explainer Strives for Both Understanding and Wisdom

The Explainer must also develop practical skills in language, vocabulary, and diction, as well as the ability to pull together adjective, adverb, phrase, verbs, and illustrations understandable to the average person. Personally, I use diagrams. I write upside down so that the person across the table from me can read it right side up. Jesus used diagrams, wrote in the sand, and was a master of prose and parable. The Explainer should do no less.

Biblical Examples of Explainers

Probably the best example of a teacher in the Bible—other than Jesus, of course—is the apostle Paul. He had, if you can imagine, been a murderer, a Jewish militant, and a persecutor of Christianity and Christians. One of his terrorist missions is described in Acts 9, when he was

> *"Yet breathing out threatenings and slaughter against the disciples of the Lord."* (Acts 9:1)

Thankfully, he experienced what all of us need—being stopped in his tracks by Christ Himself.

As he neared Damascus, he was knocked to the ground and blinded by a light; then he heard the voice of God. The Scriptures say that the fellow-terrorists who were with him,

> *"Stood speechless, hearing a voice, but seeing no man."* (Acts 9:7)

You should read how this drama unfolded, but to make a long story short, this terrorist became a saint. (Don't we refer to him as Saint Paul, after all?) He is credited with writing fourteen of the twenty-seven books of the New Testament.[53] Paul was an Explainer, a Teacher, who, as every teacher must, started with a

53 There is some debate about the authorship of some of these books, but Paul is always in the discussion as the likely author of them.

personal experience with God.

This is not theory. God is inside every true Explainer unfolding the mysteries of the kingdom of God. Every Teacher must master the writings of Paul, from the great theological concepts of Romans and Ephesians to the corrections of Galatians to the Judaizers to the Gentile prejudices in the book of Hebrews to the practical instructions to the young in 1 and 2 Timothy and Titus—everyone who wants to understand the Christian faith has to be an avid student of the letters Paul left the church.

Paul brought the Old and New Testaments together. In prison, he requested his books and parchments and poured over them. He studied for three years in Arabia before even thinking to start teaching. He interrogated the Jewish leadership, disputed in the synagogues, and stunned the philosophers on Mars Hill. He was a teacher of teachers, demonstrating for us today the need to burst out of academia into the arenas of real life because people needed the truth. They were desperate for *the* truth because:

> *"Ye shall know the truth, and the truth shall make you free."* (John 8:32)

A Word of Warning

The gift of explaining and teaching is a foundational gift. Without it we wouldn't know about any of the other giftings nor how to discover our personal Embedded Natural Abilities. Of all the Scriptures that refer to any of the seven endowments, no other gifting but that of Teacher is given a specific warning. The Explainer is such a crucial function that a warning is necessary. We already looked at it once, but let's take some time to look at it in more detail. The apostle James warned,

> *"My brethren, be not many masters [teacher], knowing that we shall receive the greater condemnation."* (James 3:1, parenthesis added)

As explained earlier, the King James word *masters* comes from the Greek word *didaskalos* meaning "teacher, instructor." (If you know anything of the British school system, teachers are often called "masters" and to this day, the head teacher is still called the "headmaster.") Note the severity of this warning in other translations:

> *"Don't be in any rush to become a teacher, my friends. Teaching is highly responsible work. Teachers are held to the strictest standards."*
> (James 3:1 MSG)

> *"Dear brothers and sisters, not many of you should become teachers in the church, for we who teach will be judged more strictly."* (James 3:1 NLT)

> *"Not many [of you] should become teachers (self-constituted censors and reprovers of others), my brethren, for you know that we [teachers] will be judged by a higher standard and with greater severity [than other people; thus we assume the greater accountability and the more condemnation]."* (James 3:1 AMPC)

People build their lives on what they are taught by the Explainer.

So why this severe warning to Explainers of truth? I think it's because people build their lives on what they are taught by the Explainer. Not only their lives, but each area of their lives—and not only each area of their lives, but also their *eternal future*. If the Explainer, Teacher, Instructor is wrong, the people will be wrong. If the people are wrong, imagine the greatness of their folly.

This is best seen in the oft-cited Scripture,

> *"My people are destroyed for lack of knowledge."*
> (Hosea 4:6a)

It is certainly true that people can be destroyed by the lack of critical data, paramount essentials, and critical, pivotal, and life-and-death-affecting information. However, in my experience, few who quote this passage know the rest of the verse and the context. Here it is:

> *"My people are destroyed for lack of knowledge:* ***because*** *thou hast rejected knowledge, I will also reject thee, that thou shalt be no priest to me: seeing thou hast forgotten the law of thy God, I will also forget thy children."* (Hosea 4:6)

Aha! There it is! The reason the people were destroyed was because they lacked vital information. But the reason they lacked the vital information was because the priests (the teachers of that day) had rejected the knowledge of God and failed to deliver His vital, life-changing instructions. Take a look at how *The Message* explains the same passage:

> *"My people are ruined because they don't know what's right or true. Because you've turned your back on knowledge, I've turned my back on you priests. Because you refuse to recognize the revelation of God, I'm no longer recognizing your children."* (Hosea 4:6 MSG)

So why did the teachers of that day reject delivering this life-changing instruction? The answer is found in the following verses:

> *"They eat up the sin of my people, and they set their heart on their iniquity.*
>
> *And there shall be, like people, like priest: and I will punish them for their ways, and reward them*

their doings." (Hosea 4:8-9)

The iniquity of the Teachers, the Explainers, was the cause! Instead of teaching the truth and nothing but the truth, they wanted to benefit from letting the people go in wrong ways. They produced an "easy" message, one that was palatable, pleasant to the taste, and non-offensive. Note the descriptive phrase, "seeing thou hast forgotten the law of thy God." Their instruction came with an absence of divine standards. And why? Why were these teaching priests unequal to their proper function? Because they were more interested in personal benefit than the truth.

Here is that verse in two other translations:

> *"They pig out on my people's sins."*
> (Hosea 4:8-10 MSG)

> *"When the people bring their sin offerings, the priests get fed."* (Hosea 4:8 NLT)

The iniquity of the Teachers was that they had turned their ministry into a business. The profit motive had taken over. They were only interested in teaching the things that appeased and kept them popular.

And what of today? I submit to you that the condition of the church today is what it is because of the industrialization of Christianity. The worldwide church—and I'm not talking about the buildings—is being designed and built on the basis of market analysis. What is the market looking for? What do people want in a church? The market-driven church only succeeds when the message they teach appeals to the market. *Yikes!* (You have no idea how much I dislike writing this, but it needs to be said. Where are the Prophets that should be calling us back to God-pleasing truths as opposed to man-pleasing messages?)

We've fallen prey to being more eager to please people than please God. Brace yourself for a word from Charles Spurgeon: "The time will come when instead of shepherds feeding the sheep, the church will have clowns entertaining the goats."[54]

If your gift is that of Teacher/Explainer, heed these warnings. Otherwise, we Christians will cease to be the salt of the earth and light to the world. Instead, we must,

> *"Preach the word; be instant in season, out of season; reprove, rebuke, exhort with all long suffering and doctrine."* (2 Timothy 4:2)

The Weaknesses and Dangers for the Explainer

Instead of listing the top five pitfalls as I did in the other sections, I'm going to list *all* the pitfalls. Because the Explainer will answer to a greater strictness, they should be wary of all that I have come across in my studies, even though that means I won't have room to elaborate on each of them in detail as I have in the previous chapters.

The Explainer, just like each of the giftings, is not without weaknesses inherent to their endowment. Here are some of them I have run into time and again:

- They can be tripped up by pride in their knowledge, for "Knowledge puffeth up" (1 Corinthians 8:1).
- They can be impatient with others not as learned as they are.
- They can be argumentative—sometimes being more focused on proving that their views are correct than discussing their points with the goal of refining the understanding of truth. They may be more interested in being the smartest person in the room than in having a sincere interest in the well-being of others.
- They can be critical of ignorance.
- They may have a tendency to show off.

54 Eph611, "Pergamos and the Mustard Seed," Ephesians611.com (Ephesians611.com, March 3, 2013), http://www.ephesians611.com/pergamos-and-the-mustard-seed/)

- They can be imbalanced in their study and, subsequently, prone to rejecting what they don't know before giving it proper consideration.
- They can be more interested in facts than concern the welfare of people.
- They can be "pie-in-the-sky" idealistic and more interested in theory than the practical.
- They may obsess over trivial details and bore those with whom they speak.
- They may miss the "God factor" in sharing solutions.
- They may lean towards depending on what they know rather than relying upon the great Teacher, the Holy Spirit.
- They can be eccentric and disorganized in their thinking and manners—fitting the stereotype of the "nutty professor."
- They may believe theirs is the highest and most important gifting, and fail to give proper respect to those with differing ENAs.
- They can become such a subject expert and thus fail to see the Big Picture over time—they miss the forest because they are obsessed with the trees.
- They can "be so heavenly minded (head in the clouds with ideas) that they are no earthly good."

Wrapping It Up

If you're a teacher, cling to the truth and be wary of your own opinions and pride. As Paul advised the Thessalonians:

> *"Rejoice evermore.*
>
> *Pray without ceasing.*
>
> *In every thing give thanks: for this is the will of God in Christ Jesus concerning you.*
>
> *Quench not the Spirit.*

Despise not prophesyings.
Prove all things; hold fast that which is good.
Abstain from all appearance of evil."
(1 Thessalonians 5:16-22)

Do these things, and your teaching will be a benefit to all and your gift greatly cherished, just as the teacher Pestalozzi's was (although I can't guarantee anyone will build a statue of you)!

Chapter Nineteen

Are You an Encourager?

A group of frogs traveled jovially through the woods, and two of them, not looking where they were going, fell into a pit.

Frogs can be cruel creatures, and this group was especially bad. Rather than helping the two out, the others looked over the edge as the two struggled to jump out and mocked their efforts. They told them they would die in that pit and there was no way they would ever get out. It was impossible.

Discouraged by their words, one of the two gave up and found a dark place to wait until he succumbed to his fate. The other, however, seemed to just try even harder to get out. Seeing his efforts, the other frogs laughed all the louder at his foolishness and scorned him all the more harshly. "Give it up!" they shouted. "There's no escape! You're destined for a horrible fate!" Then they rolled onto their backs laughing. (I told you they were horrid!)

But suddenly, the one still trying leapt high enough, caught the edge, and climbed out of the hole. Finding a stick, he helped his previous hole mate escape as well.

"Thank you so much," the defeated frog told his rescuer. "I was sure I was a goner. I gave up too easily! But you, you never quit! Why did you keep on jumping, even after I had given up? And with all the discouraging things the other frogs were saying to us? How did you keep on trying?"

"Huh?" the other frog said. "I'm sorry, I'm a little hard of hearing. I thought they were cheering me on!"[55]

One should never underestimate the power of encouraging words. They could literally help people get out of a hole and save their life!

Focus

The motivation of the Encourager is to see others reach their God-given potential.

Vocational Application

Like each of the previous gifts explained, there are vocational and employment dynamics embedded in the Encourager, the Exhorter, the Motivator. They particularly excel in sales and counselling. They can enhance the performance and accomplishments of others; thus they are good choices for management positions. They function far beyond the "if you don't work, you don't eat" incitement. Intrinsic to their gifting is the desire and ability to enthuse and inspire others to higher achievement. In a culture or social grouping where the work ethic has been somewhat overtaken by slackness, slothfulness (so named after a slow-moving animal), and lethargy, the Encourager is in great demand throughout the workforce. Those with the **E**mbedded **N**atural **A**bility to encourage and motivate others are in high demand. Who does not need encouragement, motivation, and stimulation? This certainly applies to education.

The number one enemy of sales people is discouragement, especially if their type of sales is the direct, go-get-em type. It's true that some of us are self-starters and self-motivated; however, there may be areas of life other than vocational in which we need motivation. For example, we often need encouragement in our marriage and family life. Avoidance behaviors must be

---

55 Stephen, "Encouragement Story – A Group of Frogs," Motivational Stories, December 10, 2018, https://academictips.org/blogs/encouragement-story-a-group-of-frogs/)

overcome. These fit more into this gift's Altruistic Application as we shall see.

Vocationally, Encouragers not only make great salespersons, but beyond that, they make great sales managers. In fact, many management positions will open up to them because they not only dangle goals and purposes in front of others, but also show them step-by-step procedures to reach those goals. Vocational guidance is another area in which they would shine because they evaluate the Embedded Natural Ability of others, and then inspire and instigate plans for their achievement.

Communication skills are paramount, whether on a personal level or group context. Encouragers can also see potential where others may not—in discarded products or processes. They have a high influence factor built into their ENA. Their greatest joy is in seeing the success of others in which they have played a major role. They make great counsellors.

Altruistic Application

Discouragement, depression and despair are human predicaments that are far too widespread and prevalent. A culture can be paralyzed by emotional disorders: anxiety, panic, obsessive-compulsive, post-traumatic stress, and many others. Phobias abound. Often, chemical cures for spiritual problems are sought. Perhaps the pharmaceutical industry has had too large an influence on the medical world. One prescribed pill can become a need and soon, whole chemical cocktails are required by a large slice of the populace.

Every ENA (and every one of us) is a specialist equipped to serve mankind in distinct, definite, and determined ways. The Encourager is in desperate need; they are those who, without selfish motives, will feel around the souls of others to find the cracks, the hurts, and the damage and then speak healing and inspiration to them so they can become functional again and maintain their personal ENA in full working order.

> *"Wherefore comfort yourselves together, and edify one another, even as also ye do."*
> (1 Thessalonians 5:11)

To edify means to build up, construct, and improve, whether intellectually or morally. Since God is love, He is also into doing good.

> *"The Lord is good to all: and His tender mercies are over all His works."* (Psalm 145:9)

For this reason, it should not be surprising to learn the following about ourselves:

The Encourager

In the King James Bible, the Encourager is referred to as an Exhorter. (We would probably think of them as Motivators today.) They have the natural tendency and ability to encourage others, to stimulate their faith, and inspire action to tackle a cause. The Encourager is a promoter, a cheer-er-upper, an inspirer. When everyone else is ready to quit, the Encourager is just getting started, and their motivation is contagious.

Encouragers evaluate where others are at, envision where they should be, and help them get there. They try to fill others with confidence about all they could accomplish. They often provide the holy "spurt" of enthusiasm that puts others over the top. They want to see growth and spiritual maturity in others. And certainly, among the Motivator's highest priorities is to see Christlikeness in each of their brothers and sisters. This was epitomized by the apostle Paul, who said,

> *"Oh, my dear children! I feel as if I'm going through labor pains for you again, and they will continue until Christ is fully developed in your lives."* (Galatians 4:19 NLT)

Motivators are able to detect (a better word might be *discern*) the stumbling blocks and hindrances in other's lives. They then offer energy, direction, and encouragement, urging others onward to be conquerors and winners. They also tend to be good at helping others clarify their life goals because they know how, like Paul (who was a pretty good encourager himself)!

> *"Know ye not that they which run in a race run all, but one receiveth the prize? So run, that ye may obtain.*
>
> *And every man that striveth for the mastery is temperate in all things. Now they do it to obtain a corruptible crown; but we an incorruptible.*
>
> *I therefore so run, not as uncertainly; so fight I, not as one that beateth the air:*
>
> *but I keep under my body, and bring it into subjection: lest that by any means, when I have preached to others, I myself should be a castaway."*
>
> (1 Corinthians 9:24-27)

Encouragers are incurable optimists. They visualize success wherever they look. They see the best in people—often more than people can see in themselves. They delight in the achievements of others and get fulfillment in others' successes, reveling in any small part they can play in helping them strive toward their potential.

The Motivator/Exhorter is a cheerleader, motivating, stimulating, trying to get people to be the best they could be and do the best they could do. The word *exhort* comes from the Greek word *paraklésis*, which means "comforter or strengthener."[56] Do you know who Jesus called the Comforter in Scripture? *The Holy Spirit*. (See John 14:16, 26; 15:26; 16:7.)

Encouragers have a very deep and meaningful role that parallels the work of the Holy Spirit. True Exhorters walk in tune

56 James Strong, "3874. Paraklésis," Strong's Greek: 3874. παράκλησις (paraklésis) -- a calling to one's aid, i.e. encouragement, comfort (Biblehub), accessed February 9, 2020, https://biblehub.com/greek/3874.htm)

with God's Spirit, so they, too, can help inspire the work of God on the earth. The Motivator sees great value in each person, and is excited about every one of them achieving the maximum potential God has imparted to them.

In one of the darkest moments of my life, someone spoke just two sentences to me that changed everything. I was at the end of myself. At my wit's end. I had tried everything but had still failed. I was middle-aged and could see no going forward, no hope of recovery, no future, no purpose, no forgiveness, no cleansing, no resources, nothing. I felt like life was all over for me. And to make matters worse, there was no one to blame but myself. I felt *damned.* There was no one to "cry me a river." The sun would never shine again.

And then a stranger showed up in my life. We talked for less than three minutes, and the last minute of the three brought me back to life. It was like a resurrection. All he said was, "Your best years are still ahead of you. God says,

> *"I will restore to you the years that the locust hath eaten, the cankerworm, and the caterpillar, and the palmerworm, my great army which I sent among you."* (Joel 2:25)

Those two sentences became light to my path when all I'd seen before was darkness. That's how powerful and important Encouragers are.

In that moment, the whole of God's character and nature took on a new meaning in my heart that has lasted to this very day. God is redemptive. God is forgiving. God is healing. The blood of Jesus reaches where no psychologist or Christian counselor can touch. There is absolute recovery. I started to sing anew part of Anna Waterman's song with an intensified sense of its meaning:

> Come, ye sinners, lost and hopeless,
> Jesus' blood can make you free;
> For He saved the worst among you,
> When He saved a wretch like me.

And I know, yes, I know
Jesus' blood can make the vilest sinner clean,
And I know, yes, I know
Jesus' blood can make the vilest sinner clean.[57]

Encouragers are exhorters and motivators, and they know how to turn tragedy into triumph because God not only empowers them to do so but also equips them with the stuff of God. This is the joy of the Encourager. It is explained best in Proverbs 15:

> *"A man hath joy by the answer of his mouth: and a word spoken in due season, how good is it!"*
> (Proverbs 15:23)

Additionally, Proverbs 25:11 says,

> *"A word fitly spoken is like apples of gold in pictures of silver."* (Proverbs 25:11)

Let's look at it in *The Message* for a better understanding of that proverb:

> *"The right word at the right time is like a custom-made piece of jewelry, and a wise friend's timely reprimand is like a gold ring slipped on your finger."* (Proverbs 25:11 MSG)

This is what the Encourager does.

Encouragers get others to do what they are not able to do themselves. They motivate others to function in their gifting, their ENA. That's one reason why Encouragers must understand the nature and purpose of *each* of the seven **E**mbedded **N**atural **A**bilities that God has given to us. They must know all of the gifts thoroughly, be able to identify each person's ENA, and then

57 Anna W. Waterman, Timeless Truths Free Online Library | books, "Yes, I Know!," Yes, I Know! > Lyrics | Anna W. Waterman, accessed February 12, 2020, https://library.timelesstruths.org/music/Yes_I_Know/)

They must know all of the gifts thoroughly, be able to identify each person's ENA, and then encourage accordingly.

encourage accordingly. Can you see why being an Encourager is such an important function?

They are like extra horsepower when a car struggles to get over a hill or the second wind for a distance runner. They provide the extra "courage-ment" to keep going when others may be discouraged and want to quit. Thank God for giving us the Encouragers! They know how to turn tragedy into triumph.

> *"A word spoken in due season, how good is it!"*
> (Proverbs 15:23)

Jesus the Encourager

There were many times and places in which Jesus encouraged people, but one of my favorites was when He met a woman at the local watering hole. In ancient times instead of meeting at a local bar, they met at the well. Everybody had to come there. It was the center for social interaction of all kinds. Jesus was alone. The disciples had gone shopping. And a woman who had been married and divorced five times and was now living with who knows who, showed up and Jesus asked her for a drink (of water). She was startled at the discovery that He was not a racist.

> *"The woman was surprised, for Jews refuse to have anything to do with Samaritans. 'You are a Jew, and I am a Samaritan woman. Why are you asking me for a drink?'"* (John 4:9 NLT)

Jews in those days wouldn't be caught dead talking to Samaritans. Even the disciples were shocked when they returned and found the Master talking to this woman.

If this had happened today, Jesus would have said to her

something like, "Listen, sweetheart, if you knew who I am and what I've got to offer, you would never thirst again." Let me interrupt the story for a moment to say that Jesus is the real Thirst Quencher. Unfulfilled people go through life clutching, grabbing, always reaching out for something that will satisfy their thirst, and all people are thirsty. There's not enough "stuff": not enough satisfaction in relationships, no achievement high enough in this life to satisfy. The thirst is spiritual as enunciated by St. Augustine of Hippo, when he wrote:

> Thou hast made us for thyself, O Lord, and our heart is restless until it finds its rest in thee.[58]

Back to the story. The woman runs back to town and tells everyone what had happened to her. She had found the Thirst Quencher and they could as well. And what do they do?

> *"So the people came streaming from the village to see him."* (John 4:30 NLT)

A woman, and who knows how many others that day, discovered a forgiving, cleansing power in Christ that was so effective that they would never thirst again. From that day forward, they would be full and never hungry, complete and never deficient, together and never falling apart, intact and never fragmented, strong and never weak, blessed and never cursed, whole and never broken, forward and never backward, entire and never partial. And He is that for you and me today, my friend. He comes to encourage us and lift us out of the doldrums of mere existence. He puts a fire in our bosom and will:

> *"Cause thee to ride upon the high places of the earth."* (Isaiah 58:1)

Jesus is the epitome of God walking the earth.

---

58 Augustine, *The Confessions of Saint Augustine*, public domain.

The Characteristics of Encouragers

Encouragers do the same thing today, just as that man did for me all those years ago. Encouragers remind us of who God is and what we can accomplish if we would but look to Him.

Here are a few of my other favorite characteristics of Encouragers:

Encouragers Focus on the Progress of Others

Encouragers want to evaluate where people are, know where they should be, and motivate them to get there. The following verse highlights the basic skills of the Encourager.

> *"The Lord God hath given me the tongue of the learned, that I should know how to speak a word in season to him that is weary: he wakeneth morning by morning, he wakeneth mine ear to hear as the learned."* (Isaiah 50:4)

Encouragers must be connected to God to know what is right for other people. (As with any and all of these gifts, they only work correctly when we look to God first, just like the man by the pool did to get his healing.) Then the Encourager must be skilled, educated, and know how to speak to a person who is down and needs to be lifted up. For clarity, here is Isaiah 50:4 in another version.

Encouragers must be connected to God to know what is right for other people.

> *"The Master, God, has given me a well-taught tongue, so I know how to encourage tired people. He wakes me up in the morning, wakes me up, opens my ears to listen as one ready to take orders."* (Isaiah 50:4 MSG)

Encouragers Are Visionaries and Full of Creative Ideas

> *"Where there is no vision, the people perish: but he that keepeth the law, happy is he."*
> (Proverbs 29:18)

When others have no vision, no dream to follow, no divine direction, or are simply apathetic, the Encourager will give them a holy jolt to get them moving in a worthwhile direction again. They help people figure out appropriate life goals and seek to inspire others toward their fulfillment. They have plenty of ideas. Encouragers are incurable optimists.

They believe in you more than you believe in yourself. They see beyond obstacles, limitations, and circumstances. No matter how dark the clouds are, Encouragers know the sun is still shining beyond the blackness. Encouragers see that there is a way through the wilderness, even if they know that only the other person can find it for themselves. They're not just being positive for positive's sake though. Their confident optimism is based on the sure Word of God. They never give up.

> *"Being confident of this very thing, that he which hath begun a good work in you will perform it until the day of Jesus Christ."* (Philippians 1:6)

Encouragers Are Evaluators

Not satisfied with short-lived, emotional bursts of progress, Encouragers give serious thought before giving any advice. They must detect the condition of others with a caring (rather than a critical) spirit. Their task is serious.

> *"Then shall ye return, and discern between the righteous and the wicked, between him that serveth God and him that serveth him not."*
> (Malachi 3:18)

They follow the motto, "Establish the need before you proceed."

Encouragers Give Step-by-step Directions

The mission of the Encourager is not to make overly optimistic, emotionally-based promises. Encouragers help create careful action plans. Encouragers break tasks down into human-sized incremental steps, even giving written instructions as encouraged by God.

> *"Write the vision, and make it plain upon tables that he may run that readeth it."* (Habakkuk 2:2)

Encouragers Derive Joy from Giving a Timely Word

They want to be the instrument of God that drops an encouragement that really benefits you into your mind, your thinking, and your life. For them, it is not about mere gab and chatter but specific words: "seeds" that will create positive change. You could say the Encourager's slogan is "the right word at the right time."

> *"Everyone enjoys a fitting reply; it is wonderful to say the right thing at the right time!"*
> (Proverbs 15:23 NLT)

Purity of Motive Creates Effectiveness

Here is their mission:

> *"When men are cast down, then thou shalt say, There is lifting up; and he shall save the humble person.*
>
> *He shall deliver the island of the innocent: and it is delivered by the pureness of thine hands."*
> (Job 22:29-30)

True Encouragers have no selfish motives, no manipulative intentions, no hidden agendas. Instead, they are always sincere, honest, pure, and authentic. No deceptive maneuvering, pushing or pulling, no yelling and screaming, no reaching into the pockets of another. This is what gives their words power and effectiveness. Here's a paraphrase of the verses above:

> *"To those who feel low you'll say, 'Chin up! Be brave!' and God will save them. Yes, even the guilty will escape, escape through God's grace in your life."* (Job 22:29-30 MSG)

Encouragers Emphasize Character Development

What a person *is*, is more important than what a person *does*. In fact, what we *are* deep down largely determines whether or not what we *do* will be ethical and above board. True success and progress are dependent upon long-term personal character development. Certain qualities must be in us so that true prosperity is possible. As the apostle Peter wrote:

> *"For if these things be in you, and abound, they make you that ye shall neither be barren nor unfruitful in the knowledge of our Lord Jesus Christ."* (2 Peter 1:8)

Encouragers want to see others have true success. They want to see forward movement towards the destination as each person discovers why they were born, what gifting they have been given, and how to maximize their influence in how they function for the good of others and the glory of God. This is what the Encourager deems as progress.

A Biblical Example of a Great Encourager

Encouragers are idea people. They generally think ahead of others and can see what others may fail to see. Such was the case of Barnabas, whose nickname was actually "the Encourager."

Paul wanted to visit the church leaders in Jerusalem early in his ministry (when he was still going by the name Saul, in fact), but as you might suspect, they were a little leery of welcoming this man who had been an accomplice to the stoning of Stephen and the killing of Christians. Paul wanted to share his testimony, and let them know that he, a Jewish militant, had become one of them, but they suspected a ruse to have them all arrested and imprisoned. Despite the fact that the one-time killer Saul has been dramatically converted, they were still apprehensive. The Bible tells us,

> *"They were all afraid of him, and believed not that he was a disciple."* (Acts 9:26)

What was needed was an intermediary—a mediator—who could come in and determine whether Saul was on the up-and-up or not.

Enter Barnabas. Willing to risk his own life because he believed in Saul and what God had done in his life, Barnabas went to him, heard his story, and then became his advocate to the church leadership in Jerusalem. He was the first that could see the truth of Saul's conversion and the potential he had to spread the gospel throughout the known world. He was the first who stood up for and vouched for Saul.

> *"But Barnabas took him (Saul), and brought him to the apostles, and declared unto them how he had seen the Lord in the way, and that he had spoken to him, and how he had preached boldly at Damascus in the name of Jesus."*
> (Acts 9:27, parenthesis added)

We see Barnabas exhorting again later on in Acts as well:

> *"They sent forth Barnabas, that he should go as far as Antioch.*

> *Who, when he came, and had seen the grace of God, was glad, and* ***exhorted them all****, that with purpose of heart they would cleave unto the Lord.*
>
> *For he was a good man, and full of the Holy Ghost and of faith: and much people was added unto the Lord."* (Acts 11:22-24)

Barnabas was an integral part of the early church, mentioned twenty-eight times in Scripture. While he was never mentioned as an apostle like the Twelve or like Paul, living in the shadows was never a problem for him. What he wanted, instead, was to lift up others. All he cared about was that others should fulfill their calling. What would have become of Paul if there hadn't been a Barnabas?

Furthermore, when Paul dumped John Mark because he thought the young man was flaky and unreliable, Barnabas chose to go encourage John Mark rather than stay with Paul (Acts 15:37-40). Though we never see Barnabas' name again in the book of Acts, John Mark went on to collect the teachings of Peter into the gospel of Mark, and Paul later recognized his worth:

> *"Take (John) Mark, and bring him with thee: for he is profitable to me for the ministry."*
> (2 Timothy 4:11, parenthesis added)

We need Encouragers of Barnabas' caliber today: men and women who can see where the rest of us should be going and motivate us to fulfill our callings. Surely, they will be rewarded!

The Weaknesses and Dangers of Encouragers

Just like any other gifting, Encouragers are prone to weaknesses that are intrinsic to their gifting. Here are some of them:

- They can become egotistical about what they have helped others do.

- They can begin to encourage for selfish gain instead of the will of God and the good of His kingdom, and thus, becoming manipulative.
- They can become too "pie-in-the-sky" and oversimplify problems, leading to discouragement rather than achievement.
- They may be tempted to take Scriptures out of context to suit their own ends.
- They may look at teaching as impractical and therefore, not necessary. They want to be "Rah! Rah!" all the time and ignore details and nuances of the truth.
- They are really good at starting things, but not always great at finishing them.
- They may flit from one idea to another, without truly landing on or getting any one thing done.
- They can be impatient and try to move people too far, too fast.
- They may want to take shortcuts and not do things properly, hoping for a quick "win" that will actually become a long-term loss.
- Encouragers are apt to become the dreamers of impossible dreams.
- They can fall into the popularity trap, wanting to be liked more than being effective.
- They can make undisciplined people dependent upon them and become a crutch those people cannot live without.
- They may not recognize the importance of God's timing in the realization of people's gift development, and push people to take on new responsibilities before they are really ready.
- They may be quick to speak, slow to listen, and get impatient too easily. (The opposite of James's advice in James 1:19.)
- They are prone to step in when others are moving too slowly for them and take away their chance to grow in their gifts according to God's timing by doing things

for them, rather than letting them accomplish for themselves.

Wrapping It Up

There's no question Encouragers are important to getting good things done and pushing people towards their potential. Let's watch for them and appreciate them. We're all the better for having them and encouraging them in their encouraging.

Chapter Twenty

Are You A Provider?

One of my favorite Christian heroes is not a minister, but a businessman. His name was R.G. LeTourneau. He was a simple man who had dropped out of school in eighth grade. Despite his lack of education, he was a tinkerer and an inventor. He invented the bulldozer and hundreds of other earth-moving machines, collecting more than 200 patents in his lifetime.

When he was a young man and his business was just starting to take off, he made $35,000 profit, even though the US was in the midst of the Great Depression. He thought he was really something, so rather than paying the remaining $5,000 of his annual pledge to the Christian and Missionary Alliance Church, he decided to take the money and invest it in his business, justifying that he would make even more money and could make up his giving and then some at the end of the next year. From his figuring and predictions, he would more than double his profit the next year and make more than $100,000 with the investment.

Instead, the next year he ended up with $100,000 in debt. Looking back over what he had done, he determined never to make the same arrogant mistake again. Without the money to meet payroll and with his bookkeeper ready to quit, he pledged to give an extra $5,000 for the next two years to make up for his mistake.

Over the next four years, R.G.'s business exploded. He met his pledges and then some. Looking at how much his earthmoving-equipment business was making, and how much he really needed to live comfortably, he kept increasing his giving to missionary causes until he was tithing to himself! I don't mean he kept his tithe, but that he only kept ten percent and gave ninety percent to God!

Not only that, but he and his wife founded the LeTourneau Foundation comprised of ninety percent of the stocks of the LeTourneau Corporation, the earnings of which financed Christian work worldwide. At one point, this foundation was valued at $40 million.

R.G. once told *Forbes* magazine, "I like to do two things. One is to design machines, turn on the power, and see them work. The other is to turn on the power of the gospel and see it work in people's lives." Despite running one of the biggest earthmoving equipment manufacturing companies in the world, he would drop everything and fly anywhere to speak for Christ when he was asked. He was also the only man to have been president of both the Christian Businessmen's Committee International and the Gideons International. Not only was he generous with his money, he was generous with his time.[59]

You cannot give what you do not have.

Focus

Acquiring and using wealth for constructive purposes.

Vocational Application

The Provider is a money maker who is committed to increase his or her wealth for philanthropic purposes. You cannot give what you do not have. Thus, the Provider, the Giver, must earn and accumulate assets which he or she then freely entrusts to others, so that those with different gifts can achieve their missions more effectively.

To generously donate money for good causes and the welfare of others, the Provider must enter the world of business, the world

59 Paul Lee Tan, *Encyclopedia of 7700 Illustrations: Signs of the Times* (Garland, TX: Bible Communications, 1996), 4756.

of profit, even though there are Providers who are not necessarily big money persons. Their earnings may be modest, but they limit their spending so they can share their abundance.

"If your outgo is more than your income, your upkeep becomes your downfall." Providers understand this old adage, and have a good understanding of mathematics, budgets, and accounting necessary to providing for others.

The Provider is not just focused on making money and profit, but on its purpose: giving. The Messenger gives his time and talent as does the Helper and Explainer, so the Provider directs his asset-accumulating skills to the well-being of others.

Those with the **E**mbedded **N**atural **A**bility to earn and distribute have diverse business and vocational options, so they could be involved in any kind of business that provides products or services. In addition, the Provider may work in financial planning, financial analysis, investor relations, budget and actuary analyses in insurance, statistics, banking, rating and accounting as well as the credit industry or even legal fields.

Altruistic Application

Providers look around them for opportunities to give, and understand that they have been uniquely crafted by God to bring needed support to His work on the earth. Remember that it is God who has, according to His own will, placed **E**mbedded **N**atural **A**bilities in each of us. Those **ENA**s make life provisions for us and our families for sure, but beyond that, God has an agenda for each of us to work in selfless ways, which is the essence of being altruistic. The Providers way of achieving this goal is by employing his or her gift for the benefit of others. They know how to use wealth, but it does not use them. Nothing brings them more joy than being able to give what is needed to accomplish God's tasks.

The Gift of Providing

> *"Charge them that are rich in this world, that they be not highminded, nor trust in uncertain riches, but in the living God, who giveth us richly all things to enjoy;*
>
> *that they* ***do good****, that they* ***be rich in good works, ready to distribute, willing to communicate****;*
>
> *laying up in store for themselves a good foundation against the time to come, that they may lay hold on eternal life."* (1 Timothy 6:17-19)

In the *King James Bible*, the Provider is called a Giver. In contemporary terms, Providers are better known as philanthropists who seek the welfare of others by giving generous portions of money to causes they care about. Like R.G., these people tend to not only be tithers—those who give ten percent of their income to their churches (as all of us should if we are Bible-believing followers of our Lord) —but they give in excess of that to their church, other organizations or persons whose work they want to support, ranging from feeding orphans to caring for widows to alleviating poverty, ending disease, and much more. They also give money and resources to other gifted persons to free them from their financial obligations, so they can exercise their gifting, their ENA.

Providers donate, contribute, sponsor, and provide assets to meet needs. They are usually businesspeople, like Mr. LeTourneau, who have an uncanny knack for making money. They may be witty inventors, or simply able to make wise purchases and investments that produce wealth.

True Providers don't think of this as anything special, however. Instead they admire—and sometimes virtually envy—the work of the frontline ministers whose organizations and work they support.

Again, let me emphasize we are not talking about tithing here. Tithing isn't a gift. Tithing is giving back to God the first ten percent of our increase. Some think it is only an Old Testament law. However, Jesus affirmed its continuance to the Pharisees who were tithing but omitting the weightier matters of "law, judgment, mercy, and faith." Regarding the tithe, Jesus said,

> *"These things ought ye to have done, and not to leave the other (the weightier matters) undone."*
> (Matthew 23:23, parenthesis added)

We should all tithe. Tithing is also mentioned in the book of Hebrews as something that was still going on:

> *"Here men that die receive tithes."* (Hebrews 7:8)

The Provider wants to use his or her finances to motivate and help others in their service to others, but they do not want to be manipulated or pressured into doing so. Providers love to meet the genuine and legitimate needs of others. Providers are especially elated when they discover that their giving is the answer to someone's prayers.

Jesus the Provider

The ministry Jesus did cost money. We can see this in the stories of His feeding the 5,000 and the 4,000 in Matthew 14:13-21 and 15:29-38. In fact, one of disciples was the treasurer, the one who carried "the bag." You probably guessed it already. That was Judas (John 12:4-6, 13:29).

Jesus always fed His audiences, audiences that numbered into the thousands. Normally it was part of His ministry budget. But on one occasion, Jesus asked,

The Provider wants to use his or her finances to motivate and help others in their service to others.

> *"Whence shall we buy bread, that these may eat?*

> *...Philip answered him, Two hundred pennyworth of bread is not sufficient for them, that every one of them may take a little."* (John 6:5,7)

So a miracle was needed and a miracle they got from "five barley loaves and two small fishes."

We see a similar need met by a miracle when they owed the IRS. Jesus told Peter to catch a fish that would cough up the money (Matthew 17:24-27).

Many assume Jesus was poor. Scriptural evidence says otherwise. For example, we are told Judas embezzled funds from the common purse the disciples kept together to pay for their needs and give to help others when desired. If that purse was usually empty, don't you think someone would have noticed when money suddenly disappeared? All the disciples were either businessmen or people accustomed to keeping track of money, especially Matthew who had been a tax collector. Don't you think one of them would have noticed if some of it were mysteriously missing? Not noticing theft only tends to happen when you have more money than it is easy to track, not less.

Whether we have a little or a lot, we need to be faithful to Him in all we have.

Jesus also had an entourage that traveled with Him. This included the Twelve and their families, as well as other followers, and we see no record of Jesus performing any miracles to provide for these people's needs. He also wore clothes fine enough that the Roman soldiers gambled to win them, rather than discarding them or tearing them up. Who would do that for a pauper's rags?

The God of heaven is the God of more than enough. He always creates more than He needs and has storehouses of backups, even though, if He needed something, He could just create it out of thin air. Though it's a longer discussion and off-topic here, neither poverty nor having wealth have special spiritual benefits—one is not holier than the other. There are pitfalls that go with riches, and God has no love for ill-gotten gains, but being poor is certainly no blessing either. In several places God instructs the rich. In fact, the Bible speaks more about money than any other subject except salvation. That's because money is easy to mistake for happiness and success and can easily take up mental space for the rich and poor alike that should be spent meditating on God and His Word instead. This is why Jesus warned more than once:

> *"No one can serve two masters. For you will hate one and love the other; you will be devoted to one and despise the other. You cannot serve God and be enslaved to money."* (Matthew 6:24 NLT)

Like Jesus, whether we are gifted as a Provider or not, we need to remember that the only way to serve God instead of money is to make the money we have serve Him as much as we do. Whether we have a little or a lot, we need to be faithful to Him in all we have.

The Characteristics of a Provider

As we've already seen, Providers are people who are good at making money and giving it where it does the most good. What other attributes do Providers have?

Providers See Money as a Tool

Providers believe, in some way, shape, or form, that "money answereth all things" (Ecclesiastes 10:19), and are convinced that their abilities to make and invest money wisely in others is a fundamental necessity to the success of all. To them, money is not a status symbol or a measure of their importance, it is a tool to be used to get things done, just like a carpenter uses a hammer or a saw to make a cupboard.

Providers Are Fastidious about Business Principles

They believe that money is a trust from God and must be earned, managed, and distributed according to scriptural principles.

Providers are specialists in money matters. They understand economics and know the changing financial conditions, not unlike Brutus in his speech in Shakespeare's *Julius Caesar*:

> There is a tide in the affairs of men.
> Which, taken at the flood, leads on to fortune;
> Omitted, all the voyage of their life
> Is bound in shallows and in miseries.
> On such a full sea are we now afloat,
> And we must take the current when it serves,
> Or lose our ventures.[60]

When it comes to money, the principled Providers are *not* gamblers, but understand biblical financial principles. The Provider has learned from the only trillionaire in the history of humanity, Solomon, who owned more gold than the purported 147.4 million Troy ounces in Fort Knox.[61] The wealth of Solomon makes Bill Gates, Warren Buffett, Jeff Bezos, Charles Koch, Mark Zuckerberg, and Michael Bloomberg look like financial starters. For example, from Solomon we learn to invest:

> *"Cast thy bread upon the waters: for thou shalt find it after many days."* (Ecclesiastes 11:1)

We also learn how to diversify fifteen ways in our investing:

> *"Give a portion to seven, and also to eight; for thou knowest not what evil shall be upon the earth."* (Ecclesiastes 11:2)

(I'll give you the whole lowdown on this in my upcoming book titled, *God's Way to Riches*. There are a thousand ways to poverty, but only two ways to riches: God's and man's. Man's way

---

60 William Shakespeare, *Julius Caesar*, Full Text - Act IV - Scene III - Owl Eyes, accessed January 31, 2020, https://www.owleyes.org/text/julius-caesar/read/act-iv-scene-iii#root-71646-111

61 CBS News, "Almanac: Fort Knox," CBS News (CBS Interactive, June 28, 2015), https://www.cbsnews.com/news/almanac-fort-knox/)

can get you rich but is accompanied with all kinds of sorrows. But God's way?

> *"The blessing of the Lord makes a person rich, and he adds no sorrow with it."* [Proverbs 10:22 NLT])

Providers Are Well Aware of the Dangers of Loving Money Rather than God

Providers know the dangers of pursuing wealth and accumulating nice things:

> *"But they that will be rich fall into temptation and a snare, and into many foolish and hurtful lusts, which drown men in destruction and perdition.*
>
> *For the love of money is the root of all evil: which while some coveted after, they have erred from the faith, and pierced themselves through with many sorrows."* (1 Timothy 6:9-10)

By navigating through and around financial traps that commonly ensnare others, Providers are able to bring value and worth and even glory to God's work. They have avoided the "evil eye" Jesus warned about in the Sermon on the Mount. We are warned about this evil eye three times. Here is one of them:

> *"He that hasteth to be rich hath an evil eye, and considereth not that poverty shall come upon him."* (Proverbs 28:22)

An evil eye cannot see accurately. This leads to making distorted financial decisions without the wisdom, understanding, prudence, and security of biblical principle-based decision-making. Providers make decisions on principles, not merely by financial calculations. It is never economically right to do something that is morally wrong.

Providers Love Generosity and Get Joy from Their Giving.

Providers are generous as opposed to the clutching, grabbing, stingy, and selfish use of assets that many—even poor people—often display. They love the principle laid out by Paul:

> *"He which soweth sparingly shall reap also sparingly; and he which soweth bountifully shall reap also bountifully.*
>
> *Every man according as he purposeth in his heart, so let him give; not grudgingly, or of necessity: for God loveth a cheerful giver.*
>
> *And God is able to make all grace abound toward you; that ye, always having all sufficiency in all things, may abound to every good work."*
> (2 Corinthians 9:6-8)

Providers Are Resourceful and Careful with Money

The wise know how to get value from that which others would normally overlook or discard. Waste not, want not is their view. They are also thrifty and slow to let themselves or others spend unnecessarily or wastefully. Providers are careful even with small amounts of assets. They have learned from the greatest Giver of all time,

> *"He that is faithful in that which is least is faithful also in much: and he that is unjust in the least is unjust also in much."* (Luke 16:10)

Providers Serve God, Not Money

Despite all their attention on money and assets, Providers are careful not to become asset-enslaved. The Lord Himself said,

> *"Ye cannot serve God and mammon."* (Luke 16:13)

(This concept is so important that it is in both Matthew and Luke.) Here's another version of that Scripture:

> *"No worker can serve two bosses: He'll either hate the first and love the second or adore the first and despise the second. You cannot serve both God and the Bank."* (Luke 16:13)

To Providers, pursing God is their primary aim, and acquiring money is a tool to help accomplish what God wants done. A lot of rich people are unhappy and many even suicidal. Why? Here's why.

> *"For the love of money is the first step toward all kinds of sin. Some people have even turned away from God because of their love for it, and as a result have pierced themselves with many sorrows."* (1 Timothy 6:10 TLB)

Biblical Illustrations of Providers

They are many, but let's start with the commonly, but erroneously, named "Three Wise Men." The idea that there were only three is traditionally conjectured on the basis that they brought three gifts: gold, frankincense, and myrrh. Three guys on camels also fits nicely on a Christmas card, but this entourage *had traveled eight hundred miles*. There were so many of them that Herod felt threatened. Three lone travelers talking about worshiping a supposed king of the Jews would hardly have had that effect.

> Acquiring money is a tool to help accomplish what God wants done.

If you had traveled 800 miles by camel to see a king, would you have brought a $100.00 worth of gold? That seems pretty unlikely. Instead, they brought a *lot* of gold. Jesus started off in His life with a major financial gift. These giving, providing, wise men helped create an endowment for His future ministry, as well as financed his family's escape to (and life in) Egypt.

But there were others, some of whom were women. Three of them are named in that entourage that traveled with Jesus in His ministry years I mentioned earlier.

> *"And certain women, which had been healed of evil spirits and infirmities, Mary called Magdalene, out of whom went seven devils, And Joanna the wife of Chuza Herod's steward, and Susanna, and many others,* ***which ministered unto him of their substance****."* (Luke 8:2-3)

After listing the women's names it says,

> *"And many others who were contributing from their own resources to support Jesus and his disciples."* (Luke 8:3 NLT)

There was also another Mary, the one who poured a whole pound of expensive oil on Jesus' feet (John 12:3). Acts mentions Lydia, a seller of purple, who was an important early supporter of the church in Philippi (Acts 16:14). There was Tabitha (also named Dorcas), a manufacturer of women's clothing whom the Bible describes as "full of good works and almsdeeds" (Acts 9:36). (*Almsdeeds* were financial acts of charity.) And what shall we say of the virtuous woman of Proverbs 31 who was an entrepreneur *par excellence* with real estate investments, horticultural enterprises, manufacturing, and merchandising successes? It's pretty clear God has gifted both men and women to be Providers.

The Weaknesses and Dangers of Providers

Providers are fallible human beings, just like those receiving any of the other ENAs. Here are a few of the foibles they are prone to:

- They may find pride in their giving.
- They may make the mistake of publicizing their giving, so they will be seen as great people instead of secret giving, so that all the glory goes to God.
- They could begin to believe the idea that spiritual greatness is proven by financial success (1 Timothy 6:5). It's not, of course. It's proven by servanthood instead (Mark 9:35).
- They could fall prey to manipulative appeals for finances.
- They could give to pet projects that have no eternal benefit.
- They could feed the slothful or bad practices of others by "over-giving" and so enable their bad habits.
- They could get drawn into only giving to big projects instead of the necessities of the saints.
- They could fall into the trap of giving to continue programs, instead of considering how many people are impacted.
- They might use their financial abilities as a means to popularity and influence.
- They may feel guilty, whether it be real or imagined, over having personal wealth.
- They could become hoarders. (There is an actual clinically documented malady known as a "hoarding disorder.")
- They may give to alleviate their own sense of personal guilt and responsibility rather than actually helping the needy.
- They may excuse personal luxuries even when they are exorbitant and unnecessary.
- They may give without consulting their spouse.
- They may fail to check into perceived needs and listen to trusted counselors.
- They may simply give money when they should become personally involved.
- They may adopt a temporal focus instead of an eternal one (Matthew 6:19-20).

- They may classify others into social groupings based on their financial condition.
- They may fail to properly invest (Matthew 25:14-30).
- They may fail to give "as unto the Lord" (Matthew 25:35-46).

Most of us can understand, appreciate, respect, and value those whose gift is having the ability to accumulate and distribute wealth. We have high regard for them when we observe their generosity, their kindness, their liberality, their magnanimity, and their unselfishness.

These, like each of the giftings, are a special group of people. We should not only hold them in high regard; we should pray for them. Life for them is not as easy as most believe, and their *dis*-ease is aggravated the more by our highly materialistic culture.

> *"But they that will be rich fall into temptation and a snare, and into many foolish and hurtful lusts, which drown men in destruction and perdition.*
>
> *For the love of money is the root of all evil: which while some coveted after, they have erred from the faith, and pierced themselves through with many sorrows.*
>
> *But thou, O man of God, flee these things."*
>
> (1 Timothy 6:9-11a)

Wrapping It Up

The Provider's task, as men and women of God, is to flee the very things the culture promotes with such impunity. This is why, again, this is one gift in the midst of several that is meant to work together for the building up of the entire church. Providers need to be close to those who possess other giftings and work *with* them, just as the other giftings benefit from having Providers among them. All of them work together for the edification of the whole body.

Chapter Twenty-One

Are You an Organizer?

In 1979, the United States Treasury minted a coin to commemorate the life and work of Susan B. Anthony, who had toiled tirelessly from a young age before the Civil War to stamp out slavery and give women equal rights. However, Susan had been the other half of one of the strongest social reform teams in history. If she had been alive in 1979 when that coin was minted, she would have demanded that Elizabeth Cady Stanton's head be next to her own.

The fight for the passing of the Nineteenth Amendment granting women the right to vote in America began at least one hundred years before it became a reality in 1920. Those who brought it about had been strongly involved in the anti-slavery movement and other reforms as well, but Susan B. Anthony and Elizabeth Cady Stanton stand out above all the rest.

Susan and Elizabeth were lifelong friends. Born into a Quaker family, Susan never married, but dedicated herself to seeking freedom for those around her. Elizabeth, on the other hand, was married with seven children. Wherever Elizabeth lived, there was a room in her home for Susan. While Elizabeth worked from her home, Susan did what she could not. Susan rode the rails, making speeches to groups of men and women all over the country, raising awareness for the cause. She travelled alone and spoke throughout the nation, enduring persecution and loneliness in like amounts. Elizabeth was highly educated, but had been denied in attending the college of her choice because she was a woman. Instead she had to go to a woman's college. Elizabeth was a fine speaker too, but a better writer than Susan. When they were together, Susan often tended her children so she could write. When separate, Elizabeth sent countless letters to Susan, letters full of direction outlining the next steps to take as she spoke. Elizabeth had also organized, not only the first women's rights convention in Seneca Falls, New York, in 1848, but many other gatherings as well.

Both women were strong Christians, devoted to giving women not only their rights under the law, but also the same opportunities in life and education as men, so that women could find their places in society. When Elizabeth died, Susan said that Elizabeth had "forged the thunderbolts" which she had fired. Between the two of them, it is hard to pinpoint which one was the Organizer. That may be because they worked together as if they were one person toward the same end. However, if you look very closely, you notice that while Elizabeth wrote and taught and directed, Susan organized the campaign and the thousands of gatherings in which she spoke. It is one of the hallmarks of a true Organizer to not take the credit for their work, and be able to work comfortably as a team. Susan B. Anthony had done just that. Although she and Elizabeth never lived to see the adoption of the Nineteenth Amendment, they were the ones that had fought for it most. Together they organized for a great accomplishment.[62]

Focus

The Big Picture and organizing others to work together according to their giftings.

Vocational Application

Every orchestra needs a conductor; every choir, a choirmaster. Every company needs a CEO; every army needs a general; every ship, a captain; every automobile, a driver; every train, an engineer; every airplane, a pilot in command; every team,

---

62 "Elizabeth Cady Stanton," Wikipedia (Wikimedia Foundation, March 24, 2020), https://en.wikipedia.org/wiki/Elizabeth_Cady_Stanton)

a coach; every church a pastor. I think you get the picture. Organizers coordinate and instruct subordinates in the ways in which they perform their work effectively and efficiently.

The business and vocational possibilities for Organizers are endless. Management is necessary to plan, organize, staff, direct, and control all business functions. It must include the allocation of limited resources, whether financial, technological, or human. Those with the **E**mbedded **N**atural **A**bility to organize and oversee are often referred to as "born leaders," and leaders they are.

In most businesses, there is a hierarchy of management often referred to as low, middle, and upper management. They set goals and expectations for employees to reach. There are diverse styles of management. One of the most effective is referred to as "servant management" in which the employees are the experts, and management simply aids them in fulfilling their expertise.

Organizers and managers are required to keep their organizations on track. They do this by injecting motivation, creativity, discipline, enthusiasm and providing monitoring mechanisms, so that progress is measurable. People skills are an absolute. All entrepreneurship requires these leadership skills. Ultimately, the touchstone of success is whether or not the client or the customer has been well-served.

Altruistic Application

While God has indeed created organizers and leaders, His intent goes far beyond their being limited to secular business pursuits. God has a spiritual agenda for all of us and His church collectively. The church is a group of local people who have come together to represent God to a community and do His work. They want to accomplish God's agenda, His intended ministry, to people everywhere. Not only must His work be done, but God's work must be done God's way. And believe this: He has all the details necessary. The Lord Jesus made it unmistakably clear:

> *"I will build my church; and the gates of hell shall not prevail against it."* (Matthew 16:18)

Organizers are God's way of preventing the diffusion of responsibilities—or what's called "the bystander effect." It has also become known as "the Genovese Syndrome"[63] because of the following incident.

Catharine Susan "Kitty" Genovese was brutally stabbed to death outside her apartment building in Kew Gardens in the borough of Queens in New York City. The stabbing was witnessed by at least thirty-eight persons, none of whom called the police, each assuming that someone else had already done so. The responsibility was diffused. Researchers concluded that "contrary to expectations, larger numbers of bystanders decrease the likelihood that someone will step forward and help a victim."[64] My point is not to argue the psychology of the diffusion of responsibility, but merely to point out that this socio-psychological phenomenon can cause inaction when others are present. Because individuals assume that others have already taken, or will undertake, appropriate action, they do not. God has gifted Organizers to end the diffusion of responsibility.

> The Organizer is gifted with the task of pulling us all together to work with one purpose.

God intends to have entire vanguards of Organizers at the front: pioneering, leading, and spearheading His work. When this occurs, *gestalt* occurs. Gestalt theory was derived from a German word meaning "unified whole." In psychology, "the guiding principle behind the Gestalt movement was that the whole was greater than the sum of its parts."[65] To understand the whole (the

63 Lawrence R. Samuel, "The 'Genovese Syndrome,'" *Psychology Today* (Sussex Publishers, January 10, 2014), https://www.psychologytoday.com/us/blog/psychology-yesterday/201401/the-genovese-syndrome)

64 Sandi Mann, *Psychology: A Complete Introduction: Teach Yourself* (Great Britain, John Murray Learning, 2016).

65 5PsyH, "Gestalt Psychology," *The History and Systems of Psychology*, September 4, 2017, https://psychhistoryandsystems.wordpress.com/2017/09/01/gestalt-

Big Picture) is the only way to understand the individual parts. German psychologists Max Wertheimer, Wolfgang Kohler, and Kurt Koffka, the founders of Gestalt theory, wrote that all the parts of anything could only be understood in view of the whole.[66]

This in turn leads to synergism which is the interaction of two or more parts making the effect greater than the mere sum of the separate parts (or energies). This is the concept that each part brought into proper relationship to another part causes an effect greater than the sum of the two parts.

Here is a biblical example of synergism:

> *"One shall chase a thousand, and two put ten thousand to flight."* (Deuteronomy 32:30)

You would think that if one could chase a thousand, two would be able to chase two thousand. However, in functioning together, there is an energy acting upon each other in such a way as to produce an exponential effect instead. How effective we can be if we all work together! The Organizer is gifted with the task of pulling us all together to work with one purpose.

The Organizer

> *"Let the elders who rule well be considered worthy of double honour."* (1 Timothy 5:17)

In the *King James Bible*, the Organizer is translated as *ruler*. An Organizer is someone who has the ability to see the Big Picture. They can see what the individual parts should be doing, how they should perform; and then organize, direct, control, oversee, supervise, and manage everyone as a team accomplishing specific goals.

Let me illustrate a typical situation. A woman asks for prayer

---

psychology/)

66 "Gestalt Psychology," Wikipedia (Wikimedia Foundation, January 27, 2020), https://en.wikipedia.org/wiki/Gestalt_psychology)

for an unconverted son. (Yes, we should pray with her on the spot; and even though it's difficult to find a verse that indicates that people get saved by praying, it does not do any harm to pray that they will hear the message of Jesus, as it's always through hearing the gospel that people get saved.[67]) However, we don't stop there. We give the prayer request over to an Organizer. The Organizer asks the woman how to find her son and sends a Messenger to him to communicate the gospel. If the woman says, "Oh, he knows the gospel, but he just doesn't understand it," the Organizer will answer, "Okay, I'll send an Explainer to make it clear to him." If the woman should say, "He understands it, but he doesn't feel like responding," the Organizer would reply, "OK, I'll send an Encourager to stimulate his faith then."

If a prayer request came in for a family in the neighborhood whose house burned down, the Organizer would send Helpers to help them clean up and get back on their feet. If someone were sick or injured, the Organizer would send a Caregiver to pray for, and minister to, them. (We'll be covering that gifting next.) If needed, the Organizer would arrange meals to be sent to the family, be sure the kids had rides to school, and arrange for whatever needs to be done to help so that person can rest and recover.

As you can see, Organizers are administrative coordinators or "project managers." To function well, they must be given the designated authority, the power to act, that they require. Organizers are very similar to the centurion Jesus met who said,

> *"I say to this man, Go, and he goeth; and to another, Come, and he cometh; and to my servant, Do this, and he doeth it."* (Matthew 8:9)

The Organizer sends out a person whose gifting is relevant to the need.

---

67 Prayer is absolutely necessary in every situation. Prayer is how we get specific and detailed direction from God. However, prayer can never be a substitution for obedience to God's Word nor a replacement or an alternative for the practical application and functioning of each gifting.

Jesus as an Organizer

Jesus as the Organizer trained His disciples. He sent them out to specific geographical points with a specific task, a specific message, and detailed instructions. Then He set limitations on them: no purse, no money, no suitcase, no extra shoes, no second pair of underwear, and no staff (walking sticks or trekking poles). He was training them in what I call the "No Crutch Principle." He said,

> *"I send you forth as sheep in the midst of wolves: be ye therefore wise as serpents, and harmless as doves."* (Matthew 10:16)

The Lord told them they would be accused and end up in court. Shockingly, He told them not to even try to figure out what they would say when this occurred, but that the Holy Spirit would tell them what to say. He told them they would receive what they needed to say in those instances from God. What training came from Jesus, the Leader, Organizer, and Administrator? He taught them to depend upon the Spirit of God (Matthew 10:5-20).

After they'd been sent out, they had to report back to him everything that they had said and done. Here's why I call it the "No Crutch Principle." He sent them out again, saying,

> *"When I sent you without purse, and scrip, and shoes, lacked ye anything? And they said, Nothing. Then said He unto them,*
>
> ***But now, he that hath a purse, let him take it, and likewise his scrip: and he that hath no sword, let him sell his garment, and buy one."***
>
> (Luke 22:35-36, emphasis mine)

What training! Jesus told them to have no crutches! He would be telling us today to learn that we don't need microphones, video equipment, books, hairdressers, and a bunch of helpers. He would say that we only need His message and His Spirit. Once we learn that we don't need all those crutches, we can take them and they will be our tools instead.

Before He sent them out, Jesus made sure His disciples were equipped for the task ahead by teaching them what they were supposed to do and supernaturally endowing them with the abilities they would need. Jesus was forever the Leader, the Organizer. He orchestrated the feeding of the 4,000 and the 5,000 and directed the servants in the wedding at Cana. He told His disciples what to do to find the colt He would ride into Jerusalem on the day appointed, and where to go to set up their Passover dinner together (which became the Last Supper). He handed the tasks out to those best equipped to handle them.

The Characteristics of an Organizer

Organizers Are Big Picture People

They see the whole picture, the whole task. They see where each person fits into the task at hand. Organizers provide creative outlets in which each of the other gifts can function. Organizers provide opportunity, direction, and to some measure, control. In effect, Organizers are leaders in every sense of the word.

Organizers Are Delegators

It's not the responsibility of Organizers to do all the work they see that needs to be done; it's their job to assign the appropriate gifting to that work. Organizers are delegators, turning over functional responsibilities to others, who in turn should be accountable and report back the outcomes or what is needed to complete the task.

Organizers Are Team Players

Organizers are, above all things, team players. If they have no team, they have no function. *How* things get done is just as important to them as it is that they get each task done. Did everyone enjoy the process? Were any toes stepped on along the way? Did people grow in their gifts as they worked together? If there were people getting helped through the process, were they treated well? Did the end accomplish what it was supposed to for everyone involved? These and other questions like them are used by Organizers to keep their fingers on the pulse of team morale and effectiveness.

The Buck Stops with the Organizer

Organizers often have to "take the heat" if things are handled dubiously or ineffectively. Because of this, they tend to be people who can keep track of several things at the same time. They have grace for mistakes, but also grace to get things back on track, and keep everyone in good spirits while doing it.

Organizers Are Decisive

Decisiveness is another pertinent and necessary quality of the Organizer. They will listen to everyone's opinion, but they make sure issues are resolved, tasks are assigned, and decisions are finalized at the end of the meeting. They do this by firmly relying on two things: the Word of God and a thorough understanding of the realities of each given situation. Thoroughness is giving care, and sometimes even painful attention, to details in order to assure the job is done correctly and that everyone benefits throughout the process.

Biblical Example of an Organizer

Without question, the prize for the best example of being an Organizer in the Bible (aside from Jesus, of course) goes to Nehemiah. (If you suspect you may be an Organizer, you would do well to read his entire story in Nehemiah.) Nehemiah was tasked with rebuilding the walls of Jerusalem, which had been broken down and left desolate. Its gates had been burned with fire, and the city had been left neglected for decades. The Israelites had to rebuild the walls in the midst of enemy attacks, from which they, obviously, had no walls to hide behind for protection.

It was a daunting project requiring a thorough management of available materials and workers. To get it done, Nehemiah broke the project down into smaller tasks, organized and scheduled the work, and also provided security measures for the laborers and production teams. Each task needed to be sized according to workers' abilities. It was a task like that described by Confucius when he said, "The man who moves a mountain begins by carrying away small stones." We would probably say, "You eat an elephant one bite at a time." Organizers know how to eat elephants and move mountains. They have faith, which is what it takes to move mountains (Mark 11:23).

Organizers must have something even greater than faith though. They need to have love as the fundamental motivation behind every endeavor, for

> *"Though I have all faith, so that I could remove mountains, and have not charity, I am nothing."*
> (1 Corinthians 13:2)

And, actually, all of the gifts require love to work properly—which we'll look at more in Appendix Two.

The Weaknesses and Dangers for an Organizer

Organizers are not without their stumbling blocks. Just like each of the other giftings, there are weaknesses and dangers inherent in being an Organizer. Here are some of them:

- Pride because of their authority.
- Misuse of that authority.
- Becoming dictatorial.
- Avoiding work they should do by handing personal responsibilities off to others.
- Using people to achieve personal goals rather than corporate ones.
- Seeing people only as means to achieve an end.

- Overloading certain individuals because of their willingness to serve.
- Not caring sufficiently for the well-being of individuals or their families.
- Failing to give credit where credit is due.
- Overstepping their jurisdiction.
- Failing to get proper authorization from those to whom they are responsible.
- Failure to listen to the ideas, suggestions, and input of others.
- Showing favoritism.
- Not responding to the grievances and/or needs of those they supervise.
- Not enforcing biblical or ethical standards and cutting corners to get things done more quickly or economically.
- Failing to provide adequate instruction.
- Ignoring the goals and purposes of the individuals they direct.
- Boredom when projects cease to be challenging.
- Failing to exercise patience toward others.
- Choosing to pursue promotion beyond their skill level.

Wrapping It Up

I hope that you are beginning to see the whole picture: the necessity of all of the gifts working together as one as well as the importance of each individual gift. No gifting is unimportant; no gifting is preeminent. We certainly can and should appreciate those who see and understand the Big Picture, so they can lead us into godly fulfillment of great exploits:

> *"The people that do know their God shall be strong, and do exploits."* (Daniel 11:32)

The Organizers must be sure to work *with* the rest of the gifts with a servant spirit without being bossy. Each ENA has its place and function, but they must also work in proper balance with all the others.

Chapter Twenty-Two

Are You A Caregiver?

Clarissa Harlowe Barton, better known as Clara, began serving others as a school teacher, but had to give it up when failing health forced her to move away from Massachusetts to recuperate in Washington, D. C. She worked there for a while in a patent office, but it wasn't until the Civil War broke out that she found her true calling. When a group of thirty wounded men was delivered to the Washington Infirmary after a Baltimore mob attacked them, Clara arrived promptly and continued caring for them until the last man was able to leave the hospital.

Throughout the war, she would prove invaluable to the care and healing of soldiers. Many would have died without her. It was no easy task either. In his history of the involvement of people from Massachusetts in the war, Thomas Wentworth Higginson writes of Clara:

"During the long, disastrous peninsular campaign she went to the wharves daily, when the transports arrived with loads of suffering men from the swamps of the Chickahominy, her ambulance laden with dressings and restoratives, alleviating their miseries as they were removed to the hospitals. She went with railroad cars, loaded with supplies, to those wounded in the battles of Cedar Mountain, Chantilly, Fredericksburg and Antietam. She established her headquarters once in a tall field of corn; at another time, in a barn; and at Antietam, on the piazza of an abandoned house, working day and night with the shot and shell shrieking around her, her face black as a negro's, and her lips and throat parched with the sulphurous smoke of battle." [68]

Another book would have to be written for a full record of Miss Barton's war services and life's contribution. Of course, as you probably already know, Clara Barton used the skills she'd learned over the course of the Civil War to found the American Red Cross, an organization that is always among the first responders when tragedy strikes anywhere in the world today. The tireless example of Miss Barton still inspires doctors, nurses, and Caregivers today.

Can you even imagine where we would be without such people?

Focus

Comforting the distressed.

Vocational Application

In America we rejoice at the provisions of our Constitution, our statutes and our laws. As a result we have over 1.6 million 501(c)(3) non-profit organizations. They range from NGOs (Non-government organizations) to environmental charities to animal charities, educational charities, arts and cultural charities, and religious charities. There are food banks, disaster relief charities, private foundations, fraternal organizations, and civic leagues.

In spite of all this, America places only fourth in the world of all the countries giving to charity. We are led by Indonesia, Australia, and New Zealand. Of course, it must be recognized that all charities are not directed to human need; and unfortunately, large percentages of charity-designated monies are consumed by overhead and administrative costs, with some using 90% on overhead while only 10% reaches the needy. Churches, along with many a charity, have become businesses. It would seem that we, as a culture, tend to put organizations between ourselves and real human needs. This, not to mention corruption in the systems we have created, is a frustration to the genuine Caregiver.

---

68 Thomas Wentworth Higginson, *Massachusetts in the Army and Navy during the War of 1861–1865*, vol. 2 (Medford, MA: Perseus Digital Library, n.d.), 595-596.

There was a time when the primary motive to be medical doctors was driven by compassion, humaneness, kindness, and mercy instead of financial profit. When it comes to health care, we must ask, "Where is, as Shakespeare wrote, the 'milk of human kindness?'" Where is genuine care of another to be found in a narcissistic culture that has learned the mechanism of *showing* love without loving?

Government has taken over providing cold institutional distributions in contrast with the person-to-person caring touch. Persons become a mere number. Utilitarianism rules and moral obligations perish. Governmental distribution as a pejorative mechanism has invited a "working of the system" mentality. Humanitarianism has been reduced to a political ploy, a strategy to induce votes.

In spite of the all this, a person gifted and endowed by God with as a Caregiver can still be employed in meaningful occupations. They range from frontline contact with the needy, the helpless, the poor, the hurting, the sick and diseased, the lonely and forgotten. The Caregiver wants to be the contact person, not a cog in the wheel of a system, or lost in the maze of a bureaucracy.

It is always an advantage for all persons to be vocationally involved where their Embedded Natural Ability is functioning in their job description.

Altruistic Application

Selfless application to the physical, emotional, psychological, and spiritual needs of others is the hallmark of the Caregiver. Through their demonstration of Christ's character through their actions, the Caregiver shows forth His love and mercy for all humanity. Caregivers are not turned back by difficulties and truly find joy in alleviating the sufferings of those in pain or at risk. Their life's work is completely wrapped up in their attention to this task.

The Caregiver

In the *King James Bible*, the Caregiver is termed "he that sheweth mercy" (Romans 12:8). Today we would probably say, "a demonstrator of mercy." (I use the word *demonstrator* to denote one who shows, displays, presents, or causes to be visible.) A Caregiver is someone who is sensitive to the emotional, physical, social, and spiritual well-being of others, and wants to reach out to them with support and therapeutic action.

The Caregiver can sense the feelings of others and has sincere sympathy toward those in distress, almost any kind of distress. It seems that part of the development of Caregivers, the demonstrators of mercy, is that they themselves have had to suffer in some measure which brings an increased sensitivity to the hurt and pain of others—just as Clara Barton's illness forced her into a time of convalescence, and so she better understood the needs of those who would later be in her care.

Let's get some snapshots of this from the Bible. To get the full picture, we will get our first snapshot from the *King James* camera first. Here it is:

> *"Blessed be God, even the Father of our Lord Jesus Christ, the Father of mercies, and the God of all comfort."* (2 Corinthians 1:3)

Notice that God is "the God of *all* comfort." How much comfort? *All* comfort!

Did you know that about God? He is always in favor of your recovery, your redemption, your comfort! So much so, that one of the names of God, the Holy Spirit, is *Comforter* (John 14:16, 26; 15:26; and 16:7). Don't miss this! God is the God who comforts—*everyone—always*. It is His very nature, and we do know the core of His nature, don't we? *Love!*

That's why He is the God "who comforteth us in all our tribulation" (2 Corinthians 1:4). He wants you comforted for sure. But He also wants others comforted. See more of the picture now.

> *"The God of all comfort;*
>
> *who comforteth us in all our tribulation, that we may be able to comfort them which are in any trouble, by the comfort wherewith we ourselves are comforted of God."* (2 Corinthians 1:3b-4)

Here's a summary:
- God is a God of comfort.
- God comforts us in our troubles—all of them.
- We then get to comfort others with the comfort we got from God.

This is one of the essential experiences that Caregivers get as part of their training and development. Personal experience in suffering prepares Caregivers, the demonstrators of mercy.

Let's look at another snapshot, but this time let's look through the lens of *The Message:*

> *"God of all healing counsel! He comes alongside us when we go through hard times, and before you know it, he brings us alongside someone else who is going through hard times so that we can be there for that person just as God was there for us."*
> (2 Corinthians 1:3-4 MSG)

This is remarkable. Your suffering and discomfort are *not* in vain. Let's look through the *New Living Translation* lens:

> *"God is our merciful Father and the source of all comfort.*
>
> *He comforts us in all our troubles so that we can comfort others. When they are troubled, we will be able to give them the same comfort God has given us."* (2 Corinthians 1:3-4 NLT)

Caregivers motivated to remove hurt and/or bring healing to others bring solutions to long-term problems. Caregivers are caring. Demonstrators of mercy are merciful. They have the ability to gently handle people—unless of course, firmness is necessary to help them, which it sometimes is. Even then, they are like velvet-covered steel, firm but with a gentle manner.

The Caregiver, the Demonstrator of Mercy—what accurate representatives of God!

Jesus sees others through the Caregiver's eyes. Jesus hears the cries of others through their ears. And Jesus reaches out to touch, to heal, to affirm others through their hands. Through Caregivers, the touch of Jesus still has its ancient power. The hungry are still fed; the thirsty are still given drink; the naked are clothed; the sick are healed; the depressed awakened to faith; the demonized are set free and sanity is restored.

Jesus the Caregiver

There must be dozens of places in the Gospels in which we see Jesus caring for others. He was known for His compassion. One of the most tender stories is when he brought a young girl back to life:

> *"They came to the house of the ruler of the synagogue, and Jesus saw a commotion, people weeping and wailing loudly.*
>
> *And when he had entered, he said to them, 'Why are you making a commotion and weeping? The child is not dead but sleeping.'*
>
> *And they laughed at him. But he put them all outside and took the child's father and mother and those who were with him and went in where the child was.*
>
> *Taking her by the hand he said to her, 'Talitha cumi,' which means, 'Little girl, I say to you, arise.'*
>
> *And immediately the girl got up and began walking (for she was twelve years of age), and they were immediately overcome with amazement.*

> *And he strictly charged them that no one should know this, and told them to give her something to eat."* (Mark 5:38-43 ESV)

This story is even better if you go all the way back to where it first begins in verse 22. The ruler of the synagogue comes to Jesus, asking him to come heal his sick daughter. Along the way, a woman with an issue of blood sneaks a healing from Jesus by touching Him in faith. Jesus notices, however, calls her out, but then commends her for her courage. This delayed them just long enough for a servant to come to the ruler of the synagogue and basically tells him, "There's no longer a need to come. The girl has died." Undeterred, Jesus tells the father, "Do not fear, only believe" (Mark 5: 36). They continue on with just a few hand-picked disciples, and then the above healing happens.

We see Jesus' compassion and caring in every verse of this chapter, whether it be for the worried father, the interrupting woman, the crowds pressing in around him, or even the mocking mourners—but we see it especially with the little girl. Jesus said, "Little girl, I say to you, arise." Such tender words. Then He not only heals her, but He makes sure that they feed her! (I guess being dead works up quite an appetite!) This story touches my heart every time I read it. Jesus is most certainly the model Caregiver!

The Characteristics of a Caregiver

The Caregiver demonstrates a number of character qualities.

Helpers Meet Practical Needs; Caregivers Reach into the Person.

Helpers meet more practical needs and serve them. They may volunteer at the local food pantry; rake leaves and clean gutters for the elderly; or help organize and serve tables for the church's Thanksgiving dinner for the homeless in the area. They may help the same people more than once, but their goal is usually one-and-done. "I'm here to help or serve in this one capacity—if it is not necessarily something that is ongoing."

Caregivers tend to exercise their attention on the person themselves. They feel around the person's soul, checking for cracks and hurts: mental, emotional, physical or even spiritual wounds. Helpers might be involved with a social organization or they may organize the church food pantry, or work with a nonprofit that helps the homeless of which serving Thanksgiving is only one part. They might start a group in the church to advocate for widows in the community or volunteer at a halfway house to rescue women from domestic violence or sex trafficking or overcoming addiction. The Caregiver is more inclined to help nurse someone back to health.

Caregivers Discern Real Needs versus Enabling the Weaknesses of Others

Discernment is the ability to perceive that which may not be obvious to the casual observer. As with the Helper, sometimes Caregivers seek to care, but instead, inadvertently take away the person's ability to care for themselves and by doing so enable bad behavior and irresponsibility. Many with long-term issues can be very charming in getting assistance, but aren't really looking for help as much as a handout. Caregivers learn to tell the difference and always give help, even if that help comes as a "No, you need to do this yourself."

Caregivers Operate with Compassion

Compassion is marked by a concern for the sufferings and misfortunes of others. Certainly all of the gifts operate in some degree of compassion, but Caregivers fall under the Scripture:

> *"Some have compassion, making a difference."*
>
> (Jude 1:22)

The world can be cold and cruel, unfriendly and hostile. Everyone seems to be grabbing, grasping and clutching, eager to take from us and leave us empty, scared, alone, nervous, used and abused, broken, battered, bankrupt, and often bereaved. Caregivers tend to have a kind of compassion that endures in hope, even when situations seem hopeless. They have a supernatural capacity to care. They have qualities Frank E. Graeff described of Jesus in the hymn he wrote in 1901:

> Does Jesus care when my heart is pained
> Too deeply for mirth or song,
> As the burdens press, and the cares distress
> And the way grows weary and long?
>
> O yes, He cares, I know He cares,
> His heart is touched with my grief;
> When the days are weary, the long night dreary,
> I know my Savior cares.
>
> Does Jesus care when my way is dark
> With a nameless dread and fear?
> As the daylight fades into deep night shades,
> Does He care enough to be near?
>
> Does Jesus care when I've tried and failed
> To resist some temptation strong;
> When for my deep grief there is no relief,
> Though my tears flow all the night long?
>
> Does Jesus care when I've said "goodbye"
> To the dearest one on earth to me,
> And my sad heart aches till it nearly breaks,
> Is it aught to Him? Does He see?
>
> O yes, He cares, I know He cares,
> His heart is touched with my grief![69]

From the fevered brow of a baby to the cold chilly forehead of a person lying in a casket surrounded by mourning family and friends, someone needs to be there for people when they are at the

---

69 Frank E. Graeff, "Does Jesus Care?," Does Jesus Care?, accessed February 14, 2020, http://www.hymntime.com/tch/htm/d/o/e/doesjeca.htm)

end of their rope. It is the Caregivers, the Demonstrators of Mercy, who show up. They empathize. They

> *"Rejoice with them that do rejoice, and weep with them that weep."* (Romans 12:15)

Caregivers Long to Spread Physical, Emotional, and Spiritual Healing

Caregivers do not make decisions based on personal benefit, but on the verified needs of others. They are attracted—drawn like a magnet—to those in trouble, and they want to be part of the solution to their problems. They want to release the gospel, not just for individual salvation from sin on earth, but for healing that will allow that person to be a stable, contributing member of their community.

Caregivers Demonstrate the Mercy of God.

Mercy, one of the great attributes of God, is mentioned 365 times in the Bible. Jeremiah had it right when he wrote,

> *"The Lord's lovingkindnesses indeed never cease, for His compassions never fail.*
>
> *They are new every morning; great is Your faithfulness."* (Lamentations 3:22-23 NASB)

Want to see what that looks like? Watch a Caregiver in action.

Biblical Illustrations of Caregivers

Remember the illustration Jesus used called the parable of the Good Samaritan? (You can read the story in Luke 10:30-36.)

A traveler is trekking the seventeen miles from Jerusalem to Jericho and he

> *"Fell among thieves, which stripped him of his raiment, and wounded him, and departed, leaving him half dead."* (Luke 10:30)

There he was, bleeding and dying on the side of the road. A priest—a church leader—comes by, sees the dying man, and walks on by on the other side of the road. He completely avoids the guy.

Then there came a Levite—or we might say a church worker. He takes a little closer look, but he too walks on by without any effort to help. (Interesting isn't it, what the Bible captures in phrases like "like people, like priest" [Hosea 4:9]?) Of all those who would have the highest likelihood of helping a robbed, beaten, dying man, you would think it would be the religious people, especially the religious leaders. The fact that this is not the case is indeed stomach-wrenching. (Non-Christian Christians! This is a painful truth.)

Happily, the story doesn't end there. A Samaritan—a non-racist Samaritan—came by this beaten, robbed, half-dead Jewish man. (Remember the verse we already looked at in John 4:9? "The Jews have no dealings with the Samaritans." The opposite was also true. The Samaritans had no dealings with the Jews. The animosity between these two groups was mutual, not unlike the hatred between the Serbs and Muslims in modern Bosnia, or between the Catholics and Protestants in Northern Ireland or the forever it seems, tribal wars between some of the estimated three thousand tribes of Africa.)

But not on this day, *Hallelujah!* A Jew: near death, beaten, and robbed was not cared for by fellow Jews but by an enemy, a Samaritan. Instead of forsaking him like the others, the Samaritan said OK, rolled up his sleeves, and dug in.

> *"And when he (the Samaritan) saw him (the robbed and beaten Jew), he had compassion on him,*
>
> *and went to him, and bound up his wounds, pouring in oil and wine, and set him on his own beast, and brought him to an inn, and took care of him."*
>
> (Luke 10:33-34, additions mine)

What was the difference? Compassion among other things. (It's embarrassing, isn't it, when non-Christians seem more Christian than those who profess to be Christians?) This Samaritan was a Caregiver, a true demonstrator of mercy. Beautiful! Awesome! Well done! Bravo! Splendid! Applause please!

But the story didn't end there. The Caregiver doesn't hold back. The Samaritan is not content yet. He must see this Jew back up on his feet again. Caregivers don't do things by halves. The Samaritan Caregiver had already done the trauma-reducing, life-saving, and medical response of an EMT. He had already used his donkey/jeep to provide the best ambulance service possible, moving the man from the crime scene to a safe zone. But then he does even more, a lot more:

> *"And on the morrow when he departed, he took out two pence, and gave them to the host, and said unto him, Take care of him; and whatsoever thou spendest more, when I come again, I will repay thee."* (Luke 10:35)

The Samaritan took care of business, *all* the business at his own expense plus! I say "plus" because he not only paid the current bill, but committed himself to cover any ongoing expenses until the Jewish man was whole. No excuses, no alibis, no ifs or buts, no conditions, just love and compassion for another—even when the *other* was a one-time adversary and combatant. Kinda reminds you of Jesus, doesn't it?

> *"While we were yet sinners, Christ died for us."*
> (Romans 5:8)

Can you imagine what planet Earth would be like if all of humanity cared for all the rest of humanity like this? We'd have to call it heaven on earth. Thank you, Caregivers!

Caregivers respond not only to the call for help, but to a whisper, a whimper, a groan, a sigh, or a tear. And they connect deeply and emotionally. Are they needed today? *More than ever!* Let me once again indulge in sharing the poetry and prose of days gone by. Shakespeare's *The Merchant of Venice* contains a further description of a Caregiver:

> The quality of mercy is not strained;
> It droppeth as the gentle rain from heaven
> Upon the place beneath. It is twice blest;
> It blesseth him that gives and him that takes:
> 'Tis mightiest in the mightiest; it becomes
> The thronèd monarch better than his crown:
> His sceptre shows the force of temporal power,
> The attribute to awe and majesty,
> Wherein doth sit the dread and fear of kings;
> But mercy is above this scept'red sway;
> It is enthronèd in the hearts of kings,
> It is an attribute to God himself;
> And earthly power doth then show likest God's
> When mercy seasons justice.[70]

The Weaknesses and Dangers for Caregivers

The Caregiver also has weaknesses that are inherent to their gifting. Here are some of them:

- Pride that they possess a capacity for caring that others do not
- Bitterness towards those not as sensitive to the needs of others as they are
- Resentment if not appreciated
- Over-sentimentality
- Led by emotion rather than intelligence
- Unwillingness to be vulnerable in order to heal or help
- Being overly sensitive.
- Being unforgiving by taking sides with the injured against those who caused the injury without knowing the facts
- Creating a codependent relationship with those they are helping

---

70 William Shakespeare, *Merchant of Venice*, public domain, Act IV, Scene 1, lines 182–195.

- Being possessive: taking over from the person's rightful authority
- Failing to be firm in disciplining others for their own good
- Becoming bitter toward God for allowing suffering
- Developing a savior complex
- Becoming too physically/emotionally close with someone to whom they are giving care, thus allowing a bonding that can lead to sexual temptation
- Neglecting personal, marital, and family priorities because they are busy caring for others
- Blaming others for not helping
- Failure to address spiritual needs as well as physical and emotional ones
- Trying to make themselves always look good through false humility and "always saying the 'right' thing."
- Burning themselves out
- Adopting a "martyr complex": acting as if they are sacrificing everything and that others should put them on a pedestal because of what they do

Wrapping It Up

Caregivers, like each of the other six giftings, are an absolute essential. Without them, few would be touched by, "the milk of human kindness." Few would know the real nature of God, as revealed by Jesus who was "touched with the feeling of our infirmities" (Hebrews 4:15). So go the Caregiver, the demonstrators of mercy.

Chapter Twenty-Three

A Summary

Focus: You

When you walk across the stage of time, stand at the *exist* sign and look back at your life, what will you see? My highest wish for you is that you will be able to smile, I mean smile big, and say, "I did it my way." Your way because you discovered you, the real you, the gifted you; and you took care of business, the business of lovingly blessing others by simply letting the divinely Embedded Natural Ability given to you *flow*. It's a life flow, a flow from God through you and your giftedness to others.

And what can be your expectation? You will hear a voice—calm, clear, and concise. It will be the voice of God and this is what He'll be saying to you—four declarations:

> *"Well done, thou good and faithful servant: thou hast been faithful over a few things, I will make thee ruler over many things: enter thou into the joy of thy lord."* (Matthew 25:21)

The best is yet to come. The stakes are really high! You are important! Don't let life pass you by. Live undistracted, unintruded upon, focused on being true to the *you* that God made.

Thank you for reading this book. I am dedicated to the single task of explaining the truth in its simplest and purist form to as many people in the world as possible. My mission is based on the text,

> *"Ye shall know the truth and the truth shall make you free."* (John 8:32)

I want you to be free—free to be the real you.

Please don't miss the Supplements. The first explains the Big Picture of how we should all fit into a community of other followers, respecting and working with the diversity of those with other Embedded Natural Abilities. The second takes a closer look at the intricacies of embracing God's perspective of ourselves.

God bless you!

Supplement One

The Big Picture for the Body of Christ

The Theological Context of Spiritual Gifts

> *"There is one body, and one Spirit, even as ye are called in one hope of your calling; one Lord, one faith, one baptism, one God and Father of all, who is above all, and through all, and in you all. But unto every one of us is given grace according to the measure of the gift of Christ."*
>
> (Ephesians 4:4-7)

I have referred to the body of Christ and the church interchangeably, but I think it might be time to take a moment and describe what I mean by those terms. If I say the word *church* today, many will think of organized religion or the building on the corner where we see people going in and out on Sunday mornings. While that is a widely held understanding of what *church* means, it is not the biblical one.

Is *church* a building? A structure? An organization? Not according to the Bible. In the Bible, the word *church* represents an assembly of Jesus' followers. The church is not the building, but the people who gather there. The church is people, not structures or institutions. Each follower is an individual member of that collective body.

"Ye (all of you) are the body of Christ, and (each of you) members in particular."
(1 Corinthians 12:27, additions mine)

The church is not the building, but the people who gather there.

This concept is wonderful in its application. It means that you and I are to Christ today what His body was to Him when He was on the earth. When I view you properly, that is, as a member of Christ's body, then I will treat you just like I would Christ because *you are the body of Jesus*. What esteem! What respect! What admiration! What appreciation! What reverence! What a concept!

In 1 Corinthians, we discover that there are three different groupings or "diversities" of gifts given to us, the church.

"Now there are ***diversities of gifts****, but the same Spirit.*

And there are ***differences of administrations****, but the same Lord.*

And there are ***diversities of operations****, but it is the same God which worketh all in all.*

But the manifestation of the Spirit is given to every man to profit withal." (1 Corinthians 12:4-7)

The three groups are gifts of administration, which are five in number; gifts of operation, which are seven in number; and gifts of manifestation, which are nine in number. These gifts come from the grace of God. The Greek word for both *grace* and *gift* are the same word: *charis*. It is the word from which we get the English word *charisma*, which refers to a person who has "a special magnetic charm or appeal."[71] In the Greek, it means something more along the lines of gifts that give us

71 Merriam-Webster, *Merriam-Webster's Collegiate Dictionary*, 11th Edition (Springfield, MA: Merriam-Webster, 2014), s.v. "charisma."

certain predisposed skills and inclinations, or "endowments."[72] (The Greek word *charisma* is translated as "gifts" in verse 4 above.) This passage also pronounces that there are three groups of *charismas*—or twenty-one distinct gifts in all—given to the church, listed in the following chart:

The Theological Context of Spiritual Gifts
The 21 Spiritual Gifts of the Spirit In the Church

Operation Gifts (Romans 12:6-8)	**Administrative Gifts** (Ephesians 4:11-12)		**Manifestation Gifts** (1 Corinthians 12:7-10)
The Messenger Proclaiming **The Helper** Serving **The Explainer** Teaching	**The Missionaries** Apostles **The Forewarners** Prophets **The Out-Reachers** Evangelists	Spoken Gifts	**Non-Conceptual Prayer** Tongues **Explaining Prayer/Praise** Interpretation of Tongues **Empowered Speech** Prophecy
The Encourager Exhorting **The Provider** Giving **The Organizer** Ruling	**The Church Elders** Pastors **The Church Elders** Teachers	Revealing Gifts	**Imparted Information** Word of Knowledge **Imparted Wisdom** Word of Wisdom **Identifying Spirit Types** Discerning of Spirits
The Caregiver Showing Mercy	**These Administration Gifts** are given to develop, mature and perfect the Operation Gifts, the **E**mbedded **N**atural **A**bilities **(ENA)** of each person so that they can do the work of the ministry! All ministry is categorically defined by the Operation Gifts, the ENA: Proclaiming, Serving, Teaching, Exhorting, Giving, Ruling and Showing Mercy.	Power Gifts	**Curing of Sickness** Healing **Supernaural Achievements** Working of Miracles **Imparted Confidence** Faith
These Operation Gifts Embedded Natural Abilities ENA are given before birth, by God, one to each person specifically and define his or her chief operating mode for the duration of life.			**These Manifestation Gifts** are resident in the Holy Spirit and thus are available to each person to help him or her fulfill whatever his or her personal gift is, one of those as listed in the Operation gifts, **ENA**.

* *Most Non-Bold Print In the Listing of the Giftings are from the King James Bible*

The seven gifts, or ENAs, we've been referring to are the gifts referred to in Chapters 17-22 planted by God within us in the first 270 days of our existence—before anyone had even laid eyes on us. These seven gifts are what 1 Corinthians 12:6 calls "diversity of operations." They are the abilities, the "how" of

72 W. E. Vine, et al., *Vine's Complete Expository Dictionary of Old and New Testament Words* (Nashville, TN: Nelson, 1996), 264.

God's Spirit working through us. They are divinely **E**mbedded **N**atural **A**bilities.

Though the other gifts mentioned in the chart above are not the main topics of this book, I want to take time to clarify the other two groups: the "differences of administrations" and the "manifestations of the Spirit."

The seven giftings we've been referring to are the endowments or "diversities" of operation as outlined in Romans 12:6-8. These giftings are strengths of function—not personality types, but areas in which we have Embedded Natural Abilities and preferences. We each have the ability to operate in one of these seven giftings.

The Ephesians 4:11-13 list are the "administrations" or positions of servant leadership in the church. They are often referred to as "offices."

Apostles: We most often refer to apostles as missionaries or church planters. As mentioned earlier in this book, *apostolos* means "one sent to represent another and made out of the same substance."[73] Thus an apostle or a missionary takes the substance of the church and are sent out to a different geographical location, often to a different culture or nation.

Prophets are Forewarners. They tell of impending dangers by alerting persons, peoples, churches and even nations of spiritual and moral dangers. They give forceful and cautionary advice about conduct and actions. They put people on alert, often after the same blueprint as the Old Testament prophets—with tears, crying out, and what might seem like extreme measures to those who do not understand them or their message.

Evangelists are messengers to the unconverted and teachers to all of us on how to reach others. They are the Outreachers with the primary mission of taking the gospel, the good news, to those who have not heard about the great redemption offered to mankind through the death and resurrection of the Son of God and God the Son, Jesus Christ who provided forgiveness,

---

73 James Strong, "652. Apostolos," Strong's Greek: 652. ἀπόστολος (apostolos) -- a messenger, one sent on a mission, an apostle (Biblehub), accessed February 14, 2020, https://biblehub.com/str/greek/652.htm)

cleansing, and recovery to all who will properly respond.

Pastors are Leaders, often referred to as elders, or *presbuteros* in Greek.[74] Generally there is a senior or lead pastor or elder who is accompanied by a plurality of elders who share in the responsibility, care, and oversight of a church, a local gathering of Christians. Their role is analogous to that of an under-shepherd whose responsibilities are to oversee, administrate, teach the Scriptures, and pray for the sick as indicated in James:

> *"Is any sick among you? Let him call for the elders of the church; and let them pray over him, anointing him with oil in the name of the Lord."*
> (James 5:14)

Pastors and elders are also responsible for discipline in a local gathering of Christians to assure correct doctrine, moral purity, and unity.

Teachers, in an administrative context of a local gathering of Christians, are essentially elders that are specifically appointed to instruct in various specialties of doctrine, principles of life, and life management.

It is through these administration gifts that the Holy Spirit *administrates* the Church. These gifts are not given to persons, but to the assemblies of believers. They are sometimes called the fivefold ministry or the ministry gifts, as if the offices of apostle, prophet, evangelist, pastor, and teacher are the real ministers, but they are not. They are the administers, called to release the ministry Christ has embedded in each of His people. These fivefold ministers are gifts given to the *real* ministers in the body of Christ—they are there to instruct the Messengers, the Helpers, the Explainers, the Motivators, the Providers, the Organizers and the Caregivers who are the real ministers, so they can go out into the community and be the hands and feet of Jesus. Look at the longer passage:

---

74 James Strong, "4245. Prebuteros," Strong's Greek: 4245. πρεσβύτερος (presbuteros) -- elder (Biblehub), accessed February 14, 2020, https://biblehub.com/greek/4245.htm)

"And he gave some, apostles; and some, prophets; and some, evangelists; and some, pastors and teachers;

For the perfecting of the saints, for the work of the ministry, for the edifying of the body of Christ:

Till we all come in the unity of the faith, and of the knowledge of the Son of God, unto a perfect man, unto the measure of the stature of the fulness of Christ." (Ephesians 4:11-13)

You may ask, and rightly so, "Where do these come from? And who are they?" The biblical insight that answers these questions is found in Romans 11:29 where the Bible says that the "gifts and the calling of God are without repentance." Those who occupy administrative positions are simply individuals who possess, like all of us, one of the gifts of Romans 12, but are then *called* of God to fill these administrative positions. It simply means that they are to take their personal gift and focus them back on the rest of the church members who actually do the "work of the ministry."

These "called" persons are to focus on the Messengers, the Helpers, the Explainers, the Encouragers, the Providers, the Organizers, and the Caregivers to perfect them, to improve them, to build them up so that they—the Messengers, the Explainers, the Encouragers, the Providers, the Organizers, and the Caregivers—can do the work of the ministry. And what is the work of the ministry? To carry a Message or Help or Explain or Encourage, or Provide or Organize or Give Care. This is the categorical summary of all ministry. In the *King James Version* the summary of all ministry uses these words: to proclaim, serve, teach, exhort, give, rule, and show mercy.

The Manifestations of the Holy Spirit

You've got it now. The first group of gifts, called the "operations" are Embedded Natural Abilities given to people. Although we all can do all of them in part, each of us has been given *one of them in particular.* The second group of giftings is the Administration gifts which are actually positions in the church filled by certain persons of the first group who are *called* to fill the church positions, and the focus of their gift is to help the rest of us to know, develop, perfect and use our personal giftings to help others.

As if all of this were not enough, God has also provided nine other giftings available to each of us and all of us to help us fulfill our personal mission. These are referred to as the "manifestations of the Spirit." Of them, it says, they are "given to every man [or woman] to profit withal" (1 Corinthians 12:7). They are resident in the Holy Spirit Himself, as indicated by the repeated phrase, "by the same Spirit" throughout 1 Corinthians 12. As 1 Corinthians 12 tells us,

> *"All these worketh that one and the selfsame Spirit, dividing to every man (and woman) severally as he (the Holy Spirit) will."*
> (1 Corinthians 12:11, additions mine)

They are supernatural tools, so to speak, to enhance our effectiveness. The Holy Spirit offers each of us access to all nine of these gifts to use in conjunction with our own Romans 12 gifting as we encounter situations and circumstances in which we need them to assist us in helping others. Here they are (in scriptural sequence):

1. The Word of Wisdom: Imparted Wisdom
2. The Word of Knowledge: Imparted Information
3. Faith (A supernatural faith beyond our day-to-day faith): Imparted Confidence
4. Gifts of Healing: Curing of Sickness
5. The Working of Miracles: Supernatural Achievements
6. Prophecy: Empowered Speech
7. The Discerning of Spirits: Identifying Spirit Types
8. Divers (Different) Kinds of Tongues: Non-Conceptual Prayer or Praise

9. The Interpretation of Tongues: Explaining the Prayer or Praise

Another way of seeing this group of nine is to list them in three groups of three. The first group are revealing gifts, the second are communicating abilities, and the third are demonstrations of power. Here they are organized in that manner:

1. Spoken Gifts

- Divers Kinds of Tongues: Non-Conceptual Prayer or Praise
- The Interpretation of Tongues: Explaining the Prayer or Praise
- Prophecy: Empowered Speech

2. Revealing Gifts

- The Word of Wisdom: Imparted Wisdom
- The Word of Knowledge: Imparted Information
- The Discerning of Spirits: Identifying Spirit Types

3. Gifts of Power

- Gifts of Healing: Curing Sickness
- The Workings of Miracles: Supernatural Achievements
- Faith: Imparted Confidence

There are entire books that teach about these manifestations, but our primary focus is not these, but exploring and being equipped with the endowments of Romans 12. Nevertheless, it is necessary to give some explanation of these so here goes.

The Spoken Gifts

Divers Kinds of Tongues: Non-Conceptual Prayer or Praise

There are three kinds of tongues referred to in the Bible. First there are the tongues of men, which are earthly (known) languages. There are about 6,500 of these. However, less than a thousand people speak about 2,000 of them.[75] Then there are the tongues of angels, the languages spoken by angels, whether heavenly or demonic. These are mentioned in the "Love Chapter" of the Bible:

> *"Though I speak with the tongues of men and of angels."* (1 Corinthians 13:1)

Last of all, there are "unknown tongues" referred to in 1 Corinthians 14 throughout the chapter. Speaking in tongues is non-conceptual prayer.

> *"For he that speaketh in an unknown tongue speaketh not unto men, but unto God: for no man understandeth him; howbeit in the spirit he speaketh mysteries."* (1 Corinthians 14:2)

Note that the speaking is to God, and it is non-conceptual, meaning it is not understood by the one delivering it, but is quite mentally abstract. Here's more biblical clarification:

For if I pray in an unknown tongue, my spirit prayeth, but my understanding is unfruitful.

> *"What is it then? I will pray with the spirit, and I will pray with the understanding also:*
>
> *I will sing with the spirit, and I will sing with the understanding also."* (1 Corinthians 14:14-15)

75 Infoplease Staff, "How Many Spoken Languages," Infoplease (Infoplease), accessed February 14, 2020, https://www.infoplease.com/askeds/how-many-spoken-languages)

Notice that a person can even sing and use not-conceptual words. Which of us has never needed to pray and we didn't know how, or we didn't have words to express what was in our hearts and minds? It is at those times when we still can pray with the help of God's Holy Spirit.

> *"Likewise the Spirit also helpeth our infirmities: for we know not what we should pray for as we ought: but the Spirit itself maketh intercession for us with groanings which cannot be uttered."*
>
> (Romans 8:26)

On the day of Pentecost, the Holy Spirit enabled the disciples to speak in tongues. It was a mixture of tongues for the people on the street were astonished. Note their response:

> *"Now when this was noised abroad, the multitude came together, and were confounded, because that every man heard them speak in his own language.*
>
> *And they were all amazed and marvelled, saying one to another, Behold, are not all these which speak Galilaeans?*
>
> *And how hear we every man in our own tongue, wherein we were born?"* (Acts 2:6-8)

Interpretation of Tongues: Explaining the Prayer or the Praise

Whenever a tongue is spoken as a solo, so to speak, in front of a group of listening others, it must, according to Scripture, be interpreted, so that those listening can understand the essence of what was spoken to God, and derive benefit from it. Remember that tongues is prayer or praise *to God*. Even on the day of Pentecost as referred to above, what was the interpretation of those who heard those tongues in their own language?

> *"We do hear them speak in our tongues the wonderful works of God."* (Acts 2:11)

They were hearing the praises of God.

When a tongue is spoken and there are others listening, it must always be interpreted. Otherwise, according to the Bible, those listening will think you are either drunk or crazy. Neither of these is a good idea.

> *"Except ye utter by the tongue words easy to be understood, how shall it be known what is spoken? For ye shall speak into the air.*
>
> *There are, it may be, so many kinds of voices in the world, and none of them is without signification.*
>
> *Therefore if I know not the meaning of the voice, I shall be unto him that speaketh a barbarian, and he that speaketh shall be a barbarian unto me.*
>
> *Even so ye, forasmuch as ye are zealous of spiritual gifts, seek that ye may excel to the edifying of the church.*
>
> *Wherefore let him that speaketh in an unknown tongue pray that he may interpret."*
>
> (1 Corinthians 14:9-13)

This gift comes with a warning! The Bible declares that if the person (or someone nearby) does not have the interpretation, they are to keep quiet.

> *"If there be no interpreter, let him keep silence in the church; and let him speak to himself, and to God."* (1 Corinthians 14:28)

And why? If:

> *"There come in those that are unlearned, or unbelievers, will they not say that ye are mad?"*
>
> (1 Corinthians 14:23)

> *"In the church I had rather speak five words with my understanding, that by my voice I might teach others also, than ten thousand words in an unknown tongue."* (1 Corinthians 14:19)

The answer to the abuse and misuse of tongues is not disuse but rather *proper* use.

Prophecy: Empowered Speech

One of the wonderful aspects of each of these manifestations of the Spirit is that they actually are God helping each of us be more effective. You are never alone.

Empowered speech (prophecy) is God reaching through us to others with His message.

> *"We then, as workers together with him."* (2 Corinthians 6:1)

Imagine that! God helping each of us, working together with us. What a partnership!

This particular gift is God's Spirit helping us speak and communicate to others. And it has three primary goals: to edify which means to build others up; and exhort which means to encourage others; and comfort which means to provide relief from grief or distress.

> *"But he that prophesieth speaketh unto men to edification, and exhortation, and comfort."* (1 Corinthians 14:3)

Never, never forget that *God is love.* Whenever we carry His love message to others, He offers help—big time. He empowers our speech, our message. Truth be told, empowered speech (prophecy) is God reaching through us to others with His message. Tongues, interpretation of tongues and prophecy are all spoken gifts empowered by God's Spirit help through us.

The Revealing Gifts

The Word of Knowledge: Imparted Information

Imagine the wonder of God's Spirit imparting information to you beyond that which you have studied, read, or learned. It would have been nice if this had happened every time we took a history test or an algebra exam. However, the word of knowledge (or the imparted information from God) is not a substitute for undisciplined learning. It is God transmitting information to us beyond human resources *in order to fulfill some wonderful divine intent.* This is imparted cognizance. Here is the Old Testament prediction regarding this and other Holy Spirit imparted giftings:

> *"And the spirit of the Lord shall rest upon him, the spirit of wisdom and understanding, the spirit of counsel and might, the spirit of knowledge and of the fear of the Lord;*
>
> *and shall make him of quick understanding in the fear of the Lord: and he shall not judge after the sight of his eyes, neither reprove after the hearing of his ears."* (Isaiah 11:2-3)

The Word of Wisdom: Imparted Wisdom

Wisdom is the ability to be guided by sound judgment. It is the ability to act in the best way in a given situation. One may know certain facts or information, but wisdom is the how to apply them in real life. It is the ability to respond to all life situations from an accurate point of view, and no perspective on any subject can be more accurate than God's.

It is true that a measure of wisdom can come from reason, thinking through the details, considering how best to apply actions, and life experience. That's why God gave us reasoning capability and why He says, "Come let us reason together saith the Lord" (Isaiah 1:8). Experience, our own or that of others, may be helpful, but there are two sources of wisdom on which you can always count. The first is the Bible which contains a record of God's points of view on a multitude of life-related subjects. Hence we are instructed,

> *"Wisdom is the principal thing; therefore get wisdom: and with all thy getting get understanding.*
>
> *Exalt her, and she shall promote thee: she shall bring thee to honour, when thou dost embrace her."*
> (Proverbs 4:7-8)

The second reliable source of wisdom is that which is imparted to us by the Holy Spirit directly. Mind you, this imparted wisdom will never contradict the wisdom of the Bible. God is the Author of both. This imparted wisdom is referred to as one of the manifestations of the Holy Spirit. Note the following instruction:

> *"If any of you lack wisdom, let him ask of God, that giveth to all men liberally, and upbraideth not; and it shall be given him."* (James 1:5)

> *"If you want to know what God wants you to do, ask him, and he will gladly tell you, for he is always ready to give a bountiful supply of wisdom to all who ask him."* (James 1:5 TLB)

Whether you are a Messenger, a Helper, an Explainer, an Encourager, a Provider, an Organizer or a Caregiver, imagine the value of getting wisdom from God, so you know how to best use your personal gifting!

However, we should all understand that according to the Bible, there are two kinds of wisdom and they can be known by their fruit (their outcome). The following passage will make this crystal clear.

> *"If ye have bitter envying and strife in your hearts, glory not, and lie not against the truth.*

This wisdom descendeth not from above, but is earthly, sensual, devilish.

For where envying and strife is, there is confusion and every evil work.

But the wisdom that is from above is first pure, then peaceable, gentle, and easy to be intreated, full of mercy and good fruits, without partiality, and without hypocrisy.

And the fruit of righteousness is sown in peace of them that make peace." (James 3:15-18)

The Discerning of Spirits: Identifying Spirit Types

Back of every effect there is a cause. Back of every cause there is a motive. Back of every motive there is a person. A person is a "spirit being" significantly distinct from an animal. Animals are locked into their bodies and ruled by instinct. Beavers build dams; dogs bark; horses neigh, and so forth. People, however have the ability to create, make choices, and decide. Animals will never build automobiles or computers or make moral choices. Persons, however, think and act without the reign of instinct. They are creative. This creativity was part of what God designed in Genesis 1 when He said, "Let us make man in our own image."

It is often important in life to understand what kind of person is behind a certain act or responsible for a particular outcome. Hence, we are given by God, the ability to identify, not only the *type* of spirit, but the *condition* of that spirit. There are only four kinds of spirits:

1. The Holy Spirit
2. Angelic spirits
3. Demonic spirits
4. Human spirits

Much can be understood about each of these types of spirits: their characteristics, scope of activities, limitations, and intentions.

For our purposes, it is only necessary to understand that God will enable us to discern (or identify) what or who is behind some given activity. Here is a biblical example: Jesus was explaining to the disciples His need to suffer for our sins and be killed. Peter, if you can imagine, spoke up and rebuked the Lord Jesus, saying, "This shall not be unto thee" (Matthew 16:22). Where did Peter get such an idea? Why would he contradict the Lord? We find the answer in Jesus' response when He said to Peter, "Get thee behind me Satan!" in Matthew 16:23. Jesus identified the spirit behind Peter's statements.

The Power Gifts

The Gift of Healing: The Curing of Sickness

The word *manifest* means to make evident, show plainly, display, or reveal. Each of these manifestations of the Holy Spirit are visible workings of God's Spirit. Our bodies are generally designed by God to heal themselves naturally. However, supernatural (above and beyond the natural) healing of the sick can occur in several different ways.

Sometimes a person is healed through the "prayer of faith." When the leaders of the church are called, and follow the Bible's instruction, which is to pray over a sick person, anointing them with oil in the name of the Lord, and praying the prayer of faith, here's what happens:

> *"And the prayer of faith shall save the sick*
> *and the Lord shall raise him up."* (James 5:14-15)

The Bible contains other instruction about healing too. James wrote about confessing our faults and prayer:

> *"Confess your faults one to another, and pray one for another, that ye may be healed. The effectual fervent prayer of a righteous man availeth much."*
> (James 5:16)

Jesus made it plain that those who preached the gospel would have signs following their preaching, and directed that we lay hands on people as we prayed for them to be healed.

> *"They shall lay hands on the sick, and they shall recover."* (Mark 16:15-18)

Jesus illustrated this Himself on many occasions. Once, a woman came to Him who had not been able to stand up straight *for eighteen years*. Obviously, she had a severe back problem, and needed healing.

> *"And He laid His hands on her: and immediately she was made straight, and glorified God."*
> (Luke 13:13)

The person with the prayer of faith literally prays *with the faith of Jesus*, which has immediate supernatural effect on the situation at hand.

We also exercise faith. Seven times persons were told by Jesus Himself, "thy faith hath made thee whole." These occasions included the healing of blindness, leprosy, and a woman who was losing blood continually for twelve years. We have long known we are saved by faith, but too few know that they can *be healed* by faith. Faith in what? Faith that Jesus included healing in His redemptive work on the cross. Isaiah plainly states the four benefits of Calvary:

> *"He was wounded for our transgressions, he was bruised for our iniquities: the chastisement of our peace was upon him; and with his stripes we are healed."* (Isaiah 53:5)

Peter cites the same, saying,

> *"By whose stripes ye were healed."* (1 Peter 2:24)

Unfortunately many uninformed or misinformed Bible teachers have opted to teach that these passages refer to psychological or spiritual healing only, and not physical. The proof that such is not the case is affirmed directly by Jesus.

> *"He cast out the spirits with his word, and healed all that were sick:*
>
> *that it might be fulfilled which was spoken by Esaias the prophet, saying, Himself took our infirmities, and bare our sicknesses."*
>
> (Matthew 8:16-17)

Obviously each of the nine manifestation gifts are available to all of us to help us carry out our personal gifting. It does seem, however, that some of the manifestation gifts are more directly related to some of our personal giftings. For example, a Messenger might have the greatest need for the empowered speech or imparted wisdom gifts. The Helper might need imparted information and imparted understanding. It is reasonable to also assume that Caregivers may need healing manifestations.

The Working of Miracles: Supernatural Achievements

All of the manifestation gifts are supernatural. God is supernatural. Often we need the supernatural to meet the needs of ourselves and others. So beyond those already mentioned is this diversity of miracles which God manifests to us or through us. These could include miracles of provision (food, finances, and so forth), a change in the weather; changes in circumstances; deliverances; and many others.

> Our loving God still wants to bless others through us, and is not just willing, but eager to do so.

It is easy to find any and all of the above-mentioned miracles in both the Old and New Testaments. The important issue, however, is for us to realize that our loving God still wants to bless others through us, and is not just willing, but eager to do so. Miracles often establish authenticity, and most certainly bring glory to the Lord.

The Gift of Faith: Imparted Confidence

This manifestation, the gift of faith, is God imparting faith and confidence to you so you can do what you never thought you could. Primarily faith comes from hearing and hearing and hearing. Advertisers want you to hear of their product until you have faith that you need it, and go and buy it. Jesus made it plain in His warning,

> *"Take heed what you hear."* (Mark 4:24)

Proper faith comes from two vital sources. The first is,

> *"Faith cometh by hearing, and hearing by the Word of God."* (Romans 10:17)

Belief comes from hearing the message(s) of God's Word—repeatedly! Repetition is not only the classic method of learning but the mechanism of receiving faith as well. Don't miss the Master's message,

> *"Man shall not live by bread alone but by every word that* ***proceedeth out of the mouth of God****."*
> (Matthew 4:4, Luke 4:4, emphasis mine)

What should you do with the Word of God? Know it in your head. Stow it in your heart. Show it on your face, and then sow it in the world. Know It! Stow it! Show it! Sow it!

Primarily faith comes from hearing the Word of God. In addition, there are times when each of us faces issues and challenges, and doubts our ability to meet them. When that happens, the Holy Spirit comes alongside us to impart confidence, and give us faith to do what we thought we could not do. This is delightful. Imagine the Messenger receiving imparted confidence.

Faith! The Helper, the Explainer, the Encourager, the Provider, the Organize, and the Caregiver all receive faith when they need it. How we are empowered to change the world!

How the Church Is Designed to Work

Christ is the Head of the church. The Head is the leader, the brains. The rest of us are His body designed to do today, in His physical absence, what He did when He was here. He was perfect. He performed all the gifts perfectly. Wasn't He a great Messenger? And didn't He serve? He even washed feet. And didn't He explain and teach? Didn't He motivate and exhort? Men forsook all to follow Him. And didn't He provide and give? He paid the bills and gave food for thousands. And didn't He administrate and rule? He organized not merely the Twelve, but the seventy and the five hundred and the thousands that came to Him. And didn't He care and show mercy? He healed the sick, cast out evil spirits, and blessed the children. And He did all of these perfectly.

Now we are commissioned to take His place, performing the same seven basic functions—each of us doing our part to His glory. Jesus, by His Spirit, calls and installs leaders in His church to train us, develop us, lead us, and take us forward like a mighty army. Apostles are sent on behalf of us to take the same substance of who we are to other peoples and lands. They are the "sent ones." (Remember that *apostalos* literally means, "out of the same substance as" to indicate that God sends them out like ambassadors of heaven—made "of the same substance as" the kingdom.) Prophets give us (and whole groups of churches) godly direction. Evangelists reach the lost and teach us how to reach the lost. Pastors are Jesus' under-shepherds, called to care for the local church body, and teachers are in those bodies to explain God's Word to all of us. (The terms, standards, and qualifications for these "called ones" in the local churches are clearly listed in 1 Timothy 3:1-13 and Titus 1:6-9.) The Holy Spirit also manifests Himself through us—through the "gifts of the Spirit," to help us. For example, a Caregiver may need a word of wisdom—a supernatural understanding of what to do specifically in a situation—on how to best heal another's wounds. A Proclaimer may need supernatural faith to pray for a person in a special way. (I'm sure you can think of various other examples of how the gifts of the Spirit operate.)

All of these gifts (those in Romans 12, Ephesians 4, and 1 Corinthians 12) are meant to work together in perfect order, each of us contributing its part as each of us are enabled to do so by the Holy Spirit. Oh, the power of a church functioning in their giftings, roles, and being open to the manifestations of the Spirit! What a wonderful picture of the kingdom of heaven being spread across the earth.

Far too many think of the church only as a place to meet for worship services, sermons, prayer meetings, and Bible studies. While those are good things, where are our meetings to manifest the body of Christ to our communities? Where are our meetings to gather together and do God's work?

Small ministry groups responsible to the administration gifts should cluster with their diversity of giftings to plan how to best serve and meet the needs of the people around us, both inside and outside the church. Sure, we should all be functional with our personal gifts all the time, but that shouldn't preclude us from gathering lists of needs (of people in need), and then assigning each church member to answer these needs according to his or her gift. We should send the Messenger to the lost or wayward, enlist Helpers and Servants to serve the deprived or disadvantaged, and commission the Explainer to bring understanding to the bewildered, the puzzled, the perplexed, and the confused. We should seek out the discouraged and dispatch the Encourager, and send the Provider to take food and meet the basic needs of the poor among us. To the hurt, damaged, and distressed, let's designate the Caregivers. And to make all this happen, let's yield to the leadership of our Organizers.

Then let's gather together on Sunday to worship, fellowship, learn, and rejoice that we have been part of the glorious church, the functional body of Christ bringing the real Jesus to humanity. Then let's also go the extra mile to be Jesus to our neighbors, just as Jesus instructed us to do in Matthew 5:41. And remember the parable of the Good Samaritan? Let's do it all.

But What If We Don't?

Some think I go too far when I say such things. "God is in control," they tell me. "Why does it matter what we do?" They don't seem to understand the crucial role and obligation God gave each of us when He gifted us. That is why the parable of the talents is so important (Matthew 25:14-30). It doesn't ask the questions, "How much have you prayed?" "How much have you studied the Bible?" "How large have you grown your church?" or "How many meetings have you attended at the church this month?" in order to judge who is the "good and faithful servant." Instead, it asks, "What have you done with the crucial gift(s) I have given you?"

Crucial means that the gifts are very important or vital to your life. Do you have any idea how important you are to others? If you don't exercise your gifting, what a loss! The whole universe will miss the good you could have done. Persons you would have influenced (even salvaged from the world system which is actively determined to destroy them) would be robbed of your blessing. And what about God? Would God miss you? Would God miss the good of you?

> The whole universe will miss the good you could have done.

Contrary to what theologians might tell you, the answer is yes. I want to give the theologians credit for being well-meaning, however many of them are wrong—dead wrong—at least about this. I will never forget a class in seminary where this controversy came up. The professor, a respected and wonderful man whose legacy lives on in many of us, became quite upset with yours truly for saying each of us has an irreplaceable part to play in the plans of God.

The text under question was this one:

> *"And I sought for a man among them, that should make up the hedge, and stand in the gap before me for the land, that I should not destroy it: but I found none."* (Ezekiel 22:30)

When my professor asked me what I thought of the passage, I answered, “Respectfully, sir, God was stuck.”

For that I received the biggest theological whipping of my life. “God is never stuck!” he shouted. Then a tirade ensued. Ouch, I took a beating! But remember the adage, “He that is convinced against his will is of the same opinion still.”

Sometimes God finds a “work-around.” Sometimes, it seems, He doesn’t. The fact is there is no substitute for you. Let me repeat: *You are not a copy, or a clone.* You are an original, a first edition. There is no one like you. No one can ever take your place. You are indispensable, crucial, all-important, essential, and necessary. Without you, without you functioning in your God-given capacity, others will *not* receive life-sustaining ministry God intends to give them through you.

If we are not obeying His callings, how is it that He is responsible when bad things happen on the earth?

If the Messenger does not preach the gospel—and preach it accurately—men, women, and children may be lost forever. If the Helper doesn’t serve, many could drown in loss and despair. If the Explainer doesn’t teach, many will never understand their place in God’s overall plan for the earth. If the Encourager doesn’t motivate and encourage, lives could be wasted in timidity and fear of failure. If the Provider doesn’t give, underfunded ministries will be crippled, if not aborted. If the Organizer does not administrate and lead, confusion will reign. If the Caregiver does not reach out, oh, the loss! So many would not be cared for, would remain unattended. Oh, the plight of the wounded and unhealed. If there is no one willing to step into the gap and intercede as God has called us to do, if we are not obeying His callings, how is it that He is responsible when bad things happen on the earth?

Eternity literally hangs in the balance. Once you discover your gift, heed the same urgency Jesus had when He said,

"I must work the works of him that sent me, while it is day: the night cometh, when no man can work.

As long as I am in the world, I am the light of the world." (John 9:4-5)

Did He not turn His mission over to us? Did He not declare,

"Ye are the light of the world. A city that is set on an hill cannot be hid.

Neither do men light a candle, and put it under a bushel, but on a candlestick; and it giveth light unto all that are in the house." (Matthew 5:14-15)

Please, please, never underestimate the importance of your mission. Humanity is waiting.

Supplement 2

A Closer Look

The Consequences of Not Liking Your Self

As we covered in chapter two, this is our big question: *To like you or not like you.* This is a question every one of us faces. The future well-being of our life will hinge upon our conclusion.

> *"Woe unto him that striveth with his Maker!"*
> (Isaiah 45:9)

Woe to you if you do not like yourself. The word *woe is used* 107 times in the *King James Version.* "Woe" is a crying out, a lament of caution which is often prolonged based on its urgency. It means to take care that you make no mistakes. Be alert, attentive, vigilant, prudent, discreet, and take heed. This is critical; there are three serious "woes." Big trouble is lurking behind each one.

You were your mother's baby, but God made the "you" He placed inside that baby. That's why we were taught to pray, "Our Father, who art in heaven." God made the *real you* and you do not want to be in strife with God. You will lose if you contend with the Almighty, your Maker. He made you and He's got big plans for you and for your life—plans that will take an eternity. He brought you into existence. He produced, fashioned, constructed and built you. You better like the "you" He fashioned. If not, woe! Big trouble that could last the rest of your natural life (and later) could occur. Let's look further.

> *"Woe unto him that striveth with his Maker! Let the potsherd strive with the potsherds of the earth. Shall the clay say to him that fashioneth it, What makest thou? Or thy work, He hath no hands?"* (Isaiah 45:9)

Let me paraphrase this: "Will the pot say to the Potmaker: 'Hey, You did a lousy job?' Will the clay talk back to the Potter? Will you carry on a dispute with God? Will you tell God that His hands are clumsy, and that He messed up when He made you the way you are?"

You should really *really* like yourself. You were in the hands of an Artist that makes no mistakes, the hands of a Sculptor that makes no blunders. What's the big deal? In your deepest part, you must choose to accept your "self": the self that God made—or you will decide to reject your "self": the self that God made. You will either like your self or dislike your self. Upon this fundamental foundation, your future will be determined. My advice in the strongest of terms would be for you to respond to God as David wrote:

> At your core, you need to embrace yourself.

> *"I will praise Thee; for I am fearfully and wonderfully made: marvelous are thy works; and that my soul knoweth right well."* (Psalm 139:14)

Say it every time you look in the mirror, every time you see a picture of yourself.

You can either be grateful for the way God made you or not. You will either celebrate yourself or criticize yourself. Suicide does not begin with a bottle of pills, a knife, or a rope. Self-destructive behaviors begin here. If you treat yourself the way God made you, self-destructive behaviors will not even cross your mind. At your core, you need to embrace yourself. You will rarely have to deal with depression if you do this. God loves you and you are a product of that love. Self-acceptance or self-rejection affect everything.

The person who does not like him or her self will spend the rest of their lives trying to be like someone else, always comparing themselves with others. It is thus that superiority complexes or inferiority complexes are created, depending upon with whom we compare ourselves. Instead compare yourself with God. You will not have an inferiority complex, but walk in humility, if you do that. Back to the woes.

Striving with our Maker was the first woe. Here are the other two.

> *"Woe unto him that saith unto his father, What begettest thou? Or to the woman, What hast thou brought forth?"* (Isaiah 45:10)

These are the other two woes, the one is to blame your father, and the other is to blame your mother. Some of us blame our parents for what we are. That's a bad choice. Self-rejection plus blame is still self-rejection. We must, however, come to grips with what's so "woeful" about blaming your father or mother.

The attitude we are supposed to have toward our father and mother is clear, but unfortunately not often practiced. We are instructed to "honor thy father and thy mother" (Exodus 20:12a). Honoring your father is the antithesis of indicting him for "begetting" you. Honoring your mother is the polar opposite to incriminating her for what she "has brought forth."

Your father and your mother were the conduits, the instruments, God used to bring you into the world. Anybody that had a significant role in bringing this *one-of-a-kind you* into the world should be esteemed. The rejection of your father and mother, regardless of their faults and failures, brings these "woes" into our lives. Disregarding these warnings will bring damage and destruction into our present and future lives.

"Whoso curseth his father or his mother, his lamp shall be put out in obscure darkness."
(Proverbs 20:20)

This simply means that our light, our ability to influence others the proper way, will be terminated, and we will not have a positive or godly effect on those around us, if we do not honor our parents. In contrast, if we honor our father and mother, we will not have woes but blessings. Take a look.

"Honour thy father and mother; which is the first commandment with promise;

that it may be well with thee, and thou mayest live long on the earth." (Ephesians 6:2-3)

What is the essence of these two promises? First, it will be well with you. You will have success in every area of your life; and the condition of your spirit and your conscience and your example will empower you forward. Second, you will live long on the earth. You will have fewer health issues. Your spirit and a healthy condition of mind, which comes from the proper honoring of your parents, will prompt, induce, stimulate and encourage you forward. The spiritual clutter that comes from dishonoring parents will not contribute to your physical and mental demise, so you will be set up for better success. The health of your relationship with your parents will affect the health of your body: You will live long—and well!

"O man, who art thou that repliest against God? Shall the thing formed say to him that formed it, Why hast thou made me thus?

Hath not the potter power over the clay, of the same lump to make one vessel unto honour, and another unto dishonour?" (Romans 9:20-21)

Here's the *Message* translation to help us better understand these verses.

> *"Who in the world do you think you are to second-guess God? Do you for one moment suppose any of us knows enough to call God into question? Clay doesn't talk back to the fingers that mold it, saying, "Why did you shape me like this?" Isn't it obvious that a potter has a perfect right to shape one lump of clay into a vase for holding flowers and another into a pot for cooking beans?"*
>
> (Romans 9:20-21 MSG)

What are the woes of not liking you? I want you to grasp this. I submit to you that you will have *an artificial sense* of inferiority. You'll have an *artificial* inferiority complex. You will think something's wrong with you when it's not. And an artificial sense of inferiority is as devastating as if it were earned for real. So, what are the woes of not liking you? I have quite a list.

1. You will blame God and/or your parents.

Number one, you will end up blaming God or your parents, or maybe both. When you reject yourself, when you don't like you, you're going to blame somebody. You may blame God because He's your Maker; or your father because he brought you forth, and you got ties to him. Or it's your mother. So the first woe is that you will end up blaming God and/or your parents for what you are that you don't like.

2. You will be bitter towards God and/or dishonoring towards your parents.

If you blame God, you'll become bitter. If you blame your parents, you will not have the ability to honor them. And so, every time Father's Day or Mother's Day comes around, you know you have to do it, but you don't feel like it. In reality, we should feel like it 365 days of the year, not just one.

3. **You will assume God doesn't like or love you.**

If you don't like you, since God made you, you will assume that God doesn't like you either. You will also assume He doesn't love you. Of course, this leads to a tremendous sense of being alienated from God and leads you into having an inability to trust Him in other aspects of your life.

4. **You will assume others won't like you.**

If you don't like yourself, why would you think other people will like you? You probably won't, and that's not a nice way to live.

5. **You will hide or disguise the real you.**

It gets worse. When we assume that others will not like us, we then hide or disguise the real us, the real you. This could lead to an abnormal shyness or social withdrawal. You may try to make up someone you think people will like. You will work at presenting yourself in a certain way in hopes that you will be accepted because you think people don't like you. Of course, this leads to an artificial existence. As a result, clothes and appearances can become paramount. How one appears to others becomes all important.

6. **You will create a caricature of you that you think others will like.**

You will manufacture a new you that you think other people will like. To do this, you'll check out what things people like or dislike, and then shape yourself, so that they will like you. In the process, you distort the real you. This is essentially the dynamic that occurs with peer pressure. The pressure to conform to the group around you in order to be accepted drives out a sense of personal identity. Individuality gets lost. As a result, perfectionism can become compulsive.

7. You may compensate through materialism.

You will seek certain kinds of compensations to make up for the fact that you don't like you. It could be through things. You think that if you have "stuff," it will help you feel better. You'll go shopping more often and buy more stuff because you don't like you. In the end, selfishness, not self-love, may become the driving factor.

8. You will experience abnormal sensual temptation.

A person who does not have an authentic self-like will tend to look for love and acceptance in all the wrong places. The emptiness caused by self-rejection begs for someone (or something) to fill that gap. All people yearn for someone to care for and love us; and someone to see our value and affirm us. However, if you do not like your self, you will attempt to fill the void by grasping at virtually anything that has the appearance of acceptance by others. Consequently, those with concealed evil and selfish motives can become attractive. You will think you're being accepted by them, when what is really happening is that you are entering into a potentially abusive situation. Lust has many disguises for love. Lust impersonates affection.

As you spend massive amounts of time making yourself physically attractive, you may falsely imagine that if someone is attracted to you physically, they must really like the *real you*. This is incredibly dangerous. If your body is not for sale, don't advertise it. Whatever you advertise is what buyers seek. Show off your body, and you will attract those interested merely in those parts. Yuck. They'll be coming after you all right, but for immoral and dishonest reasons.

After being used or abused in the "dating context," you get discarded for someone else. Discarded! How degrading! Your already low self-esteem is further reduced and demeaned. Sex is a poor substitute for self-assurance.

9. You will not have genuine self-respect.

Respect is showing esteem, regard, reverence, and admiration for another person. Without self-respect one loses a proper sense of dignity. Factually speaking, you are royalty of the highest order, a son or daughter of the Most High God. You were designed for nobility and grandeur, character and poise. These attributes engender respect. Respect is not snobbishness. We are not speaking of being a spoiled, pampered brat, but rather seeing yourself properly and accurately with confidence, faith in oneself, and self-regard. Without self-respect, you will mistreat yourself in hundreds of ways.

10. You will not believe you are worthy of respect (but will seek it anyway).

If you do not like you, you will not believe that you are worthy of respect, even though you seek it anyway from other people. Do you understand the pain of not liking yourself? Of thinking you're inadequate, inferior, and that there's something wrong with you? You may feel like you are always missing something. I want to affirm to you, my friends, that God never intended that you live the rest of your days thinking ill of yourself. We're going to see how to recover from this in a few moments. You might cover it up. You might hide it. You might mask it. You might put some kind of veneer over it on the outside, but inside you think you're unworthy, unloved, unliked, and unsought. And I'm not sure that we can tally up the pain that comes from this condition.

11. You will secretly believe your critics.

Secretly, secretly, not openly, you will mentally side with those who make fun of you, mock you, despise you, point their finger at you, ridicule you, and even call you names. The internal fortitude that comes from liking yourself is no longer there; and so when the enemies come in (as they invariably will) with various mental attacks, the ability to withstand them is not there.

Why? Because you don't like you either. So you hardly blame others for doing the same, even though you might openly do so.

12. You will side with the Adversary against yourself.

You need to understand a little bit about the Devil.

> *"And I heard a loud voice saying in heaven, Now is come salvation, and strength, and the kingdom of our God, and the power of his Christ: for the accuser of our brethren is cast down, which accused them before our God day and night."*
>
> (Revelation 12:10)

First of all, he really hates you, more than you can even understand. He has this name—the accuser of the brethren—and he once had access to heaven. His access was legal. God was legally obliged to listen to him—until Calvary, where he was defeated and cast down. Satan no longer has access, and God is no longer obliged to talk to him. Before that though, the Devil was always accusing the saints. And now, after Calvary, he is cast down, but he is still carrying on that same activity. He may no longer have access to the ears of heaven, but he is making up for it by continually assaulting the ears of men.

He is constantly pointing his finger at you. Satan, the Devil, is your adversary. Like a roaring lion, he's walking about the children of men, and *he wants to devour you*. Remember that. *We are called upon to resist him steadfastly in the faith.* What faith could that possibly be? It certainly includes faith in your own personal worth and value. He accuses you in an effort to shake you from liking yourself. He is God's archenemy, and since you are the creation of God he wants to get to God *by getting to you*. Don't let him.

You may be wondering, *Where do all those crazy ideas I get come from about how bad I am, and how worthless I am?* They come from your adversary, the Devil. Note this Scripture about self-opposition:

> *"In meekness instructing **those that oppose themselves**; if God peradventure will give them repentance to the acknowledging of the truth;*
>
> *and that they may recover themselves out of the snare of the devil, who are taken captive by him at his will."* (2 Timothy 2:25-26, emphasis mine)

> *"Gently instruct those who oppose the truth. Perhaps God will change those people's hearts, and they will learn the truth.*
>
> *Then they will come to their senses and escape from the devil's trap. For they have been held captive by him to do whatever he wants."*
>
> (2 Timothy 2:25-26 NLT)

If you do not like you, you will be functioning against yourself. Notice how we get into the condition of opposing ourselves, speaking ill of ourselves, and thinking evil about ourselves. How do we get to the point "not liking" ourselves? The recovery for this state is to get out of the "snare of the devil." It is the Devil that wants you not to think of yourself the way God thinks about you. When you don't like yourself, you're really siding with the your adversary.

13. You will view others as competitors.

Rivalry is the natural inclination when we do not like ourselves. No one wants others to be better than, higher than, more popular than, or smarter than us. You will compare yourself and consciously or unconsciously live in tension with others. Your ability to genuinely be congratulatory to others will be impaired. You may be able to weep with those who weep okay, but rejoicing at the success of another becomes more difficult. You don't want to be outdone. This can even influence you to search out others that you can dominate. You look at them as inferiors so you can feel superior. A non-genuine acceptance of ourselves will cause you to view others through biased eyes.

14. You may not be able to get along with your siblings.

No grouping of persons should be more bonded than family. That bonding begins with a father and a mother, indissolubly attached to each other by the covenant bond of marriage. That bonding extends to each child, with the mother and father equally attached and securely joined to each of them. Such bonding includes respect, esteem, and honor, as well as a commitment toward one another. That same attachment should extend from a child to each brother and sister. "We be brothers" is a phrase indicating the strongest of attachment and association. According to the Bible, one of the purposes for a brother is to have someone you can count on when trouble comes.

> *"A brother is born for adversity."* (Proverbs 17:17b)

> *"A friend is always loyal, and a brother is born to help in time of need."* (Proverbs 17:17 NLT)

The Message translation says, "Brothers stick together in all kinds of trouble." Not liking one's self not only interferes with liking a sibling, but it gets projected onto a brother or sister as well. Psychological projection is the act of placing undesirable feelings or emotions onto someone else, rather than admitting to, or dealing with, them. When a person projects, they are not being responsible for their own feelings; instead they put them on another. Competition turns to rivalry; rivalry turns to contention; contention turns to hatred. A Cain and Abel scenario may develop to one degree or another.

> *"And Cain attacked his brother, Abel, and killed him."* (Genesis 4:8 NLT)

15. Your sense of happiness will rise or fall based on the affirmations others give or do not give you.

If you don't like you, the only thing that helps you is if somebody comes along and says something nice about you, so you end up trying to negotiate ways to get as many people to like you and say nice things about you as possible. Otherwise, you get depressed. This is, again, one of the problems of peer pressure. Peers may endorse bad behavior and that may make you feel good. However, it's artificial because inside, if you really liked you, it wouldn't matter even a little what anybody said about you. You would know that "their own master will judge whether they stand or fall" (Romans 14:4, NLT), and would not be enthralled to the opinions of others.

In the Bible, Jesus put it this way:

> *"How can ye believe, which receive honour one of another, and seek not the honour that cometh from God only?"* (John 5:44)

When you don't like yourself, you also don't like what God made you to be. This introduces self-destructive dynamic in your life.

16. You will tend to be a people pleaser.

Everybody's opinions will be more important to you than yours or the opinions of God. This is not a healthy way to live: always worried about what somebody thinks about you. You will become subservient to others, whether they are right or wrong. Others will shape your life. You will be open to being manipulated, dominated, and controlled by others. Your self-confidence will be undermined, and you will constantly worry about what everyone else thinks. Your own convictions will dissipate. When others catch on to this, they will treat you like a doormat. Your natural impulse will be to hide your true feelings and lie and only share what you think others want to hear. You will have to develop a built-in public relations department. This is a tortuous way to live, and all because you don't like yourself.

17. You will not find satisfaction from within.

You were designed to be happy from the inside out: satisfied and wholly complete.

> *"The backslider in heart shall be filled with his own ways: and* ***a good man shall be satisfied from himself.*** *"*
> (Proverbs 14:14, emphasis mine)

You were designed to be happy from the inside out.

If you like you, *genuinely like,* yourself, you will have this inner source, this fountain of joy within you. We call it joy. We call it happiness. It's an exultation of your inner spirit that comes from genuine harmony with yourself. If you don't like you, that fountain of joy doesn't exist, and you spend the rest of your days in restless pursuit of compensations for that joy.

18. You will not have peace.

How could you possibly have peace if you don't like you? How could you possibly have this inner tranquility? This calm? This cool? This collectedness? Confidence? This interior condition that "Hey, I'm all right. I really am somebody."

The lack of peace in anyone's life is most troubling. Peace is referred to 429 time in Scripture. Thirteen of the fourteen New Testament letters begin with an expression of the desire for peace to the readers. Seven times God is referred to as the God (or Lord) of peace: Romans 15:33, 1 Corinthians 14:33, Romans 16:20, 2 Corinthians 13:11, Philippians 4:9, Hebrews 13:20, 2 Thessalonians 3:16. Jesus is known as, "the Prince of Peace" in Isaiah 9:6. Jesus came to:

"Guide our feet into the way of peace." (Luke 1:79)

Jesus said of Jerusalem,

"The things which belong unto thy peace...are hid from thine eyes." (Luke 19:42)

May this not be true of us! Genuine self-acceptance is one of those things that "belong unto your peace."

19. You will not have joy.

You were designed by God to have so much joy that you would shout about it (Psalm 32:11, 35:27, 132:9, 16) You were designed to have so much joy that you could not contain it. It would make you sing. The Christian way is a joy-filled way. There are some who *profess* to be Christians who look like they were baptized in lemon juice. They have faces so long they look like a saxophone. These fakes give Christians a bad name. God is a happy God, and His people are a joyful people of whom it is said,

"Therefore with joy shall ye draw water out of the wells of salvation." (Isaiah 12:3)

God is a happy God, and His people are a joyful people.

Without the natural and exuberant joy of the Lord, mankind will go looking for it elsewhere. That's why amusements attracts us. Amusements are the entertainment of those who will not think. Muse means to think, and amuse means not to think. Amuse means to divert the attention. Our amusements are distractions. Thus we have these games, whatever they are, to stop us from really thinking, because we have this inner lack.

20. You will not have contentment.

Contentment is pretty elusive these days. One of the primary dynamics in most advertising is to stir up discontentment with whatever you have, so that you will develop a "felt need" for the product being advertised. The advertiser plays up your inadequacies and your fears in order to get you to spend your money, thereby transferring the wealth of your pocketbook into theirs.

Contentment is realizing that God has already provided everything you need for your present happiness. If you don't like you, how could you ever be content?

> *"But godliness with contentment is great gain."*
> (1 Timothy 6:6)

21. You may live an artificial life attempting to compensate.

To *compensate* means to make up for a lack, especially for something that is unwelcome or unpleasant. Compensation as a psychological mechanism means to make up for some real or imagined deficiency. Imagine the waste of life, energy, time, talent, and treasure attempting to make up for an *imagined* deficiency. An entire lifetime can be wasted. How could you ever come up with an equivalent for the real you? Impossible! You end up competing with yourself, trying to prove to yourself that you are somebody—that you really are something. It's one of the "woes" of self-rejection.

22. You will have rejected the real you.

To not like yourself is to reject the real you. What a disapproval! What a bondage! What a suffering! What a self-inflicted wound of unworthiness! What self-abuse! What self-hatred! What self-annihilation! What a suicide by installment plan! What a sin against one's self! What an entrance into an illusionary world! What a wrong moral judgment! What treason! What a discarding of value! It is the mistake of all mistakes! It is the wrong of all wrongs!

23. You will tend to imitate others you admire.

You will try to be like those you think are likeable. You will make judgments based on mere appearances. If you spend your life trying to be like other people, guess what? There's nobody left to be you, the real you, the remarkable you. Who will be you? The whole universe will be robbed of the blessing that you were intended to bring to it by just being your self!

24. You will develop varying degrees of self-hatred.

Last week I sent my wife a beautiful sunset picture taken over the Atlantic Ocean. I attached the caption, "You think this is beautiful? Look in the mirror!" If I could, I would do the same with you.

If you hate everything about you, you need to understand with certainty that your judgment is severely impaired. Self-loathing to any degree is the same as siding against God's view of you. And by the way, in case you haven't figured it out yet, God is always right! He doesn't hate you. He loves you! Because He is not a respecter of persons, He says to you exactly what He said to Jeremiah:

> *"Yea, I have loved thee with an everlasting love: therefore with lovingkindness have I drawn thee."*
> (Jeremiah 31:3)

My best advice to you is to get on God's side, and love you!

25. You will subconsciously develop self-destructive attitudes.

Stop being a traitor, a traitor to yourself. Self-destructive behaviors will start cropping up in your mind, in your thinking. When you don't like you, you turn on yourself. Thoughts turn to attitudes, attitudes into feelings, and feelings turn to actions. Negative thoughts = negative attitudes = negative feelings = negative actions. Negative actions are actions that destroy, no matter how incremental their process. One cigarette after another is one coffin nail after another. One drug after another is the destruction of thousands of brain cells after other thousands. I like what Shakespeare warned about alcohol: "Oh, that men would put an enemy in their mouths to steal away their brains!"[76]

There are many self-destructive behaviors: overeating, undereating, drug abuse, social suicide by alienating yourself from others, overspending, refusing rest and sleep, and so on. These destructive dynamics, both consciously and unconsciously, sabotage the soul. Many focus their attention on the *perceived* worst parts of their lives. Persons often see themselves through their *perceived* deficiencies, thus inducing pathologies, dysfunctions, addictions, learning disabilities, mistakes, sin and dark realities.

26. You will speak evil.

Your self-talk will be contaminated. What you say to yourself about yourself is important. A person who does not like themselves, says, "I'm no good." They don't say it out loud for other people to hear maybe, but then again, they might.

If you know somebody who's outwardly like this, you ought to declare an emergency over that person. They need you to give them the message about how to start liking themselves instead. They will say things like, "I'm dumb. I can't do anything right." They trash themselves. The pain, the pain of soul that builds and builds and builds under this assault of words has a snowball effect. Over time, their self-destructive behavior will get worse.

> What you say to yourself about yourself is important.

But isn't this "just talk?" No! Words have power.

"Death and life are in the power of the tongue."
(Proverbs 18:21)

76 William Shakespeare, *Othello*, public domain, Act 2, Scene 3.

The more evil you speak to yourself, the more evil will increase in your life. You may ask, "How so?" We are taught that "faith comes from hearing, and hearing through the word of Christ" (Romans 10:17 ESV) and we have no trouble understanding that hearing the Word of God will build our faith. When you speak the Word, you reinforce it to the increasing of your faith. The more you say something, the more you believe it.

> You end up believing what you say to yourself.

Commercials play the same message over and over and over again. Why the repetition? Because the more you hear that you need their product, the more you will believe that you do and go buy it. Similarly, the words you say to yourself (whatever they are) will affect the condition of your soul. You end up believing what you say to yourself. If you speak evil to yourself, you will believe that evil. If you speak good, you will believe the good.

This is so important that I want you to at least see some scriptural truths about this:

> *"The tongue of the wise useth knowledge aright: but the mouth of fools poureth out foolishness."*
> (Proverbs 15:2)

> *"A wholesome tongue is a tree of life: but perverseness therein is a breach in the spirit."*
> (Proverbs 15:4)

> *"Whoso keepeth his mouth and his tongue keepeth his soul from troubles."* (Proverbs 21:23)

> *"What shall be given unto thee? Or what shall be done unto thee, thou false tongue?"* (Psalm 120:3)

> *"Thy tongue deviseth mischiefs; like a sharp razor, working deceitfully."* (Psalm 52:2)

"Keep thy tongue from evil, and thy lips from speaking guile." (Psalm 34:13)

27. You may lose all hope.

Hopelessness is despair without a glimmer of optimism. Despondent, desperate, depressed: these are not happy words and certainly not healthy conditions of the soul. It may seem like the whole world is against you, and nobody cares. If you feel this way, please read the rest of this book. Make sure you grasp the four steps on how to enthusiastically like yourself. God cares for you.

28. You may wish you were never born.

The Bible tells a story about this. Job was the central character. The circumstances of his life were exceptionally negative. He did not understand why these awful things had happened to him. Instead of blaming his environment, he blamed himself and got to the place where he wished he'd never been born.

"And Job spake, and said,

Let the day perish wherein I was born, and the night in which it was said, There is a man child conceived.

Let that day be darkness; let not God regard it from above, neither let the light shine upon it.

Let darkness and the shadow of death stain it; let a cloud dwell upon it; let the blackness of the day terrify it.

As for that night, let darkness seize upon it; let it not be joined unto the days of the year, let it not come into the number of the months.

Lo, let that night be solitary, let no joyful voice come therein.

Let them curse it that curse the day, who are ready to raise up their mourning.

Let the stars of the twilight thereof be dark; let it look for light, but have none; neither let it see the dawning of the day:

because it shut not up the doors of my mother's womb, nor hid sorrow from mine eyes.

Why died I not from the womb? Why did I not give up the ghost when I came out of the belly?"

(Job 3:2-11)

Job basically was saying, "Just forget about my birthday. Forget about the fact that it ever happened. Let the day be darkness. Let not God regard it from above, neither let the light shine upon it. Get it out of the calendar, let there be no joy–don't celebrate my birthday. It's a cursed day. I wish I had been born dead!" The psychological condition presented to us in these verses is not unlike many in our culture, and sorrowfully, even some Christians who don't like themselves and wish they'd never been born.

29. You will be tempted to medicate yourself.

There is no chemical cure for a spiritual problem. Mind-altering drugs may mask a problem for a short time, but they cannot cure. For example, guilt is a spiritual problem, and can only be resolved completely by spiritual principles and their application. The guilt on a person's soul cannot be chemically removed.

It is beyond the scope of this writing to be definitive on this subject but a few things must be mentioned. The Bible predicts and describes conditions that will exist when the world collapses. Drug dependence is one of them.

"For by thy sorceries were all nations deceived."

(Revelation 18:23)

The actual word translated "sorcery" in the KJV is the Greek word, *pharmakeia,* from which we get "pharmacy" and "medications."[77] In other words, entire nations will be deceived into using drugs. America seems to be one of those nations. But a nation is only deceived if the people are deceived. How could such a condition be produced? The answer is to be found in the money trail. Here is what the Bible teaches:

> *"They that will be rich fall into temptation and a snare, and into many foolish and hurtful lusts, which drown men in destruction and perdition.*
>
> *For the love of money is the root of all evil: which while some coveted after, they have erred from the faith, and pierced themselves through with many sorrows."* (1 Timothy 6:9-10)

Let's look at the facts:

- These people are money-motivated.
- This money-motivation produces temptation.
- This money-motivation produces snares.
- This money-motivation produces stupid desire.
- This money-motivation produces hurtful results.
- These desires damage other people.
- These other people are destroyed.
- The root cause is love of money.
- It causes people to leave biblical principles.
- The results are many sorrows.

This is the drug story of our day. Unfortunately this does not only apply to street drugs, but to mind-altering prescription drugs too. Watch out. There is no chemical cure for a spiritual problem.

There is no chemical cure for a spiritual problem.

77 James Strong, "5331. Pharmakeia," Strong's Greek: 5331. φαρμακεία (pharmakeia) -- the use of medicine, drugs or spells, accessed February 16, 2020, https://biblehub.com/greek/5331.htm)

30. If unchecked you may think of suicide.

Instead of suicide on the installment plan—one cigarette after another, one drug after another, one drink after another, one hit after another—some want to end the whole deal. This comes from not liking yourself.

Plato quoted Socrates as saying that suicide was desertion, and that mortals were soldiers of the gods, and suicide was akin to a soldier running away from his post, and "therefore the destruction of divine property."[78]

Those that don't like themselves and reach this extreme mental, emotional, and spiritual state don't even know that they have a post, a mission, a responsibility, a joyful enterprise. They don't know they have an important function. The truth about them has been obliterated. At the root of the issue is a strong dislike of themselves. It is so strong that their life becomes meaningless, hopeless—an endurance contest until the weakened will cannot endure it any longer. And Satan, the hater, the destroyer, wins; and self-murder is still murder. Woe!

God is on your side even when you are not.

The answer to this problem is to think correctly about yourself. You will know when you've arrived, because you will be joyful, enthusiastic, exuberant, cheerful and energetic. How will this come about? You have a chance to change your thoughts about you: change to God's thoughts about you. They are the facts. They come from the Holy Bible. They are the truth. It is time to end the pains of life that are based on illusions and false ideas of life. When you do, your pain will go away. Depression will vanish. You will have better things to do than fight with yourself. God is on your side even when you are not. He is always *for* you, never against you. Why not join Him for,

"If God be for us, who can be against us?"
(Romans 8:31)

78 George Howe. Colt, *The Enigma of Suicide* (New York et al.: Simon & Schuster, 1992) 146.

There are more details about this matter in an ebook entitled "How To Like Yourself" available as a free download at NothingButTheTruth.org

My Prayer for You

I wish you could understand how deep is my anxiety for you and all who have never met me. How I long that you may be encouraged, and find out more and more how strong are the bonds of Christian love. How I long for you to grow more certain in your knowledge and more sure in your grasp of God Himself. May your spiritual experiences become richer as you see more and more fully God's great secret, Christ Himself! For it is in Him, and in Him alone, that men will find all the treasures of wisdom and knowledge.[79]

79 J. B. Phillips, "The New Testament in Modern English", 1962 edition, published by HarperCollins., Colossians 2:1-3

IF YOU'RE A FAN OF THIS BOOK, PLEASE TELL OTHERS...

1. Post a 5-star review on Amazon.

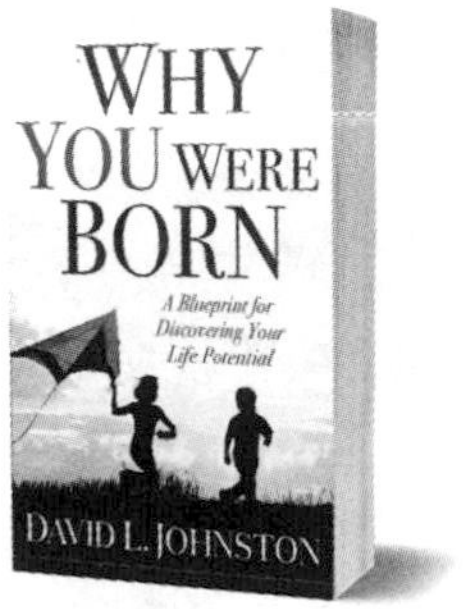

2. Write about the book on your Facebook, Twitter, Instagram, LinkedIn, or any social media platforms you regularly use.

3. If you blog, consider referencing the book or publishing an excerpt from the book with a link back to our websites. You have permission to do this as long as you provide proper credit and backlinks.

4. Recommend the book to friends, family, and AD caregivers—word-of-mouth is still the most effective form of advertising.

5. Purchase additional copies to give away to others or for use by your church or other groups.

Learn more about the authors or contact them at www.NothingButTheTruth.ORG

ENJOY THESE OTHER BOOKS BY DAVID JOHNSTON

How You See Yourself – The Source of Your Struggle and How to Conquer It!

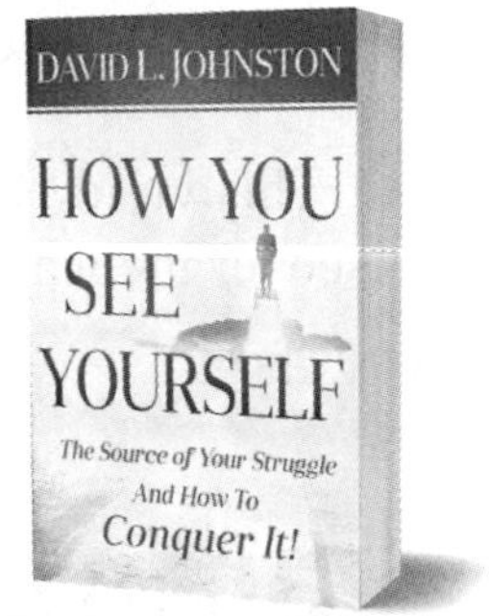

We are hindered from being the best version of ourselves, the version God intended. We are prevented by this insidious thing called iniquity. Iniquity is mentioned 334 times in the Bible, yet so many remain oblivious to its significant and negative impact on everyday living. Iniquity is the ancient term for narcissism. It's what turned a good angel, Lucifer, into the devil… "***thou wast perfect in thy ways from the day thou wast created, till iniquity was found in thee***" (Ezekiel 28:15).

It's one of the four reason Jesus went to the cross… "***He was bruised for our iniquities***" (Isaiah 53:5). It's why Jesus was sent… "***to bless you, in turning away every one of you from his iniquities***" (Acts 3:26).

As you journey through the pages of this book you will not only identify the problems iniquity imposes upon us, but you will also discover the solutions.

This book will help you discover:

- How iniquity contributes to mental illness
- How iniquity causes divorce and destroys households
- How conquering iniquity will cause your prayer life to flourish
- How you can finally live without fear and regret
- How to embrace the benefits that come from being free from iniquity and the way it robs you of your God-given potential!
- How iniquity is different from sin

MORE BOOKS BY DAVID JOHNSTON

The Inaugural Address that Changed the World

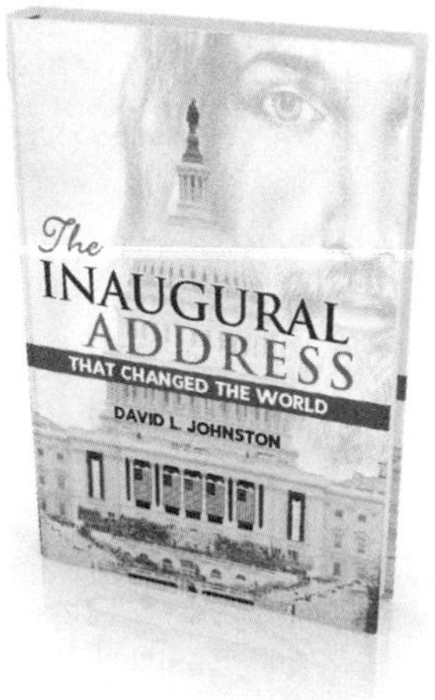

An Inaugural Address is a speech which marks the beginning of a new administration, rulership, or government. It is intended to inform the people of the incoming leader's intentions, springing from his or her personal values. I refer to the Sermon on the Mount as the Inaugural Address of Jesus, where he disclosed His intentions, values, policies, procedures and budget, all with the motivation of love, which is, in fact, the core of His message and mission.

About Us - Nothing But The Truth Ministries

NOTHING But The Truth

Dedicated to the single task of explaining the truth in its simplest and purest form to all peoples of the world.

People matter. YOU matter! Truth is the substance of all wise decision-making. So it's important to know the truth – about you, about why you were born, about every aspect of your life. Truth is wonderful, even when sometimes it may not seem comfortable.

This site is dedicated to sharing God's truth with you – truth that you can apply to your daily life; your relationships, your finances, your choices, your future.

Visit our website at
www.NothingButTheTruth.org and
www.KingofKingsChurch.us.
You can order these books at www.NothingButTheTruth.org
or wherever you purchase your favorite books.